P9-CDC-132

Back up your argument with sound research!

Who Says? The Writer's Research shows students HOW to do research in today's digital age and explains WHY research is essential to their academic work.

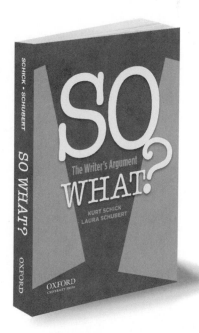

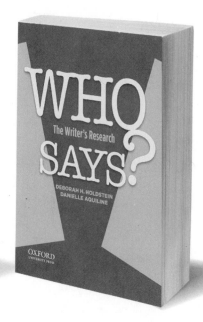

Package and Save! Save your students 20% when you pair *So What?* with *Who Says?*. Order using package ISBN: 978-0-19-937204-1.

Contact your Oxford University Press representative or call 800-280-0280 for details.

So What?

THE
Writer's
Argument

Kurt Schick
Laura Schubert

both of
James Madison University

New York   Oxford
Oxford University Press

Oxford University Press publishes works that further Oxford University's
objective of excellence in research, scholarship, and education.

Oxford   New York
Auckland   Cape Town   Dar es Salaam   Hong Kong   Karachi
Kuala Lumpur   Madrid   Melbourne   Mexico City   Nairobi
New Delhi   Shanghai   Taipei   Toronto

With offices in
Argentina   Austria   Brazil   Chile   Czech Republic   France   Greece
Guatemala   Hungary   Italy   Japan Poland   Portugal   Singapore
South Korea   Switzerland   Thailand   Turkey   Ukraine   Vietnam

Copyright © 2014 by Oxford University Press.

Published by Oxford University Press.
198 Madison Avenue, New York, New York 10016
http://www.oup.com

Oxford is a registered trademark of Oxford University Press

All rights reserved. No part of this publication may be reproduced,
stored in a retrieval system, or transmitted, in any form or by any means,
electronic, mechanical, photocopying, recording, or otherwise,
without the prior permission of Oxford University Press.

Library of Congress Cataloging-in-Publication Data
Schick, Kurt, 1964-
    So what? : the writer's argument / Kurt Schick, Laura Schubert, both of
James Madison University.
        pages cm
    ISBN 978-0-19-994907-6 (pbk.)
    1. English language--Rhetoric--Study and teaching.   2. Report writing--
Study and teaching (Higher) I. Schubert, Laura. II. Title.
    PE1404.S337   2014
    808'.0071'1--dc23
                                                                    2013037249

Printing number: 9 8 7 6 5 4 3 2 1
Printed in the United States of America
on acid-free paper

contents

preface

ACADEMIC WRITING confounds many college students—not because they lack sophistication, but because of the natural expertise that they already possess. Decades of real-world language use have taught them that authentic writing involves a genuine audience, purpose, and context—all of which school writing seems to lack.

So What? The Writer's Argument approaches college reading, writing, and argument as scholarly activity and situates students as apprentice scholars. *So What?* gives writing a real audience, purpose, and context by teaching apprentice scholars authentic styles, organizing structures, and persuasive moves that they can use in writing classes and beyond. This book introduces students to many of the thought processes, motivations, and strategies that scholars use to answer questions, to solve problems, and to defend their ideas.

To the Instructor

Professors, employers, and politicians agree that college students should learn to write well, but not everyone agrees how or why. Should writing classes prepare students to write in their majors? Should we teach writing skills for the workplace, or for citizenship? Should we focus on the processes of writing or critical thinking, or on various types and technologies of writing? Which approach will have the greatest impact?

Learning argument accomplishes many of these outcomes at once. By blending communication with problem solving, argument prepares students to use language and thinking so they can participate effectively in their academic, civic, and professional communities. As writing scholar David Fleming explains, argument teaches a process of "reasoning with others."

Still, teaching argument doesn't magically solve a challenge that writing teachers and students inevitably face: motivation. What kinds of authentic arguments can students make while in school? How can they discover something interesting to argue about when academic writing often seems like regurgitating the words and thoughts of others? Too often, students cannot imagine significant reasons for writing other than for a grade and some blurry sense of audience and purpose. Left without reasons to care about their writing, students (and their readers) are often left wondering, *So what?* Students and faculty need an approach that teaches argument as useful and meaningful.

The Scholarly Apprentice Model

Our solution is not to separate academic writing from the "real" world but to teach it as an authentic activity. We invite students to participate in scholarly argument, to apprentice alongside their scholarly mentors (professors) who use writing to understand the world and engage with others. Our apprentice model elevates students by treating them as colleagues. Redefining students as scholarly apprentices invites them to become active citizens of the scholarly community from which they often feel disconnected.

This book seeks to open students' eyes to the notion of the academy— a place where scholars debate, create, and communicate knowledge. *So What?* treats students as apprentices with less experience and knowledge but with equal potential to contribute to the vibrant conversations that characterize higher education. Given the opportunity to create knowledge—for themselves and sometimes for others—students are more likely to make what they're doing matter.

The apprentice-scholar framework in *So What?* gives students a meaningful way to view academic writing, one that they can use to understand the technical moves of argumentation. Rather than defining argument only as persuasion, designed primarily to change people's minds, we teach students how to use argumentation to create knowledge, promote understanding, and bridge differences—the way scholars do. Scholarly argument seeks to enlighten, to open new areas of discussion, and to advance society, not primarily to convert or persuade.

In addition to motivating students and legitimizing their work as apprentices, by training them to think like a scholar, *So What?* teaches students habits of mind that will benefit them personally and professionally. While we champion the vision of the classical liberal arts, we also recognize students'—and society's—demands for practical education that prepares graduates to transition quickly and smoothly into the workforce. We believe the most transferable skills that students can learn through argument are not specific genres of writing or technical knowledge but scholarly habits of mind that writing teachers can model and teach.

Transferability

Recent studies indicate that introductory writing classes may not bring as many long-term benefits as we once imagined. Students do not automatically "transfer" what they learn into their major studies ("near" transfer), nor do they always apply the skills and understanding to new contexts outside of school ("far" transfer).

To improve transfer, we must imagine learning outcomes that can be woven through the curriculum—skills, habits, and knowledge that will be relevant across different situations. Recently, organizations of writing teachers and professors (the Council of Writing Program Administrators, the National Council of Teachers of English, and the National Writing Project) developed an inventory of "intellectual and practical" Habits of Mind that "will support students' success in a variety of fields and disciplines" (http://wpacouncil.org/framework). *So What?* reinforces these habits through each chapter:

- **Engagement**—"a sense of investment and involvement in learning." We introduce scholarly argument as a means of engagement and the writing process as an investment worth students' time and effort. We present argument as a tool to discover, communicate, and revise what we know, think, and believe.
- **Curiosity**—"the desire to know more about the world." We encourage students to follow an inquiry-based writing process, inspired by questions, careful reading, and analysis. Apprentice scholars learn how to discover compelling questions and problems and situate their arguments within scholarly conversations.
- **Openness**—"the willingness to consider new ways of being and thinking in the world." A chapter on finding credible sources helps students select sources carefully and prioritize ones that are more stable, reliable, and credible. Arguing in conversation with sources helps students to understand the value of enlarging their perspectives.
- **Creativity**—"the ability to use novel approaches for generating, investigating, and representing ideas." Our chapter on creating a compelling thesis explains that behind every relevant, significant, and original thesis is a compelling, challenging, and controversial question or problem awaiting a creative response. Descriptions of stylistic choices throughout the book encourage students to approach writing creatively.
- **Metacognition**—"the ability to reflect on one's own thinking as well as on the individual and cultural processes used to structure knowledge." An organization chapter shows students how to structure arguments to meet their audience's needs, and another chapter on finding faults provides practice in scrutinizing reasoning. Many of the exercises throughout the book stimulate students' metacognitive thinking skills.

- **Persistence**—"the ability to sustain interest in and attention to short- and long-term projects." Several of the chapters encourage students to investigate issues exhaustively and to defer conclusions until weighing all evidence and assumptions. Practicing scholarly argument as case building helps students see knowledge building as an iterative process.
- **Responsibility**—"the ability to take ownership of one's actions and understand the consequences of those actions for oneself and others." A chapter on using sources models how to design arguments by responsibly borrowing and building on the words and thoughts of others. Responsibility can also be developed by collaborating with others, as writers often do in a classroom that focuses on argument.
- **Flexibility**—"the ability to adapt to situations, expectations, or demands." Our style chapter (and explanations throughout the book) maintains students' focus on the craft of writing, developing a toolkit of options that can be adapted for particular audiences and purposes.

Contents

So What? progresses **from higher order concerns** (such as support and organization) **to later order concerns** (like citation and punctuation), while addressing style throughout. The first chapter explains the point of scholarly argument and provides guidance for improving the writing process. In the next few initial chapters, students learn how to read arguments effectively and how to find good sources. From Chapter 5 forward, we explain how to develop and organize arguments for various purposes and audiences, teaching students how to support arguments with evidence and sources, how to rethink arguments, and how to present them effectively.

Our approach to argumentation continues the classical and modern rhetorical tradition, owing heavily to Aristotle, Cicero, and

Stephen Toulmin. While we do introduce some fundamentals of rhetoric (stasis questions, appeals, fallacies, genre, and style), **we do not overwhelm students with unnecessary technical jargon or theory.** We also do not attempt to introduce every scholarly style or genre, or even specific disciplinary research techniques; rather, we attempt to teach students how to learn these things for themselves by providing them with heuristics and tools that help them think like writers and scholars.

Features

- CHAPTER CHECKLISTS forecast the key topics for each chapter.
- CONSIDER THIS activities embedded in each chapter provide opportunities for students to reflect on the book's content and style and on their own writing.
- TRY THIS exercises allow students to practice or investigate what they learn immediately via short exercises that can be used in class or as homework.
- WHAT'S NEXT features conclude each chapter with activities and assignments that help students transfer and apply what they've learned into other classes and beyond school.
- APPENDICES at the end of the book provide quick guides for peer review and collaboration, and for organizing arguments. Students can refer to these guides to complement their writing and reading process.

We have attempted to write in a style that would be straightforward and engaging. In doing so, we risk oversimplifying complex theories and practices of argument that scholars have been developing and debating for the past 2,000 years. As a selection and interpretation of that tradition, the book is itself a kind of argument. We anticipate that both students and instructors will find points of clarification and points of disagreement with our work. Indeed, we hope that readers will use the book to generate discussion, debate, and inspiration for further investigation.

To the Student

Many new college students either think that they already know how to write well (because teachers told them so and they believed it) or they cannot write well (because teachers told them so and they believed it).

However, most students who were "good writers" before college eventually discover that whatever formulas they mastered previously cannot guarantee their success in college or beyond. For example, knowing how to write research reports or five-paragraph themes with correct grammar and citations will not necessarily enable you to perform the following tasks:

- For your environmental science class: Write a public policy recommendation on hydraulic fracturing ("fracking") for natural gas based on current laws, economic factors, and scientific research.
- For your boss: Write a memo justifying why your team cannot complete a project on time in accordance with your client's contract.
- For your local planning commission: Write a letter requesting a zoning exception so you can build an addition to your house that violates existing code.

Each of these tasks would require you to adapt your argument for a different audience, purpose, topic, and type of writing. The good news is that you can learn to be a more adaptable writer by studying and practicing the kind of arguments that scholars use to discover, improve, and communicate ideas.

Similarly, learning more about argument can help students who have struggled with writing in the past. The most important challenges of writing in college or in the workplace are not grammar and punctuation (though those are also important for many readers). Good writing is not just pretty words and sentences but carefully crafted ideas. **The hardest part of producing good writing is finding something significant and compelling to write about.**

So What? will teach you how to invent and present significant, compelling arguments. The core lessons will teach you how to discover controversies or public problems to argue about, plus patterns of organizing and supporting arguments that address those controversies. Mastering these techniques will help you find something substantial to write about in almost any situation.

Creating arguments to solve problems that matter to others is a powerful and valued skill in college and in the workplace. Why not seize the opportunity to learn these essential habits of mind now? Your professors, through years of study and practice, have mastered the arts of argument in the subjects they teach. Take advantage of your apprenticeship with these master scholars. As you learn their craft, you can build the kind of expertise that makes college worth your investment.

acknowledgments

THE AUTHORS WISH TO THANK many colleagues for their excellent contributions, including Emiline Buhler, Kathy Clarke, Jared Featherstone, Karen McDonnell, Paige Normand, Justin Thurston, and Jim Zimmerman. Our sincere thanks to our wise editor Frederick Speers, his assistant Talia Benamy, and our illustrator Craighton Berman.

We appreciate the help of many outside reviewers in strengthening the manuscript, including Clark Draney, College of Southern Idaho; Christopher Ervin, Western Kentucky University; Jeff Pruchnic, Wayne State University; Brooke Champagne, University of Alabama; Greg Hagan, Madisonville Community College; Danielle Zawodny Wetzel, Carnegie-Mellon University; Megan Swihart Jewell, Case Western Reserve University; Cheryl Edelson, Chaminade University; Dave Badtke, Solano Community College; Andrew Higl, Winona State University; George Cusack, University of Oklahoma; Gina Weaver, Southern Nazarene University; Susie Crowson, Del Mar College; Anthony Cavaluzzi, SUNY Adirondack; Joe Musser, Ohio Wesleyan University; Tisha Turk, University of Minnesota-Morris; Brian Walter, St. Louis College of Pharmacy; Michael Morgan, Bemidji State University; Jessica Gravely, Prairie State College; Eileen Abrahams, Schenectady County Community College; Eleanor Welsh, Chesapeake College; Andrew Scott, Ball State University; and Stephanie Mood, Grossmont College.

We received invaluable feedback from many students in our first-year writing classes, especially Nathan Boone, Taylor Coats, Danielle Camiso, Erin Dooley, Kaitlyn Keyser, Jordan Lewis, Nick Love, Liz Mott, Will Mullery, Laura Nettuno, Jessie Seymour, Olivia Smithey,

Tyler Young, Cameron Yudkin, and also outstanding suggestions from tutors in our University Writing Center.

We are also indebted to our past teachers and mentors who instructed and inspired us, particularly Jim Corder, Becky Howard, Bob Jacobs, Robert Keys, Joseph Petraglia, Gary Tate, Robert Carballo, Patricia King, Jay B. Landis, Janet Martin, Gretchen McTavish, Kenneth Morefield, Virginia Schlabach, and Beverly Schneller.

Finally, we want to thank our families for their encouragement, patience, and wisdom. We are especially grateful for their support and care, and for cheering us on.

CHAPTER **one**

Why Do We Argue

chapter checklist

- What's the point of writing in college?
- What do arguments achieve?
- How can we use writing to improve our lives?
- How and what do scholars write?
- How should apprentice scholars approach writing in college?

For many students, academic writing seems awkward or pointless. Even if you've been a successful writer in school, you have probably encountered some assignments that ask you to do things that don't make much sense. What's the point, for example, of endlessly practicing five-paragraph essays? Why, you might wonder, must I use MLA citation format for my bibliography? Why does my teacher demand six sources (only two of which can be from the Internet)? And *so what* if I use Wikipedia?

We wrote this book to reveal the motivations behind academic writing and to help you understand how practicing argument, in particular, can teach you things that will be useful to you in college, in work, and in life. Writing can be empowering: it gives us a voice and an opportunity to say something meaningful and significant. When we write about something, we stretch our minds and we learn more deeply. When faced with a writing task, we have the potential to change the world in some small way, even if it's just to inspire or pester or provoke one reader, and to change our own minds about something. Writing and arguing are *active*, and they can even be fun.

So, What's the Point of Scholarly Writing?

You may not realize this, but you're already an expert communicator. You were using language before you could walk. And despite criticisms that "people don't read or write enough these days," we actually do so more than our ancestors ever did. With Google, Facebook, Wikipedia, Twitter, and text messaging at our fingertips, many of us consume and produce writing constantly, with sophistication that we're still trying to understand. So, although we might not read books the way our grandparents did, we may very well be the best information foragers and social networkers who ever walked this planet.

Our natural expertise may also be the reason why academic writing seems so baffling at times. Decades of real-world language use has taught us that authentic writing involves a genuine audience, purpose, and context—all of which academic writing seems to lack. What's the point, for example, of writing a paper about the deeper meanings of Shakespeare for your English teacher, who likely knows and cares more about literature than many students ever will? Or, why should a teacher really care about students' opinions on, say, legalizing marijuana? In either case, the reader or writer may be left wondering, *So what?*

A Scholar's Work—in College and Beyond

The *So what?* question can only be answered if you understand how and why scholarly writing works as a genuine form of communication, with real audiences and purposes. To begin, you should know that higher education has two interrelated functions:

- to *communicate* and
- to *create* knowledge.

Professors not only teach; many are also professional scholars who, in various ways, work to investigate humanity's endless supply of unanswered questions and unsolved problems. In fact, human progress depends upon posing and answering such questions, from the most broad and consequential ("How might humans live together peacefully?") to the specific and seemingly obscure ("How does climate change affect the migration patterns of Ruby-Throated Hummingbirds?"). Scholars, such as professors and other researchers, are experts at advancing what we know by investigating such questions. What's potentially exciting about college is that you might have an opportunity to learn from professors who literally "wrote the book" on the subjects you're studying.

College will provide you with an opportunity to *apprentice* as a scholar. Just as an artist, mechanic, or teacher might practice under the mentorship of an expert, you will learn how master scholars discover and communicate knowledge. As an apprentice, you can begin making sense of how and why scholars use writing to expand the bounds of human understanding.

Why Bother?

By now, you might be wondering how you might reasonably be expected to "expand the bounds of human understanding." After all, aren't you mostly in college to learn what others have been discovering for the last few thousand years—or simply to get a good job? Who ever said that you wanted to become a professional scholar, anyway? How will all this make you a better citizen, professional, or worker?

Our answer: **You'll use the skills, knowledge, and habits that you learn as an apprentice scholar throughout college and in your personal and professional life.** As an undergraduate student, you won't really be expected to cure cancer, end world hunger, or design an income tax system that actually makes sense, but rather to *practice* some of the skills that are necessary to do such things.

TRY THIS ➤ Set Some Goals for Yourself

TRY THIS exercises like this give you an opportunity to practice or investigate chapter content.

For this exercise, seek outside expertise to help you set some goals for developing as a writer. Chances are good that you have friends or relatives who are established in the workplace (or maybe you have extensive work experience yourself). Whether or not they attended college, working professionals know something about what characteristics contribute to a successful career. They might even be in a position to hire new employees. Call or e-mail a few of them and ask the following questions:

- What skills would you look for when screening applicants?
- What do you think are the most important things for me to learn in college?
- What's the role of writing and continued learning in your work?

Scholarly Habits of Mind

Whether or not you plan to become a professional scholar, developing the skills and habits that scholars use can help you succeed in college

4

and beyond. For example, you'll be more likely to notice what others overlook, to solve problems creatively, and to make decisions independently. People who are well educated, either by schooling or by years of life experience, exhibit habits of mind that others can learn. Your apprenticeship will teach you how to think like a well-educated person. How, you might ask, do well-educated people think?

- Well-educated people **make decisions carefully and take their time**. They appreciate that the world is complicated, that there's more to most issues than meets the eye, so they understand the importance of studying an issue from multiple viewpoints, gathering as much information as possible before rushing to judgment.
- By practicing scholarly argument, well-educated people learn that they must **carefully explain and support their conclusions for others to scrutinize**. They understand that their readers won't let them off the hook with half-baked assertions, judgments, or decisions.
- Well-educated people know that **everyone's perspective, including their own, is limited**. That's why educated people practice critical thinking, which involves looking carefully for errors in reasoning.

People who are well-educated about how arguments work can craft logically sound, persuasive cases that benefit them personally and professionally. For example, citizens rely on their critical thinking skills when they spot the tricks that politicians use to get their vote or that advertisers use to entice consumers to buy things they don't really need. A company's CEO thinks like a scholar when she compares competing business proposals and selects the most viable and profitable option. A physical therapist thinks like a scholar when he develops an evidence-based treatment plan that will withstand the scrutiny of a health insurance company. An entry-level worker thinks like a scholar when she builds a bulletproof case for a pay raise. And so forth. The point is that whether or not you see yourself as a scholar, thinking like one can make you more successful in college and beyond.

CONSIDER THIS ➤ Nonsexist Language

Occasionally, we'll pause so can you reflect on the content of the chapter, your own writing, or the stylistic choices we've made while writing. These mini-lessons should remind you that whenever you read, you should pay close attention not just to *what* you're reading about but also to *how* it's written. Even if you disagree with the decisions a writer makes, it's worth your time to stop, study, and collect a few more tools for your writing toolkit.

For this reflection, consider why we alternate between using "he" and "she." Most academic disciplines now advocate or require that scholars use nonsexist language. A common but confusing question is how to use third-person pronouns. Decades ago, writers would always use masculine pronouns (he, him, his) unless referring to a specific female person. To support equality, scholarly writers eventually adopted *gender-neutral* language by using "he/she" or sometimes "s/he." Because these versions seemed clunky, nowadays many writers alternate between "she" and "he" as we have chosen to do in this book.

What do you think of our decision? Can you think of better ways to be gender neutral? Do you think this really matters? Why or why not?

A Fresh Look at Your Old Writing Process

Writing can help you develop educated habits of mind, but only if you're willing to adopt a writing process that is more flexible and complex than what you've probably used in the past.

Inexperienced writers use a simplified process for good reasons. Remember, when you first started driving, how difficult it was to think about turning, accelerating, braking, and navigating roads, signs, and traffic all at the same time? To avoid information overload and to simplify the academic writing process for students, teachers often require a formula that looks something like this: First, pick a topic. Then, research the topic, as needed. After reading a lot of sources, create an outline and write a first draft. Finally, revise, edit, and submit the paper.

In theory, this process works reasonably well because it forces students not to skip steps and because it's easier to learn a complicated process by concentrating on one part at a time.

However, experienced writers usually don't write in such a formulaic, straight line. Scholars typically follow a more *recursive* process—that is, they move back and forth among the stages, oftentimes repeating steps multiple times and at different points in their process. Although they typically do some planning before they begin, scholars also allow drafting, revision, and peer feedback to reshape their ideas. Throughout the writing process, they improve and focus their ideas by imagining different audiences and purposes and by finding potential gaps in their arguments.

Learning to use a more complex writing process might seem overwhelming, but scholarly writing takes practice and persistence. Inexperienced writers sometimes have an unrealistic and unattainable view of writing—that good writing happens magically for the lucky few, with little effort—as though you're either born a good writer or not. Here's the good news: **effective writing is not a magical or natural talent**. It can be explained and learned.

Remember, too, that college professors expect you to *apprentice* as a scholar, not to become professors or professional writers. Keep your goals within reason, and don't let scholarly writing intimidate you. Like learning to drive, it might seem awkward and frustrating at first, but becoming proficient may be easier than you think.

To develop your writing ability, you only need four things:

- knowledge,
- practice,
- feedback, and, most important,
- motivation.

These key ingredients can help you become a more effective writer in college and beyond.

CONSIDER THIS ➤ Habits and History

For this reflection, use the following questions to help you think through how you typically write for school assignments. Be honest.

1. What, if anything, do you do before you start to write a draft? Do you freewrite or use an outline? How do you generate ideas?
2. What conditions do you prefer while writing? Do you like to write at a desk, or maybe in bed? By hand or on a laptop? What time of day do you do your best writing? Do you need quiet, or does background noise or music help you focus?
3. What do you do with your first draft? What kinds of changes do you typically make before handing it in?
4. How did you learn these strategies and habits? Why do you write this way?

The One-Draft Wonder

Despite how hard teachers try to improve students' writing process, research indicates that most new college students write one draft and make few changes before submitting their writing for a grade. For practical purposes, novice scholars often hand in their rough drafts.

Why do so many students still trust their one-draft wonders? Efficiency.

If, based on your own experiences, a single draft and some light proofreading have given you the results you want (an acceptable grade or a completed assignment), then why would you expect big rewards from multiple drafts? And if no one has ever taught you how to draft and revise effectively, how could you be expected to do so?

Most writers can achieve *some* success without much planning or revising. As long as investing the bulk of your time and energy in drafting yields the results you want, that's okay for now. But if you're like us, when you encounter difficult writing projects (like a twenty-page research paper, or a short but complex argumentative essay), you will need a process that includes careful planning and lots of revision.

So our first writing process lesson is this: Adapt your writing process to fit the particular writing situation. **Experienced writers don't write the same way every time, and neither should you.**

If your teacher assigns a short argument and you can effectively organize your ideas in your head without making an outline beforehand, then go ahead. If you can write an effective short-response paper the night before it's due in one draft, that's okay. But before you think your one-draft wonders will always work in college, think back to when you first learned algebra. You probably thought "showing your work" was pointless, at least at the beginning. When the problems became more difficult, though, you learned that you could no longer solve them in your head. You needed a more complex process to solve more complex problems. The same is true in writing.

Toward a Better Writing Process

So, what does a more complex writing process look like? We'll begin by breaking the writing process down into four parts: discovery, drafting, revision, and editing.

- *Discovery* includes tasks such as choosing a topic, identifying the right questions to ask, finding and processing outside sources, organizing ideas, and so forth.
- *Drafting* generates the first version of a complete draft.
- *Revision* involves significantly adding, deleting, or rearranging chunks of text or content.
- *Editing* polishes paragraphs and sentences for style, formatting, grammar, and so forth.

We assume that since you're in college, you're willing to invest serious time and energy into your studies. Still, you can only afford to spend a certain amount of time and effort on a given assignment. Thus, the four parts of the writing process are inversely proportional to each other: **The more time and effort you spend drafting, for example, the less time you have to invest in discovery or revision.** To represent these proportionalities vividly, we might use a pie chart like the one shown in Figure 1.1.

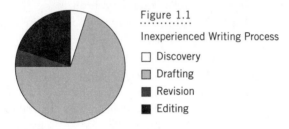

Figure 1.1

Inexperienced Writing Process
☐ Discovery
◻ Drafting
■ Revision
■ Editing

What would a pie chart of your typical writing process look like?

Of course, these portions are not scientifically precise, but the pie chart can help us imagine the typical writing process of a one-draft wonder writer who spends most of her time drafting and editing, leaving little to invest in discovery or revision.

An Experienced Writer's Process

In contrast, for complex tasks, experienced writers try to balance the elements of the process, spending more time before and after drafting to develop and refine their writing. In fact, experienced writers often spend much *more* time thinking (discovery) and rethinking (revising and editing) their writing than on creating their first draft because they realize that writing is closely connected to thinking. They use writing as a tool to understand complex concepts and to clarify their perspectives on issues. Researchers have also discovered that more experienced writers do not always write in a straight line, from discovery to drafting to revising to editing; rather, they move back and forth among stages.

How might the one-draft process hinder your development as a writer? What are its potential costs? First, if you love your draft too much, you won't want to change it. After all, if the majority of your investment is drafting, then you probably won't want to redo that work, even when it's not very good. More important, **if you only write one draft, you lose the opportunity to revise and expand your thinking**—to re-envision your argument, to understand your subject matter more completely, and to discover new and better ideas.

With the one-draft wonder, you also risk selling yourself short because most educated people equate good writing with good thinking. And vice versa: Readers think poor writing results from careless thinking. In many classes, writing will be the only window professors have into your thinking, so you need to use every opportunity to represent your reasoning powers well.

You might find it useful, then, to experiment with some other economical ways to invest your time and energy. For example, if you begin thinking about an assignment as soon as you get it, maybe even jot down ideas as they occur to you, then you can add discovery time with little cost. Similarly, a fifteen-minute visit to your instructor's office to talk about plans for the paper can pay big dividends: if you change your topic or misread the assignment at that early stage, you haven't already "wasted" time drafting, right? Scholars do this, too, when they discuss an idea for a research article or a conference paper with a colleague who can help them brainstorm and develop a research plan. Another good time investment is using your campus writing center, where you should be able to get help during any stage of the writing process. All of these strategies save drafting time by helping us organize to avoid later problems. In fact, for some scholars, drafting takes the *least* amount of time because they do most of the hard thinking and problem solving before they compose their first paragraph and after their first draft is complete.

Set Priorities and Adapt Your Process

Experienced writers don't feel locked into a linear process, but they do set priorities when drafting. Following writing scholars Paula Gillespie and Neal Lerner, we divide these priorities into "higher order concerns," such as content development, focus, and organization, and "later order concerns," like grammar and formatting. Experienced writers address higher order concerns first, not just because they're more important, but for efficiency. For example, before you edit a paragraph to make sure your writing is clear and correct, you should make sure that the paragraph effectively develops necessary content. If a paragraph presents information that is off topic or restates information that you already covered, then you may need to revise it. Why waste time tweaking sentences that might later be removed or substantially changed?

Another way to save time is to think carefully about your audience and purpose so you can adapt your writing process according to the needs of each particular situation. You will be frustrated if you assume that chemists write the same as economists, that every professor in your major will follow the exact same grading criteria for every assignment, or that every job will require the same kind of writing tasks. By experimenting with different strategies, you can assemble a writing toolkit to use when you encounter new or difficult writing situations. Throughout this book, we'll present many ways of interpreting, handling, and excelling at various writing tasks.

Practicing Argument

Now let's talk about one of the main tools that scholars use to communicate and solve problems—*argument*, which happens to be a crucial but often confusing feature of scholarly writing, and is therefore the focus of this book.

When you hear the term "argument," you might first think about kids squabbling over whose turn it is to sit in the front seat of the car, or you might imagine you and your parents fighting over how late you can stay out. "Argument" may also conjure visions of TV lawyers presenting their case before a jury, or senators debating over the particulars of a new energy regulation. For us, the term "argument" signifies a tool that helps us explain *what* we think and *why* we think so. Arguments influence what our audiences know, believe, or act, and they can also clarify or enhance our own thinking.

Scholarly arguments contain elements of everyday arguments, including the following:

- **Scholarly arguments have real purposes based in problems that interest the participants.** In Chapter 3, we discuss common categories of problems, for example: "How should we interpret X?" "What caused Y?" "What should we do about Z?" Each of these questions prompts a different kind of scholarly investigation and a distinct kind of argument designed to answer the question.
- **Scholarly arguments address a specific audience.** Unlike some school writing that seems to be intended for no particular reader, scholarly arguments always address a specific group of people, often defined as a specialized academic *discipline*—for example, chemical engineers or US Civil War historians.
- **Scholarly arguments belong to larger conversations, histories, and contexts that determine the rules for what counts as a good argument.** Lawyers use established courtroom procedures, rules of evidence, and precedence to build a case. Similarly, to establish new knowledge in a discipline, scholars must know what methods of reasoning are typical, what kinds of evidence are acceptable, and what other scholars have already said about the subject.

Along with the similarities between scholarly and everyday arguments, there are also some important differences to keep in mind:

- **Scholarly arguments pursue ideal purposes.** Unlike arguments on the playground or (sometimes) in politics, scholars use arguments to seek truth and justify discoveries, rather than merely to "win." Because winning isn't the ultimate goal, *how* we argue is just as important as *what* we argue about. In fact, in college you will often be judged more on how you develop and defend your ideas than the ideas themselves. For instance, in a literature class, your professor will evaluate your interpretation of a poem based on the evidence you provide to support your thinking, rather than whether you arrived at a single "right" answer. Remember, your goal in college is to apprentice as a knowledge-maker. The "product" of this learning is not so much *what* you make as learning *how to make.*
- **Scholarly arguments address sophisticated, demanding audiences.** Scholars will expect that you examine your subject from different angles, that you anticipate other perspectives or counterarguments, that you validate your evidence, and so on.

Beginning in the next chapter, we discuss strategies that you can use to make sense of complicated scholarly arguments. You'll learn more about how scholars design arguments and how you can break them down to see exactly how they work.

A Note about *Rhetoric*

This book carries on an educational tradition that's over two thousand years old, a tradition in which you've participated all your life, whether you've known it or not. That tradition is the study of *rhetoric,* the investigation of how persuasion and communication work. Studying and practicing rhetoric was important as far back as the early democracies of Greece and Rome, whose citizens used various kinds of argument to solve problems, settle disputes, and build consensus. Throughout this book, you'll learn elements of rhetoric that will help you ask compelling questions, select reliable sources, dig for better data, and recognize weak or deceptive arguments—all of which will make you a better reader and writer.

We've already been building up to the first lesson about rhetoric: To be an effective communicator, you should always **pay careful attention not just to the content of what you read but also to the author and his audience and purpose.** These elements—writer, audience, and context—are the main elements of what we call the *rhetorical situation*. Rather than seeing writing simply as lifeless words and ideas on a page (or on a computer or mobile screen), scholars think of reading and writing as social activities—a conversation that involves real people and human motivations.

For example, let's consider the rhetorical situation of this book. We, the coauthors, are experienced college writing teachers. We also tutor writers from all over campus, so we've helped thousands of students with all kinds of writing in many different subjects. Knowing that about us can help you understand where we're coming from and maybe even trust us more than, say, your friend or relative, to give good advice about college writing. Wherever you, our intended audience, are right now, we are thinking about you as we write, trying to explain ideas in ways that will make sense, seem interesting, and be most useful to you.

You should also try to imagine our motivations and context. Why did we choose to write this book? On the one hand, writing is part of our occupation. To be successful in a college like ours, professors must publish. For us, though, writing this book is more than just a job. We're especially interested in the *problems* that this book attempts to solve:

- What are the most important things that students should know about writing in college and in life?

- How can we present those topics in fresh and interesting ways?
- How can we translate our expertise in writing and rhetoric into something that's useful for students who may not like to write and probably have never formally studied rhetoric?

The Rhetorical Situation

An easy way to remember the various elements of the rhetorical situation is to ask yourself the investigative questions that reporters and detectives use: *Who?*, *What?*, *When?*, *Where?*, *Why?*, and *How?*

Any time you are reading an argument, you need to ask yourself questions that fall under these primary categories:

Who (Author, Audience)?
- Who is the author or publisher of this text? What might readers already know about the author that might influence what they think of the text itself?
- Who is the intended audience? Are there others?
- What is the intended audience's background and demographics (age, gender, income, education, political preferences, etc.)? What do they value? What assumptions or biases might they have about the topic?

What and How (Subject Matter, Argument, and Style)?
- Does the argument contain an explicit or implied thesis?
- How much (and what kind of) background information does the author present?
- How are the arguments and evidence organized? Are there headings or different sections? What do these different sections suggest about the purpose of the text?
- What kinds of evidence or examples does the argument rely on? Are there any outside sources quoted or cited? How does the

author use these sources? To build credibility? To corroborate findings? To dispute ideas or discount other arguments?

- How does the text establish the author's credibility to make such an argument?
- What kind of tone do you notice? Is it serious, funny, sarcastic, scholarly, arrogant, immature . . .?
- What words stick out? What hints do they give you about the author's purpose and audience?
- What design elements are used? Does the design seem informal, playful, ordinary, formal, technical . . .?
- How does the argument use charts, images, or other visual elements?
- What kind of citation style does the author use?
- Are there footnotes or endnotes? What purposes do they serve?

When and Where (Context)?

- Where and when was the text published? What difference might that make to an audience?
- If the text is on the Internet, what is its domain (for example, .com, .edu, .org, .net, or .gov)? What does the domain suggest about who might be funding the publication or endorsing it? What does the domain suggest about the text's credibility, reliability, purpose, and audience?

Why (the Writer's Motivation—So What?)

- What is the author's purpose and motivation? What catalyst prompted her to write?
- Why is this an important topic? What are the larger consequences and implications for the audience?

You can apply these questions to any reading or writing situation. Let's start with how to interpret the rhetorical situation of college writing assignments.

From Academic Writing to Scholarly Writing

One of the most confusing things about college writing is that it sits somewhere between typical high school writing (academic writing) that displays your understanding of knowledge discovered by others, and writing published by experienced scholars (scholarly writing) that creates and communicates new knowledge. Both situations use arguments, but usually high school arguments are less authentic because you're not really trying to convince your audience of anything, while scholarly arguments have the authentic purpose of justifying new discoveries to a specific scholarly community.

Argumentative "moves" are the common ground of both academic (that is, student) writing and scholarly writing. Five-paragraph essays and high school research reports may seem formulaic and oversimplified, but these kinds of writing can teach some of the fundamental moves that scholars use, such as case building, reasoning, scrutinizing evidence, and so on. (In fact, the five-paragraph essay is loosely based on a more sophisticated classical argument that we discuss in Chapter 8.) The purpose of your scholarly apprenticeship is to help you transition from academic to scholarly writing, so while in college you will practice elements of both, often displaying what you know and creating new understandings at the same time.

Envision Your Purpose and Audience

Because scholars in most disciplines use writing to communicate their discoveries, another challenge of college writing is that it comes in many forms—from scientific research articles to business case studies to artistic analysis papers. You probably won't write in every class, but you may very well write more often than you have before in classes other than English. These writing tasks will have different purposes, audiences, and writing styles, so there aren't clear-cut rules or go-to formulas for every scenario. Instead, you'll need to make informed decisions by interpreting your professors' assignments thoughtfully and looking for clues in the assignment that suggest its rhetorical situation and a smart approach to take. The sections that follow provide some features to think about.

Writing with Purpose

As an apprentice, you can assume that most writing assignments will ask you to blend academic and scholarly purposes: to showcase your knowledge and understanding of subject matter while also using critical and creative thinking to develop some fresh understanding. Your professor might provide clues for the assignment's purpose by using specific terms to focus your attention, such as:

- *analyze*—to take something apart to see how it works
- *evaluate* or *critique*—to judge something according to established criteria
- *interpret*—to examine something's meaning, implications, or significance

Whenever professors use less specific terms like "discuss" or "examine," ask them to clarify or provide some strategies for how to meet their expectations.

To figure out what a specific writing task calls for, ask yourself:

- What could this kind of writing achieve?
- What could this argument do for readers?
  - ○ Would it try to persuade the audience to adopt a new position?
  - ○ Would it enlighten them and give them new ideas to think about?
  - ○ Would it defend a controversial interpretation?

Regardless of your writing task's central aim, professors usually expect you to demonstrate what you're learning in class. Here's where you'll need to use a little gamesmanship, because you'll often find yourself explaining something to someone who already knows more than you do about a subject, or arguing a point to demonstrate that you know how to build an argument. Keep in mind that you're *practicing* scholarly writing—just as in a sport—so your professor wants to see you make specific moves. Like a coach watching a football team run a new play, your professor is observing from the sidelines, expecting to see you demonstrate the strategies and skills you've been learning. Knowing this makes clear why you should elaborate your ideas and explain concepts, even ones your professor already understands. You need to convince your professor that *you* grasp the concept, and explaining it allows you to illustrate the intricacies of your understanding.

The paper that best demonstrates learning is the one that you could not have written before taking a course. Write that paper.

To successfully demonstrate learning, it can be helpful to exaggerate scholarly moves: Refer to key terms in the textbook or mention important theories or topics covered in class. We're not saying you should just regurgitate information to the point where you dilute your own voice and thoughts. You can connect your ideas to concepts you've been studying in ways that display your new knowledge. Scholars must also "overexplain" what they're talking about sometimes because their subject matter is often so specialized and their discoveries are so original that even their expert peers need extra help to understand. Connecting prior knowledge to new ideas helps audiences understand arguments more easily.

Even when it's "just practice," writing for your professor provides an opportunity for you to engage with a real audience and to get more immediate and helpful feedback than professional scholars typically receive. Seize opportunities to interact with your scholarly mentors by asking questions in class, visiting during office hours, and paying careful attention to written feedback. This experience conversing with professors and interpreting and meeting their demands can prepare you to impress future employers who might not clarify their expectations so explicitly and give feedback so generously.

Writing for Your Professor

An argument's purpose also depends on its audience, so it's important to decipher an audience's disposition and their needs. You can imagine your audience metaphorically as a dartboard, with the bull's-eye representing your target audience and the surrounding rings signifying secondary and tertiary audiences (other readers who could also benefit from your work). Apprentice scholars usually aim for professors as their primary target audience. This is because professors can stand in for the scholarly community by identifying credible sources, asking relevant research questions, and suggesting an appropriate style and format for your discipline.

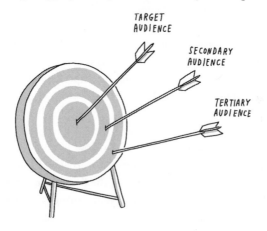

TARGET
AUDIENCE

SECONDARY
AUDIENCE

TERTIARY
AUDIENCE

Writing for Others

Alternatively, some professors will ask you to consider your classmates as your audience, in which case you can write for peers who have a similar level of expertise and experience as you. Just as scholars use "peer review" to improve and validate their work, you may have the opportunity to give and receive feedback from fellow apprentices.

Sometimes, professors will ask you to imagine addressing "real" secondary audiences. For example, you might investigate tax reform and write an evaluation or proposal argument in the form of a blog post, a letter to your legislator, or an op-ed piece for your local newspaper. Each of these assignments would prompt you to consider distinct audiences, purposes, and styles. Even if you don't actually publish your work for an outside audience, such writing can be fun and useful practice—and you can still look for places where publication may be possible (for example, in your student newspaper or an undergraduate research journal).

Undergraduate and even graduate students often write for an audience of no-one-in-particular, which can leave their prose flat and uninteresting. When experienced scholars have something important to say, they try to imagine specific audiences early and often during the writing process by asking themselves:

- Who would care about my topic and findings? Who needs to know what I've learned? Who can act on what I've found?
- What writing styles will those readers expect and find persuasive?
- What publications does that audience read?

Make It Matter

Experienced scholars not only consider who would care about their argument but also **why it matters in the first place**. Thinking carefully about the larger implications of your writing task—how it relates to your course's learning objectives, your personal goals, and other classes—can give you a clearer rationale for doing the work. Having a sense of the *So what?* can also help you make smart decisions. For example, ask yourself:

- Why might my professor have assigned this?
- What does she hope I'll learn from doing this?
- How does this assignment relate to the readings we've discussed in class or other course material?
- What skills or habits of mind might this assignment help me practice, and how could these help me later?

22

> **CONSIDER THIS ➤** Using First Person
>
> For this reflection, consider the appropriateness of using the first person in scholarly writing. We argue that professors really want to hear what you think. However, teachers have probably warned you not to use "I" in formal academic writing. So, you might be wondering,
>
> - How am I supposed to express my thoughts without using the first person?
> - Can I ever use "I" in college writing? If so, when?
> - When might it be inappropriate to use "I"? Why?
>
> Considering what we've said so far, how do you think we'd answer these questions? What have you been taught before, and what do you *really* think?

Identifying the purpose, audience, and larger significance of a writing task can help you make decisions about content, length, organization, and writing style, among other things. Plus, you'll gain greater insight into the authentic reasons for writing, which can increase your motivation.

So What?

Scholars read and write arguments to investigate three basic questions:

1. How do we know what we know?
2. Why do we believe what we believe?
3. How can we improve what we know and believe?

Remember throughout your scholarly apprenticeship that most professors want to hear what *you* think. They will encourage and expect you to demonstrate your knowledge, to exercise your critical thinking skills, and to take some intellectual risks. Typically, they don't want you to regurgitate old knowledge and reuse familiar formulas. We hope you'll take them up on the challenge, using argument as a tool to discover, communicate, and revise what you know, think, and believe.

Now that you more fully understand the purpose of arguing in college and the benefits of adopting a more flexible and complex writing process and a rhetorical thinking approach, you might be wondering about the fundamentals of argumentation. In the next chapter, we introduce you to the ways that arguments work in college and in life. We explain how arguments get to the bottom of problems and controversies, and how they use research and evidence to answer significant questions. We describe how to locate weak spots and assumptions in arguments in order to make a compelling case. And we reveal how effective arguments are built on a strong basis of agreement with shared knowledge, values, and beliefs. This overview will give you a strong foundation for creating arguments that matter—those that answer the important *So what?* question, connect with audiences, and improve our understanding of the world.

What's Next

"What's Next" features will help you transfer and apply what you've learned into other classes and beyond school. Take what you've learned in this chapter and write responses to the following prompts.

1. **Seeing Yourself as a Scholar.** Write a 1,000-word essay that introduces your intellectual interests and motivations to your instructor and your classmates. Use the following questions to get you started:

- Think back on previous writing assignments and try to remember one that you liked the most and one that you liked the least. What inspired or discouraged you? What motivates you—or *might* motivate you—to write?
- What do *you* want to know more about? What questions inspire you most? What beliefs do you want to interrogate and understand? Identify some significant questions—related to your major or to your life—that spark your curiosity.

2. **Real-World Publishing.** Imagining a public version of a college assignment can give you a clearer vision of its purpose and audience. For example, you might imagine a geology paper that compares agricultural practices that caused the 1930s Dust Bowl with current conditions in the Great Plains published as:

   - a feature article in an Oklahoma newspaper
   - a letter of warning to the Department of Agriculture
   - a *National Geographic* or *Smithsonian Magazine* article

Now, write a paragraph that identifies a potential "real" publication venue for each of the following arguments. Explain how you would adapt the assignment for the new audience and publication. It might be useful to examine a real publication for clues about style, format, and design.

- What could an assignment in communication studies that reviews research on how distractions (like texting) affect students' studying be published as?
- What could an autobiographical essay that describes significant events in your life be published, in whole or in part, as?
- What could a psychology assignment that examines the symptoms of posttraumatic stress disorder on veterans of Iraq and Afghanistan be published as?

CHAPTER two

How Do We Argue

chapter checklist

- How do arguments work?
- How can apprentice scholars identify significant arguments that motivate them to write?
- What are the elements of arguments, and how do we build them?
- How do we locate underlying assumptions, gaps, and weak spots?
- How does inquiry inspire argument?

In simple terms, arguments explain *what* we think and *why* we think so. A thesis states what we think, and the rest of the argument shows why. More specifically, arguments can be defined in two different ways:

1. By their function, or what they do: Compelling arguments respond to questions or problems that seem urgent, controversial, or

significant to writers and their audiences. They help us create and communicate answers and solutions, and they influence us to modify what (or how) we know, believe, think, or act.

2. By their form, or how they're structured: Arguments are comprised of four main elements: a claim, support, linkages, and some explanation of why the argument matters.

Where Do We Find Arguments?

Arguments originate from a *catalyst*: a gap or imperfection, an unknown answer, or an unsolved problem that matters to the writer. The catalyst could be as simple as an employee facing financial difficulty or as complicated as the federal deficit. We build arguments that respond to these significant, practical or theoretical controversies.

Let's consider some examples from school and the world beyond that illustrate how arguments can be used to solve a problem or answer an important question.

- **Scholars** use arguments to explain and improve our world. In recent years, for example, increased occurrences of school shootings in the United States have led us to wonder, *Why do these tragedies occur? What causes people to do such terrible things? What might be done to prevent future violence?* Researchers in psychology, sociology, criminal justice, and other disciplines conduct investigations and build arguments to help us understand and address problems like these.

- **Government and military intelligence experts** use arguments to inform politicians. Analysts piece together information from limited or incomplete sources, compare different versions of what might be happening, make judgments, and draw conclusions about what they think. Their answers help to justify foreign policy actions of all kinds.

- **Criminal trial lawyers** use arguments to establish guilt or innocence. Juries decide questions of guilt or innocence based on the cases presented by prosecution and defense attorneys in the courtroom. The justice system seeks the truth about the case, but regardless of what actually happened, the verdict determines a defendant's fate.
- **Scientists** discover evidence through research, which others use to build compelling cases for new laws or regulations. For instance, in the 1920s, a German scientist posed the research question, *What diseases might be linked to cigarette smoking?* Other scientists conducted follow-up research and gathered mounting evidence of the dangers of smoking, which eventually led governments to require health warnings on cigarette packaging.

These examples illustrate a defining feature of arguments: All arguments—whether they intend to solve practical problems or simply deepen our understanding of an issue—**begin with a question or uncertainty and use some method of investigation and case building to arrive at a conclusion**. That is, honest jurors, politicians, and scholars examine the evidence *before* drawing conclusions.

Clearly, arguments have significant implications when they influence decisions that affect people. In government, such decisions can determine whether programs receive funding or soldiers go to war. A trial can determine a defendant's freedom or death. Arguments can carry serious ethical consequences that writers and audiences must weigh.

What about Scholarly Arguments?

Right about now, you might be thinking that some scholarly arguments you've read or heard about don't seem all that significant, practical, or urgent. In the examples we listed earlier, the issues are clearly important to the world. In contrast, oftentimes scholars work

CONSIDER THIS ➤ Starting with Questions

For this reflection, consider the following: We believe the scholarly approach of case building increases the chances of finding the truth or the best decision/answer possible. However, this process (starting with a question and withholding judgment until investigation is complete) might be different from how you have been taught to develop arguments:

- When you write, when do you come up with a thesis?
- When were you taught to consult sources?
- How do you think the writing process might affect scholars' ability to discover accurate information, to think objectively, and to build ethical arguments?

in such narrow specializations that their work seems insignificant or impractical to people outside their scholarly community. However, such work is significant and compelling to those writers and their audiences. In fact, a scholarly community signals the importance of such work by publishing arguments for everyone to hear.

Of course, scholars don't always address problems of great urgency or practical significance, but even when their work is theoretical or esoteric, their arguments respond to a catalyst that matters to them and to their audience. For example, scholars might:

- discover a disciplinary question that puzzles them,
- feel aggravated by a problem in their teaching,
- vehemently disagree with another scholar's findings, or
- notice something new that contradicts previous experience.

Such catalysts compel scholars to investigate and to write arguments for others in their field to consider and build upon.

Here are examples of arguments that scholars make to each other:

- A literary scholar, on the basis of textual evidence, biographical information about an author, and historical information about the time and place of a publication, argues for a new interpretation of a famous novel.
- An education scholar, on the basis of theories about learning and results of experimental teaching, argues for a new method of effective instruction.

Apprentice scholars can feel more motivated and be more successful when they identify similar gaps and imperfections. If you can find a catalyst that really interests you—something you want to figure out—you can get a taste for what it's like to solve a scholarly puzzle. The next few chapters explain how to discover catalysts that ignite your curiosity. Finding a *reason* to write (beyond the I-need-to-pass-this-assignment excuse) will help you develop as a scholar. It might even feel less like practice and more like something that *matters*.

Inquiry-Based Argument

As you may recall from the first chapter, scholars use arguments to seek truth and justify discoveries that result from careful investigation. This means that scholars often don't know their thesis when they begin writing, but rather *discover* it through investigation and research. Their process is guided by inquiry—an attempt to gather information and create understanding.

For example, consider the smoking example that we cite earlier in the chapter. When scientists initially questioned the health effects of cigarette smoking, they began their research process with a question or a hypothesis; they suspected that smoking might not be good for us. *After all,* they thought, *you're inhaling smoke.*

By investigating piles of medical records and discovering that many people suffering from lung cancer were, indeed, heavy smokers, scientists began to assemble irrefutable evidence that built a case against smoking. As evidence of cigarettes' danger mounted, the US government's warnings (or arguments) grew proportionally stronger, from a statement in 1966 that sounded more like opinion ("Cigarette smoking may be hazardous to your health") to statements of fact like we see now ("Smoking causes lung cancer, heart disease, emphysema, and may complicate pregnancy").

In other words, the thesis intensified as the evidence became stronger: "We *suspect* this might be hazardous . . ."; "We *think* this is dangerous"; "We *know* that cigarettes can kill you!" The thesis, which originated in a question, became more "certain" and convincing as the support accumulated.

TRY THIS ➤ Explore Current Inquiry-Based Arguments

For this exercise, explore the arguments surrounding a current social or political issue that interests you, such as the local food movement. Read a few popular sources, like newspapers or magazine articles, and at least one scholarly article, and then discuss the following in class:

- Who are the various stakeholders in this issue (for example, individuals, organizations, and governments who have a vested interest in the matter)? What are their concerns? What arguments do you hear them making?
- What questions or controversies do these arguments raise?
- What characteristics of your community (context) promote or limit these discussions? For example, arguments about the local food movement might be different if you live in a farming community or a large city. What economic or cultural factors might influence the stakeholders? What is the dominant political affiliation, and how does that affect people's views on the issue?

Implications

The smoking example demonstrates how arguments can gradually change the way we think about issues over time. What we know, think, and believe evolves through investigation, new experiences, and persuasive arguments.

If you don't think that arguments can influence what we know, think, and believe, consider the effects of:

- arguments made by civil rights leaders who changed how we think about equality
- arguments made by feminists who influenced the way American families function
- arguments made by activists who demanded health care reform
- arguments made by respected mentors who inspired you to question a previously held opinion

These examples illustrate that inquiry and argumentation (the results of investigation, discovery, and thinking) have tangible effects on our daily lives. Can you think of more examples of arguments that have influenced what you know and how you live?

Indeed, the best arguments are the ones that have important *implications*—consequences or effects that answer the "*So what?*" question. For instance, arguments can inspire readers to reconsider their position, to modify their behavior, or to open themselves up to another possibility. Or arguments can evoke a change in the writer herself: for example, when she develops a deeper understanding of an issue or problem, when she encounters new viewpoints, or when she experiences the peace of mind that comes from justifying her beliefs and values. A change can occur in the audience if they become willing to adjust their thinking, to compromise, to find a new solution, to investigate further, and so on.

As with an argument's catalyst, implications can be stated explicitly or inferred by the reader. Sometimes we tell audiences how and why our arguments matter so they won't miss the impact. Research articles often begin with a section that contextualizes the study's significance (called a Research or "Literature" Review) and conclude with a section that discusses the larger implications for the research findings. Whether or not we tell our readers outright how and why our arguments matter, we at least hint at some implications so they're not left to wonder, *So what?*

Compelling arguments have significant implications that not only change what audiences think but also inspire follow-up questions and arguments. In this way, the process is circular (see Figure 2.1). For example, we might read a *Science* magazine article that concludes that we are less happy when our minds wander. One implication of this argument might be that we should pay more attention to what we're doing while we're doing it. Discovering this might lead us to ask, "What techniques can we use to quiet our mind?" Now, we have a catalyst—an inspiration for research that might ultimately lead to an argument about the benefits of meditation. See how the process works?

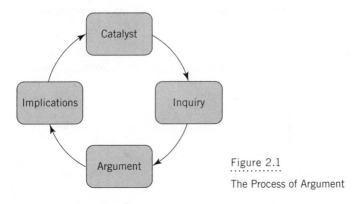

Figure 2.1
The Process of Argument

Can you imagine how this cycle helps knowledge to evolve?

TRY THIS ➤ Use Precise Vocabulary

For this exercise, take a break from the chapter's content to examine and experiment with some language choices that writers make.

We have attempted to write this book in an engaging, straightforward, and informal style. That includes not overwhelming readers with technical jargon or unnecessarily complicated words. However, you'll notice that we occasionally choose less familiar terms to express precise meaning. (In a previous section, for example, we described some scholarly work as "esoteric.")

Part of what makes language marvelous—and writing potentially fun—is gathering a deep pool of available vocabulary. Whenever you read, keep a dictionary or smartphone app handy so you can acquire new words for your own use.

Beware, though: Scholars who use big words just to sound smart do no favors for themselves or their readers. If we need a complex word to convey a complex idea, that's fine, but often we don't.

Effective writing is deliberate and precise, not overcomplicated.

What do you think of our choice to use "esoteric"? What other words or ways of expressing this idea would work as well or better? To reflect on the effects of using sophisticated vocabulary, experiment with the following:

1. Write a simple sentence.
2. Consult the thesaurus to rewrite the sentence with more sophisticated words.
3. Revise the sentence to strike a tasteful balance between sophistication and clarity. Then, compare with a peer and defend your word choices.

How Do We Build Arguments?

Imagine an argument as a bridge between a writer and reader. The **thesis** is the roadway, built by investigation and thinking. The road will not stand alone without displaying our investigation and thinking for readers to scrutinize. We must build **supports** to hold the road up and **linkages** to tie everything together, as in the suspension bridge drawn below.

The thesis is our argument's central **claim**, a debatable or controversial idea that we're proposing to our audience. A thesis can be stated explicitly or implied. Although it often appears in the beginning of an argument, sometimes we state our thesis most clearly in the conclusion, because that's what it really is: the conclusion or result of our investigation and thinking. Sometimes the thesis can be more like a hypothesis (used in scientific method), when it's a tentative thesis that needs to be tested and validated through investigation and argumentation.

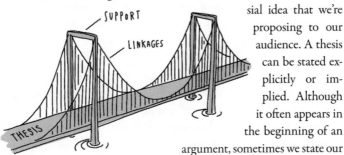

Supporting Claims

Because claims are controversial or open to question, we pair them with some kind of support that our audience will trust. The basic structure looks like this: [Claim] because [support]. For example,

> **Claim**: "You should keep reading"
> because
> **Support**: "this chapter will be really useful."

In everyday arguments, we call this kind of support a "reason," but a reason is actually another kind of claim that our audience might question (like "this chapter will be really useful").

Rather than relying only on reasons, scholars seek the firmest, most well-developed supports they can find, ones that critical audiences will trust. The three most common categories of support used by scholars are evidence, verification, and illustration.

Evidence includes anything we can observe. During an experiment, for example, we might observe a chemical reaction or response from a plant that we're investigating. We can also use evidence acquired through personal experience, as when we witness an event or observe a film or work of art. When writing a literary analysis, we can use quotations from a poem or novel as evidence for our interpretation. As we discuss in Chapter 6, we typically use evidence to activate our audience's sense of logic or reasoning.

Verification includes things we can look up. Students often support arguments by summarizing, paraphrasing, and quoting from scholarly articles or books to corroborate their claims. Lawyers reference laws and legal precedents as verification. Scholars rely on established theories and previous research to verify their work. Verification often determines the credibility of an argument.

Illustrations involve things we imagine. For example, we might offer a hypothetical example or fictional narrative to support our thesis. Like other illustrations, figures of speech such as analogies and metaphors can evoke an emotional response from the reader.

- Evidence is a **primary source**, something that you can collect and analyze yourself.
- Verification is a **secondary source**, which means someone else has already analyzed or interpreted the evidence.
- Illustration is an **original source**, one that you create or borrow for a particular argument.

Table 2.1   KINDS OF SUPPORT

EVIDENCE Something you can observe	VERIFICATION Something you can look up	ILLUSTRATION Something you can imagine
• Empirical data • Personal experience • Textual evidence	• Previous research • Law or precedence • Established theory	• Fictional narrative • Hypothetical example • Analogy or metaphor

When might these different kinds of support build credibility, activate reasoning, or evoke emotion?

Of course, some kinds of support can cross over into more than one category. For example, sometimes personal experience can be used as evidence but also carry emotional impact. A hypothetical example can either evoke emotion or activate reasoning. Sometimes empirical data or statistics can build credibility. What's most important is that we think carefully about what the support should accomplish: *Do we want it to build credibility, activate reasoning, or evoke emotion?* We select the appropriate kind of evidence for our specific purpose.

Evidence tends to be the strongest kind of support because we trust most what we can observe. Evidence connects most clearly and certainly with reality and truth. Evidence also works well for different kinds of audiences, whereas verification is usually based in a specific culture. For example, the US Constitution would provide convincing verification for an audience of US citizens, but probably not for Canadians. Likewise, sociologists might not trust or find relevant the theories and research used by literary scholars. As the most speculative form of support, illustrations can evoke the most inconsistent but potentially powerful effects on audiences. We discuss ways to support arguments in much greater detail throughout the rest of the book.

For an argument to be successful, our audience must agree with or accept the support we present. Whenever an audience doubts or considers our support controversial, the bridge collapses. Sometimes collapses occur when the audience doubts the accuracy of evidence or misunderstands an illustration, but most commonly, supports fail when we haven't linked them properly to our claims.

Linking Support to Claims

Linkages connect supports and claims together. A linkage, also known as a premise, explains the "because" part of an argument. Often, these linkages go unstated, but they are always present, whether or not we make them explicit. For example, we might argue that people shouldn't smoke because smoking is unhealthy. The unstated or assumed linkage is that people should not do unhealthy things.

You might think that linkage is obvious or "common sense," and so it doesn't need to be stated explicitly, but you've probably heard what can happen when you assume. In this case, we shouldn't assume that linkage is "obvious" or uncontroversial because lots of people who know the risks of smoking do so anyway. Countless doctors and government officials have warned people about the dangers of smoking, yet many people continue to smoke. Why? Because many people disagree with the notion that people should not do unhealthy things. For them, the linkage is open to question—a claim that needs support.

Linkages are just as important to arguments as claims and support. In fact, a distinguishing characteristic of scholarly argument is the extent that scholars go to scrutinize linkages and make them visible. That's why scientists use elaborate statistical calculations in their research: to validate the strength of linkages between evidence and the conclusions of investigation. In Chapters 6 and 7, we explain more fully how to design and test the linkages between claims and support.

Table 2.2   ARGUMENT ELEMENTS AND THEIR FUNCTION

ELEMENT	FUNCTION
Catalyst	The argument's inspiration, such as the question or problem that prompted the argument
Thesis or central claim	The debatable or controversial idea
Support	The evidence, verifications, and/or illustrations used to defend the claim
Linkage	An explanation of how a support holds up a claim
Implications	The consequences, effects, or larger significance of an argument

Can you imagine how these elements come together to form an argument?

An Everyday Argument

To illustrate the basic components of an argument, let's consider an example of an everyday workplace argument. Like many everyday arguments, this example begins with a claim supported by reasons. But remember, reasons are actually claims themselves—debatable statements—not evidence, verification, or illustration. As soon as the reader or listener disagrees with a reason, we must provide better support.

Everyday arguments like this are actually claims stacked on top of other claims. This kind of argument can work when we argue with friends or acquaintances who share a lot of background knowledge, but whenever we encounter points of disagreement, we must support our claims with evidence, verification, and/or illustration. We must eventually base the argument on something that we agree about, that's not open to question. This is especially true with arguments written for a demanding, sophisticated audience. In a later section, we'll show how a scholarly argument does just that.

Let's imagine a scenario where an employee is feeling financially strapped, so he approaches his boss to build a case for a pay raise. The dialogue goes like this:

EMPLOYEE: "I deserve a raise." (*thesis*)
BOSS: "Um, so do I. But why should I give *you* more money?"
EMPLOYEE: "Because I work hard, I'm indispensable, and I'm underpaid." (*reasons*)

The employee's argument should seem familiar, since the layout resembles the kind of argument that most of us learned in high school. His main claim, or thesis, asserts that he deserves more pay. To support his thesis, the employee gives three reasons that he thinks his boss will accept. **Effective arguments always build on some basis of acceptance or agreement.** If the boss agrees that her employee is hard working, indispensable, and underpaid, she's likely to give him a raise (if she has the authority to do so, her budget allows, and so forth). However, as we can see from the dialogue, the argument only works if the boss accepts the reasons provided. Note that the employee has not yet offered evidence or verification to support his claims:

BOSS: "I agree that you're a hard worker, but tell me more about how indispensable you are."
EMPLOYEE: "Well, I have more experience doing this work than anyone else in this office, and I'm a good problem solver." (*more reasons*)
BOSS: "Can you give me some examples of problems that you've solved that nobody else could?"
EMPLOYEE: "Sure. Remember that time …?" (*evidence*)
BOSS: "Okay, so now I see how you're a hard worker and sometimes indispensable. But so is everyone else. Why do you think you're underpaid?"
EMPLOYEE: "Because other employers keep offering me more money."
BOSS: "Can you show me some of those job offers?" (*verification*)

40

Getting to the Bottom of Things

Notice how difficult it may be to get to the "bottom" of an argument? Whatever reasons the employee provides, the boss can always dig deeper, asking for more support. With an especially complicated or controversial argument—or when addressing a demanding audience—this process might go on for a long time before reaching the bottom or finding some basis of agreement.

Let's look at that original argument once more in a graphic format that highlights how its structure can unfold (see Figure 2.2).

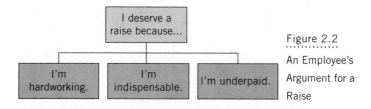

Figure 2.2

An Employee's Argument for a Raise

Notice that the employee's three reasons are really claims.

Again, if the boss agrees with the basis provided, she might be persuaded. If not, the employee must dig deeper to build a stronger, more elaborate foundation for her argument, like the one shown in Figure 2.3.

Thus, we can imagine a brick building, where the thesis must rest on a strong foundation of support. Any block that's doubted or not accepted by the audience can cause the argument to teeter or crumble like a tower of blocks (think of the game Jenga). As we provide better reasons and more evidence to meet the needs of our audience, the basis of our argument grows larger.

In scholarly arguments, we drill down until we find much more solid ground to support our arguments. You can see how an everyday argument might work when both the person arguing and the audience share a lot of background knowledge. But in the workplace

Figure 2.3

An Employee's More Developed Argument

Can you imagine what evidence or verification the employee could use to support his claims?

example, the employee might need to provide evidence of his work productivity or examples of his contributions. Or he may need to verify that he has received job offers from other companies. His foundation would have been stronger if he had built these supports into his argument from the beginning.

Learning to anticipate and meet the needs of a demanding audience (the way scholars try to do) can help you make more compelling and convincing everyday arguments, too.

TRY THIS ➤   Assemble the Elements of an Argument

For this exercise, practice building the elements of an argument. To identify a catalyst, brainstorm with other students about a problem that you've observed at your school. Develop a thesis to resolve the problem and think of what kind of support would convince professors or administrators to implement a solution. Then create a block structure like the one above to represent how you could present your proposal.

Making Assumptions

Assumptions are any elements of the argument that either the writer or the audience are thinking but not saying. Assumptions can include things such as

- evidence, verification, or other background knowledge that we assume our audience already knows ("You've seen my work, so you already know I'm a good problem solver")
- values and beliefs ("You value hard work") or
- the catalyst or implications of our argument ("You know I've been struggling financially, and you can imagine how much harder I'll work if I get a raise").

In arguments, assumptions always lurk below the surface, like the immense base of an iceberg that is much larger than its visible top. Indeed, what's assumed in an argument is greater than what's said or written. That is to say that **assumptions make up the bulk of the total argument**, even though they're typically hiding, unstated, below the surface.

Of course, we always have to make some assumptions when creating an argument because we can never say everything we mean. In everyday arguments, we often leave most of our assumptions "submerged" when we argue with people we know well. We can rely on shared background knowledge, familiar culture, and so forth. When the employee in our everyday argument example provides reasons disguised as support, he is making assumptions. In this case, however, he wrongly assumes that his boss will not question his reasons or need additional support.

When we engage in scholarly arguments, we're arguing with strangers—readers who don't know or trust us already and who will scrutinize our arguments carefully. (In fact, rigorous scholarly "peer reviews" are normally "double blind"; that is, the author's and reader's identities are not known to each other during the editorial process.) Scholarly arguments therefore seek to be as complete as possible so that readers can critique our work. Scholars know that writing is different from speech: we can't clarify, reword, add more detail, or respond to objections once we've published or "turned in" the argument. So we work diligently to ensure that our support is as solid and complete as space allows, that our linkages are clear, and that our "bridge" is fortified.

One way to avoid making assumptions is to make our unstated assumptions (reasons, catalysts, prior knowledge, and so forth) explicit. Metaphorically speaking, we raise as much of the argument above the water as we can.

"Above-Water" Arguments

Since arguments have the power to change our minds, behaviors, beliefs, and actions, scholars scrutinize their arguments carefully. As an apprentice, you might find the task of finding and fixing faults in arguments daunting, but your goal is to become a skeptical reader who isn't persuaded easily. You might think that your arguments will become too long or overexplained. But scholars leave little to chance. Every sentence in the argument is there for a reason, whether it be to prevent an objection, to answer a question, or to fully explain a controversial point. As much as is practical, we make our support and linkages visible to our audience: **Arguments that anticipate disconnects—that is, objections and unshared assumptions—have the best chance for changing our audience's mind.**

Taking the time and space to design a complete argument that will satisfy a skeptical audience usually pays off. Doing so not only helps us persuade readers, but we're also more likely to understand our subject in more depth and detail.

TRY THIS ➤ Build Support

For this exercise, take what you learned about making assumptions and apply it to a hypothetical situation.

1. Imagine that you're a teenager who wants to stay out later than usual for a party, but you need to persuade your parent to let you do so.
   a. What claims and support might your audience accept?
   b. What unstated assumptions must your audience share for your argument to work?
2. Now imagine that you're the parent, trying to convince your teenager that staying out late is a bad idea. What support and shared assumptions would make your argument work?
3. Based on how you answered 1 and 2, where are these arguments most likely to break down? What are the potential sources of disagreement or unshared assumptions?

Find the Right Mix

For apprentice scholars, the hardest part of college writing is imagining how much is safe to assume and how much must be made explicit. In other words, how much of our iceberg do readers need to see? As a general rule, **increased controversy requires increased explanation**. A truly "original" thesis will contradict what the audience already thinks, so we have to work harder to earn their agreement.

Here are three of the most common rookie mistakes made by apprentice scholars:

1. **Arguing the obvious.** That is, arguing about something the audience already knows or agrees with. Here, the writer wastes lots of effort supporting a conclusion (thesis) that really doesn't need to be argued.

2. **Arguing without support.** That is, underestimating how controversial a statement is—stating something *as though* the audience already knows or agrees with it when, in fact, they don't. Rookie writers often use unsubstantiated claims to support an argument.

3. **Supporting without arguing.** Sometimes apprentice scholars present evidence, validation, or illustrations without telling the audience what point they're trying to make. Expecting that your audience will reach an unstated conclusion is a trick that works fine in everyday arguments, advertising, or politics. (For example, advertisers expect that handsome men can "sell" products to women.) However, experienced scholars state their claims clearly and explicitly.

So how do we know whether we're making these mistakes?

- **To avoid arguing the obvious:**

a. **Read more.** When scholars think they have an original idea, they review other scholars' work to make sure that their research question or tentative argument isn't old news. (We discuss Research or Literature Reviews more in Appendix B.) You can do the same by consulting scholarly sources; if you find lots of sources that have made your argument already, you might need to find a new angle.

b. **Ask an expert.** A good shortcut is to ask a scholarly mentor, such as your instructor, if the idea seems fresh and interesting. She'll tell you if she's already read too many papers about a tired subject like raising the drinking age.

- **To avoid arguing without support:**

a. **Highlight your argument.** Read your draft and mark the thesis and supporting claims in color (on your computer or with a highlighter). Then review the parts that aren't highlighted: *Do the claims need more support? Is there anything that your audience might question?*

b. **Consult a reader.** Ask a trusted classmate, writing center tutor, or your instructor to review your draft with an eye for assertions that need more evidence or explanation.

- **To avoid supporting without arguing:**
  a. **Use topic sentences.** Like mini-thesis statements, topic sentences can alert your reader to the reason or claim that you're about to develop. Good writing doesn't always need topic sentences, but they can help weary readers (and you) keep track of your points. We discuss more organizational strategies in Chapter 8.

  b. **Search for stranded support.** Make sure that you have clearly linked your claims and support together. *Is it clear what point you're trying to support with that evidence?*

So What?

Arguments use evidence, verification, and illustration (what is known or invented) to support claims (what is unknown or controversial). In effective arguments, the writer's catalyst and the implications for the audience converge to answer the question: *So what?* (See Figure 2.4.)

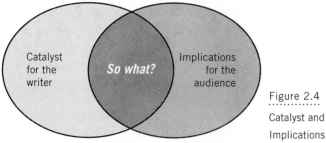

Figure 2.4
Catalyst and Implications

Can you imagine arguments where the writer's and audience's motivations overlap?

two   How Do We Argue?

Now that you know that arguments are a complex network of cata-lysts, claims, support, linkages, assumptions, and implications, you might wonder how you can read arguments carefully enough to detect all of these features. Indeed, before we give any more advice on develop-ing compelling arguments, we'll offer useful strategies for reading, analyzing, and responding to arguments. Responsible scholars wait to advance their own arguments until they have fully listened to what others have said. In order to develop persuasive arguments, we must first discover the most reasonable answers and the best courses of action for our audience. These pursuits require us to read others' words accu-rately, precisely, and critically. After all, our own thinking might be flawed, and it's certainly limited, so we need to take into account the intellectual work of others. Chapter 3 describes techniques that you can use to become a stronger reader—so that you can deeply under-stand others' arguments (both what they say and how they're con-structed) and be ready to participate as an informed apprentice scholar.

What's Next

Take what you've learned in this chapter and write responses to the fol-lowing prompts.

1. **Practice Q & A (Question and Argument).** Integrate the various parts of an argument by creating an outline or graphic that devel-ops one of the following questions:

   - What major should I choose?
   - Which profession should I pursue after college?

   a. State your tentative answers to the question in the form of a thesis. For example: "I should major in [Biology, Business, or Basket Weaving] so that I can get a job that is profitable and prestigious."

48

b. What kinds of support would you need to convince a friend or relative who thinks you should decide something different? Can you think of some evidence, verification, and illustrations that would answer the question more definitively?

2. **Writing and Researching in Your Discipline.** Interview a professor in your discipline to learn about writing and research practices in your field. Then, write a two-page summary of your professor's comments. Some sample questions that you might consider asking are as follows:

- What is the purpose of research?
- How do scholars think and analyze in this discipline?
- What "moves" (such as explicitly stating the thesis early in an argument or using personal opinion to support a claim) do you expect students to make in their papers? What features do you value most in student writing?
- How do scholars in our discipline write? What does their writing process look like?

If you were to present this interview to an audience, you could add a photograph of the person being interviewed or a video or audio clip. Can you think of ways that this might make your presentation more persuasive? Do you think this would add something substantive or just add unnecessary ornamentation?

CHAPTER **three**

How Do We Read Arguments

chapter checklist

- What are the benefits of becoming a better reader?
- How do we read texts as models for designing effective arguments?
- How do we read rhetorically?
- How do we identify and analyze an argument's central controversies?
- How do we read multimedia arguments?
- How do we respond to arguments?

In their daily routines, scholars read much more than they write. As an apprentice, your primary means of learning will be reading other scholars' work. Sure, you'll spend plenty of time listening to lectures or participating in class discussions, but much of your learning will be on your own, reading books or articles assigned by your professors.

This chapter presents strategies that will help you read more efficiently and effectively—that is, so you can remember, comprehend, and analyze what you read with greater success. Just like showing your work in algebra or spending more time with discovery or revision when writing, these techniques may seem awkward at first. But practicing will help you to develop expertise and confidence so that you can work smarter.

Why Read?

You can probably imagine the benefits of becoming a more efficient and effective reader. Reading provides most of the information that you write about, and it's difficult to write about something you don't understand. In fact, many of the problems we see with student writing aren't really writing problems at all, but rather challenges that students have with the demands of college-level reading. Even expert writers struggle when trying to explain difficult content, so before we write about a source, we have to read it carefully enough to understand its argument thoroughly.

Equally important, reading provides models. Every time you read, you should intentionally notice how each argument exhibits the choices of its author, how effectively (or ineffectively) it achieves its purpose. Models can help you learn new vocabulary, sentence structure, style, and persuasive strategies that will gradually strengthen your reading and writing skills.

You may already think of yourself as a good reader. Nowadays, we do read a lot, but we read differently than our parents or grandparents did. Immersed in electronic texts, most of us have become good (though we could always become better) at "surfing," or literally, skimming along the surface of the Web. With some tweaking, the skills you use to quickly browse websites or Wikipedia will also help you handle the volume of reading that you will likely encounter in college.

However, success at surfing may also conceal a weakness. Have you ever been reading for a long time and then suddenly realized that you can't remember what you just read? Have you ever been overwhelmed by trying to make sense of a long, complicated article or book that you were assigned? While you may excel at skimming, you may not be as good at remembering, comprehending, and analyzing what you've read.

Reading requires concentration, engagement, and a quiet mind— all of which are difficult to maintain in our highly distracting society that values technology, multitasking, and immediacy. These priorities have the potential to overload our brains, which is what Nicholas Carr argues in his provocative article entitled "Is Google Making Us Stupid? What the Internet Is Doing to Our Brains" (an excerpt of which is located in the back of this book). Carr summarizes the views of neuroscientists, psychologists, sociologists, and writers who believe that the Internet's scattered, fast pace threatens our ability to concentrate and think deeply. We all can relate to Carr's distracted reading experience. For many of us, if something isn't highly captivating with flashy graphics, bright colors, short snippets of text, and lots of pictures, it won't hold our attention for very long. This is unsettling, given the fact that complex problems and grueling tasks require deep concentration. If Carr is correct, then we need to think carefully about how the Internet affects how we process information.

Practicing reading can train your brain to slow down, to focus, and to move beyond surface-level thinking. These habits of mind are essential for us to be productive members of society. We need doctors who can think through a diagnosis carefully and deliberately, without losing concentration at the drop of a hat. We need senators who can debate an issue at length, without succumbing to distraction. Furthermore, we want these habits of mind to come naturally, which requires practice. Reading is like a fitness class for your brain.

Most scholarly apprentices need additional techniques for handling the demands of college-level reading. Even if you're a confident, effective reader, you should consider trying some reading strategies.

If you're like most college students, you'll need to pay more attention to how you read so you won't waste time or fall behind.

Reading Strategies

The first lesson in strategic reading is to **have a clear, specific purpose in mind every time you read.** Your professors and other scholars rarely read something without a purpose; typically, they read because they're curious about a problem or subject in their field, or they want to keep up with the latest discoveries, trends, or research methods. As an apprentice, you will get to practice the same active approach to reading that scholars take, one that is fueled by curiosity—the desire to know more about the world—and the impulse to respond. To keep your purpose in mind, ask yourself the following questions. You might even write these questions on notecards, which you can reference and answer each time you're reading something for class, asking yourself: Why am I reading this, and what do I want to get out of it?

- Am I reading to get a basic idea of what this is about?
- Am I reading to learn and fully understand a concept?
- Am I reading to analyze or criticize something?

Your answers should determine your reading pace, place, and approach. For example, if you're searching through the library or Internet databases to find sources for a paper, you might only need to scan them to decide whether you should invest more time in reading. When you find sections of a book or article to be useful, then you can layer on deeper reading and analysis techniques. Bottom line: **You shouldn't read everything the same way.**

To get the most out of your reading, you'll need reading techniques that focus on concentration and repetition. If your mind is not actively engaged and you don't review what you've read, you won't remember it, let alone be able to comprehend or analyze new information and difficult arguments. Brain research indicates that **repetition enhances memory**. The more times you think about information or ideas, the better they stick. Also, repeating the information in a slightly different way each time increases your level of comprehension. So, in order to enhance and monitor your concentration, reading experts advocate a reading process that involves three different phases: previewing, reading, and reviewing.

Previewing

1. **Before you read something, scan the table of contents, headings, tables, images, and key words** so that you can formulate tentative answers to these questions:

   a. What are the main ideas?
   b. What is the writer trying to accomplish?
   c. How does this reading connect to the course I'm taking?

2. **Then, skim quickly through the whole text**, refining your sense of the main ideas. Speed up or slow down according to how well you already know the information that you're reading. Move quickly through information that you know well, but don't skip anything or you might miss a key element needed to get the big picture. Don't skim more than one or two minutes without pausing to review what you've just covered.

Reading

Once you've previewed the text, you're ready to begin reading as you normally would, except now you can read much more quickly (probably twice as fast) with greater comprehension because you already know most of what the text is about. As you're reading, try the following techniques:

1. **If you encounter a confusing paragraph, stop** and try to work out what the author is saying. Write down or talk out the points

you understand. Then, skim ahead to another section to see whether the new information helps you better understand what isn't making sense. Write down questions that you have, which you can return to during the reviewing stage.

2. **Take notes while reading**. To amplify your ability to remember what you read, take notes as you go along. Begin with notes about what the text is about. Create an outline or just write down key words and phrases in the margins. You might also be tempted to highlight or underline important passages. This technique works sometimes, but you'll find that writing while reading improves concentration more than just coloring over it. Taking notes will help you concentrate and remember what you learn because writing (especially by hand) activates different parts of your brain. Rewriting information in different words will also deepen your understanding of what you read and will also be good practice for paraphrasing and summarizing.

3. **Write down your reactions to the argument**. Record questions, thoughts that come up while reading, and your response to the writer's ideas. You can make note of these reactions in the margins of the text, in a notebook that stores all of your notes, or on your smartphone or tablet. You can even download apps that assist in this process. For instance, dictation apps turn recordings into written text, so you can record yourself talking out your thoughts and then return to them later.

Reviewing

Lost concentration presents the biggest obstacle to remembering and comprehending what you read. Whenever you forget what you just read, you've lost concentration. That's why we suggest reading and reviewing in a continuous loop. Whether you pause every few minutes, every page, or every paragraph, **stop reading and recall what you just read**. If you can accurately recall what you just read, then continue. If not, you've only wasted a few minutes of effort, so go back and read and review again.

Research suggests that **repetition needs to happen in fairly quick succession after you first learn new material**. If you wait longer between reading and studying new material, you'll basically be starting over, which means you'll waste time and energy having to learn the material again from the beginning.

Remember, these reading techniques are meant to focus your attention. You can also **improve concentration by limiting distractions**. Every time you stop reading to answer a text message, to check social media, or to have a conversation with a friend, you break concentration. Consider finding a quiet place and turning off your cell phone while you study—or better yet, disconnect from your wireless network. You'll end up getting better results in less time than if you allow yourself constant interruptions. You might even discover what reading was like before Google.

Even if you use the techniques we've advocated so far to maintain concentration while you read, making sense of long and complicated arguments takes practice. Part of the problem, obviously, is that most scholarly articles are written for experts, not apprentice scholars. If you lack the deep background knowledge and specialized vocabulary that expert scholars rely on to understand scholarly work in their field, you'll have to work harder to keep up. But as you gain experience, you will gradually accumulate the necessary knowledge and learn to recognize the moves that scholars make to support their conclusions.

Reading Rhetorically: Reading to Discover *How It Says*

As you read more scholarly writing, you will begin to see texts not merely as unquestionable, lifeless, purely objective collections of facts and ideas, but as part of conversations that writers and their audiences use to create and recreate knowledge—and you will begin to participate in that discussion yourself. Closely studying an argument's rhetorical elements can deepen your understanding of its message.

To read and analyze a text rhetorically, we break down the argument to see how it works, without judging or agreeing or disagreeing. The guiding questions of analysis are as follows:

- How is the argument designed?
- What choices did the author make in designing the argument?
- Why did she make those choices?

For example, why did she choose to open the essay with that particular illustration, or why did she choose that kind of evidence? Analyzing texts this way helps us read other writers' work as models for our own. In the next section, we will discuss additional rhetorical elements to examine while reading.

So What? The Catalyst, Purpose, and Implications

As we discussed in Chapter 1, authors write because they are responding to some catalyst: a problem, question, or gap in understanding. Something *motivates* them to write. Maybe they read something and disagreed with the author's argument. Or they discovered a problem that needed a solution. Or they became curious about a question. Something happened. We can better decipher a writer's catalyst if we ask ourselves: *What happened? What is this writer responding to? Where did this idea originate? Why did this topic matter to him?* Whether or not the writer explains or implies a catalyst, effective arguments usually leave clues about the author's motivation to write.

If the catalyst is the cause of the argument, the purpose is its desired effect: what the writer hopes his argument will accomplish. In general, arguments influence how our audiences think or act, so an argument's purpose will be to modify the knowledge, beliefs, or behavior of the reader. Implications involve the larger consequences of an argument: its indirect and unforeseen consequences that go beyond the immediate purposes.

Let's consider an everyday example. Someone becomes irritated about teenagers speeding through her neighborhood (*catalyst*), so she writes a letter to the editor of her local newspaper to raise awareness of the problem (*purpose*). After reading the published complaint, the chief of police sends a patrol car to the neighborhood to set up a speed trap (*implication*).

Now for a scholarly example: A professor who tutors in a writing center notices many students who seem to obsess too much over "later order" concerns in their writing, such as grammar, punctuation, and citation formatting (*catalyst*), so he experiments with different tutoring techniques that shift students' focus to higher order issues, like designing compelling arguments. He shares the results of his investigation in a journal read by faculty at other writing centers, hoping to enhance their tutoring practices (*purpose*). A few readers hold workshops for faculty across disciplines who want to improve how they teach writing, and the tutoring techniques get translated into strategies for teaching peer review in business courses, science labs, and so on (*implications*).

TRY THIS ➤   Practice with the Catalyst, Purpose, and Implications

In this exercise, take what you've learned and try to imagine two or more possible catalysts, purposes, and implications for each of the following examples. Compare your results with a classmate.

- An editorial that criticizes a local politician
- A cigarette package that warns about the health risks of smoking
- A college academic department website
- A consumer survey that polls residents about their spending habits
- An in-class exercise in which you practice thinking about catalysts, purposes, and implications

---

Author and Audience

Knowing something about an author's credentials and background can give us insight into his assumptions, motives, biases, and credibility. We might do some digging into authors' backgrounds (by searching online) to learn about their expertise and what else they've written. We might also search for information about their political, personal, and community affiliations, if we think these factors might influence their argument. Similarly, we imagine the argument's intended audience—their background and demographics (age, gender, income, education, political preferences), values, assumptions, and biases—because all of these elements can influence the writer's choices and the audience's reaction.

CONSIDER THIS ➤ Yourself as the Audience

In this reflection, think about what factors could influence your interpretation of an argument. What are your values, assumptions, biases, and background? What demographics do you belong to (age, gender, income, education, political preferences)? How might these factors affect how you interpret and respond to arguments? For example, how might your perspective on arguments differ from someone significantly older or younger than you?

Genre

Argument genres are like literary genres, such as a play, poem, or novel. They're recognizable because they're designed according to unwritten "rules" or conventions that audiences expect. Genres often use similar kinds of support, writing styles, and organizational patterns. For example, an editorial (*genre*) typically comments on a controversy of public concern (*catalyst*) in order to change public opinion (*purpose*). Or, a warning label (*genre*), in response to a known health risk (*catalyst*), cautions consumers about the dangers of using or misusing a product (*purpose*).

When we recognize an argument's genre, we know its purpose, and we can evaluate it according to established, though often unwritten, rules and expectations. For example, as a moviegoer, when you watch a horror movie, you expect to be scared and startled, maybe even disgusted by blood and gore. You might also get some drama and humor, but like all genres, the horror movie has to follow the rules, mostly, or audiences will be disappointed. There's nothing worse than a comedy that isn't funny or a mystery with no surprises. Later chapters discuss scholarly expectations for appropriate styles, organizational patterns, and so on for genres of scholarly writing.

Context

In some situations, once you understand an argument's genre and content, you've read enough. But we've all communicated and miscommunicated enough to know how important the context can be. For instance, have you ever shown up to a party and realized that you were terribly overdressed? The style you wore last time was clearly too formal for this occasion. The context changed, so your choice was no longer appropriate.

An argument is also influenced by its larger context: where and when it was written. When reading something written long ago or far away, we may not be able to fully understand a text's meaning or purpose unless we know something about the time period, culture, community values, controversies, current events, and so on. Thinking about these elements gives us a richer picture: We can see more of what is going on in the background of the argument.

Identifying the Controversy

To help you identify what an argument is really about, concentrate on finding, detangling, and categorizing the main controversies or points of disagreement that the argument addresses. You'll notice that most complex controversies involve multiple issues, but they can fall into at least one of five categories (see Table 3.1).

Complicated arguments often involve several controversies. Categorizing those controversies can help us sort out points of agreement

Table 3.1 CONTROVERSY CATEGORIES

CONTROVERSY CATEGORY	QUESTIONS THESE ARGUMENTS ANSWER	EXAMPLES OF EVERYDAY ARGUMENTS AND SCHOLARLY ARGUMENTS
Existence or fact	*Is it true? Did it happen?*	• Does Country X have nuclear weapons capability? How do we know? • Do scholarly apprentices struggle with the demands of college-level reading?
Definition or interpretation	*Does this case fit the definition? How do we interpret this information?*	• What kinds of weapons does Country X possess? • What kind of reading problems do college students have?
Cause, consequence, or circumstance	*What caused this? Was it intentional? Are there extenuating circumstances?*	• What prompted Country X to develop nuclear weapons? • Why do college students struggle with scholarly readings?
Evaluation	*Is it right or wrong? Is it serious enough to warrant our attention?*	• Do Country X's nuclear capabilities pose an imminent threat to global security? • Do students' reading difficulties present a serious obstacle to learning?
Jurisdiction, procedure, policy, or action to be taken	*What, if anything, should we do about it?*	• How should we respond to Country X as a nuclear threat? • What actions might professors and students take to improve reading skills?

What controversy are you currently debating with friends, and which category would that issue fall under?

and disagreement so we can seek a resolution more efficiently. The controversy categories are generally *sequential* or *hierarchical*: until we agree about the facts, definitions, and interpretations (what's happening and what it means), there's no sense in finding solutions (enacting policies and procedures). Let's consider an everyday example and then something more scholarly.

Here's an everyday example: Let's imagine that you're arrested for murder. (Ok, this isn't such an everyday example after all—but stay with us here.) During your trial, the first controversy that must be resolved is what actually happened—the facts of the case. If the prosecution does not have enough evidence to establish that, for example, you were the person who stabbed your [girlfriend, boyfriend, spouse, companion, or partner] to death, then you will go free. Once the prosecution establishes that fact, then they must establish that your actions fit the legal definition of murder. The cause (motive) and circumstances might affect the definition: Was it premeditated? A crime of passion? An accident? And the definition—first- or second-degree murder, involuntary manslaughter, and so forth—will determine the penalty or action to be taken according to the law.

In your trial, it doesn't make sense to skip steps and decide whether you should get the death penalty before we determine whether you were the person holding the knife. Indeed, that's why many countries, including the United States, base their justice systems on the presumption of innocence (innocent until proven guilty)—to guarantee citizens due process before enforcing penalties. The process doesn't always work, but would you rather face a lynch mob?

And here's a scholarly example. Political scientists take interest in constitutional matters and how they affect public policy. Before addressing a policy like gun control, they often go back to the US Constitution for guidance (verification). And before interpreting how the Constitution defines the gun rights, legal and political scholars would check an important fact: What does the Constitution actually say? Unlike a criminal trial where the facts are obviously controversial, you might think that the literal wording of the Constitution would never be in question. In everyday conversations, it often is. For example, you've probably heard people say something like "The Constitution guarantees my right to life, liberty, and the pursuit of happiness." Well, that's wrong. That phrase is in the Declaration of Independence, which was signed by delegates to the Continental Congress, not ratified by the states. Facts that can easily be observed or verified are simple enough, but consider controversies about the existence of something as complicated as climate change.

With regard to gun rights, the Second Amendment states that the "right of the people to keep and bear arms shall not be infringed." Long before scholars can discuss policies and regulations, they must investigate what that statement means. Several factors affect that meaning, including what the founders may have meant by that language, the circumstances of the original context versus today, legal precedence, and so forth. And if we can ever agree on a definition, we must address jurisdiction before we can discuss policy: What jurisdiction do states or federal governments have to regulate firearms? Can your college ban guns on campus?

As you can see, these categories of controversy can help us methodically navigate complex issues to get at what we call the heart of the matter or sticking point—the main controversy. After all, arguments are designed to *resolve* controversies, so we can argue more effectively and efficiently if we can settle what we already agree about and direct our attention (argument) toward what matters most. As we discuss in Chapter 5, the main controversy is where we can find a compelling thesis.

TRY THIS ➤ Analyze an Argument Rhetorically

For this exercise, read an essay and then write a rhetorical analysis: an essay that examines an argument's rhetorical situation in order to understand the author's choices. Follow these steps:

1. Read the essay "Is Google Making Us Stupid?: What the Internet Is Doing to Our Brains" by Nicholas Carr (which is published in the July/August 2008 issue of *The Atlantic*, a magazine that analyzes current cultural, global, and technological issues). You can find an excerpt of this essay on pp. 262–269 in this book.
2. While reading the article, analyze the argument's rhetorical elements (purpose, audience, author, genre, and context). Refer to the list of questions on pp. 16 and 17 for guidance on completing a thorough analysis. Also, take note of the controversies that Carr addresses. You might even list five to ten of the main issues he discusses, and then categorize them according to the kind of controversy they are (existence/fact, definition, cause, evaluation, and jurisdiction/policy).
3. Write a three-page rhetorical analysis of the article. Your goal is to fully describe the argument's rhetorical situation and to explain *how* the text makes its argument. You can write for an audience of peers who have already read Carr's essay (so you don't need to summarize the article). For assistance organizing your essay, read ahead in Chapter 8.

A Guided Reading of a Scholarly Argument

Now that you have a firm grasp of how to read rhetorically, we're going to layer in analysis techniques that you can use to locate and understand an argument's elements (the fundamental features we describe in Chapter 2). In the next section, we will walk you through the steps of reading a scholarly argument, with an eye for an argument's catalyst, thesis, support, linkage, and implications. We recommend that you use these techniques whenever you read scholarly work; in fact, you can reference the table on p. 70 whenever you're reading an argument. Before we begin, read the article "A Wandering Mind Is an Unhappy Mind" by Harvard psychologists Matthew A. Killingsworth and Daniel T. Gilbert (reprinted in this book on pp. 257–261). Then, follow along in the essay as we model the analysis.

Identify the Catalyst

As we're reading Killingsworth and Gilbert's article, we have to ask ourselves three important questions, in order to identify the catalyst:

- What initially motivated Killingsworth and Gilbert to investigate the connection between mind wandering and happiness?
- What gap in research or unanswered question prompted their attention?
- Why did *this* problem or question matter to these psychologists?

The researchers cite two pieces of information that stirred their curiosity and led them to hypothesize, or tentatively claim, that mind wandering might interfere with happiness. We can locate these statements in the first paragraph of the article. Can you find them?

If you still can't figure out the researchers' catalysts, look for an important clue in the introduction by asking yourself:

- What is the research question?

Identifying what prompted Killingsworth and Gilbert's investigation helps us understand how and why they developed their hypothesis, and how this led them to investigate people's thoughts and feelings. The catalysts and hypothesis that we detected are shown in Figure 3.1.

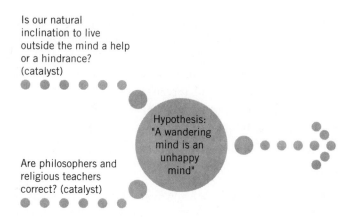

Is our natural inclination to live outside the mind a help or a hindrance? (catalyst)

Are philosophers and religious teachers correct? (catalyst)

Hypothesis: "A wandering mind is an unhappy mind"

Figure 3.1

The Catalysts and the Hypothesis in "A Wandering Mind Is an Unhappy Mind"

Do you notice how the psychologists' hypothesis responds to the catalysts?

Identify the Central Claim

To locate the article's central debatable statement (hypothesis), we focus our attention on the introduction. Sometimes a scholarly argument will state a thesis, instead of a hypothesis, which is just a more definitive statement. To locate the thesis or hypothesis, we ask ourselves:

- Where is a potentially controversial, overarching idea that Killingsworth and Gilbert will need to support?
- What is the title of the article? Does that give us a clue about the article's thesis?

We can also look for the thesis in the conclusion, since this is a research article. Oftentimes research articles answer their research questions at the end, after they have described their methods and results (a scholarly research article is outlined in Appendix B). In this case, Killingsworth and Gilbert restate their thesis in the conclusion, but this time with more certainty because they have validated their hypothesis. After we locate the thesis, we can evaluate the argument's support.

Identify the Support

While we typically find an argument's catalyst and thesis early in an argument (and perhaps again at the end), the body of the argument usually contains the support. To find the support, we look for examples of evidence, verification, and/or illustrations that hold up the thesis. In the case of "A Wandering Mind Is an Unhappy Mind," we notice that the support is primarily evidence, in the form of empirical data (statistics), which provides "the results of observation and experimentation" (*Oxford English Dictionary*). When we diagram the elements of the argument, we see a strong base of support (see Figure 3.2).

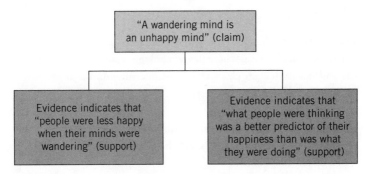

Figure 3.2

The Elements of the Argument in "A Wandering Mind Is an Unhappy Mind"

What are some possible implications of these findings?

CONSIDER THIS ➤   Missing Support

For this reflection, find one claim in "A Wandering Mind Is an Unhappy Mind" that isn't supported with evidence, verification, or illustration, and think about why the authors did not offer support. In order to understand this choice, ask yourself:

- Where was this article originally published?
- Who is the original audience, and what background knowledge would most readers have?

   Then, compare your answers with a peer and discuss the following:

- When writing, how do we decide whether claims, evidence, and linkages are open to question and therefore need support?

   Develop a list of criteria for assessing whether we need to support claims.

Identify the Linkages

Finally, we can identify examples of linkages in the *Science* article when we look for places where the psychologists connect their statistical findings with their claim that "a wandering mind is an unhappy mind." To find these, we ask ourselves:

- Where do Killingsworth and Gilbert explicitly discuss the connection between their thesis and their research results, in order to tie up any loose ends?
- Where do they help readers interpret their statistics?
- Where do they correct potential misunderstandings that readers might have about how their data led them to conclude that people are less happy when their minds wander?

We can usually spot linkages at the end of paragraphs because that's an effective place to remind readers explicitly how support verifies, illustrates, or provides evidence for a claim. As is common in many research articles, Killingsworth and Gilbert help readers interpret their data, so that we can see how they have drawn their conclusions. Recognizing linkages helps us connect their hypothesis and support, so we are more likely to understand that most people are emotionally affected by mind wandering.

Identify the Implications

A scholarly argument's implications may be stated or implied. If they are stated, we usually locate them in the conclusion. But Killingsworth and Gilbert do not explicitly address the consequences of their argument or suggest specific changes readers should make (like learning to become more focused). To identify unstated implications, as yourself:

- What are the consequences or effects of the argument?
- What is the larger significance of the argument? Why does it matter?

Deciphering an argument's implications helps us discover what the writer wants us to *do* if we are moved by the argument (see Table 3.2). We can also identify questions for further research, issues we might take up in our own writing, and other potential "leads" (catalysts).

How Do We Read Multimedia Arguments

Many arguments that we encounter on a daily basis include multimedia elements. Often a picture, graphic, sound clip, or video can be more persuasive than words alone.

Advertisements, social media, television, and websites are only a few of the sources of multimedia messages we encounter. We use

Table 3.2   IDENTIFYING AND INTERPRETING A SCHOLARLY ARGUMENT'S ELEMENTS

ELEMENT	QUESTIONS TO ASK YOURSELF	PLACES TO LOOK
Catalyst	• What gap, problem, or unanswered question prompted the writer's attention? • Why did this problem or question matter to this writer?	The introduction
Thesis or central claim	• What is a potentially controversial, overarching idea that requires support and directly responds to the catalysts? • What is the title of the article?	The title, introduction, and conclusion
Support	• What evidence, verification, and/or illustrations hold up the thesis?	The body paragraphs
Linkage	• Where does the writer explicitly discuss the connection between a claim and support, in order to tie up any loose ends? • Where does the writer correct potential misunderstandings that readers might have about the link between the claim and support?	Near the end of all paragraphs and in the conclusion
Implications	• What are the consequences, effects, or larger significance of the argument (stated or implied)? • Is there a call to action?	The conclusion

How might this table help you read complicated arguments?

many of the same principles to examine visual arguments that we would to analyze and evaluate print-only arguments:

- Who is the author? Who is the intended audience?
- What is the controversy or debatable claim?

- What support does the argument contain?
- What is the purpose of the argument?
- How does context affect its meaning?

The strength of multimedia arguments—their vividness—can also be a weakness. Vividness makes these arguments memorable or "sticky," as advertisers say, and vividness can also evoke emotional responses easily. Ironically though, because multimedia elements like images are often used as illustrations rather than evidence or verification, they must assume a lot in order to work. Claims and linkages are often more implicit, so we must ask ourselves:

- What is missing from this argument? What has the author left to my imagination?
- What connotations, symbolic meanings, or cultural assumptions am I supposed to supply?

Let's examine the following visual argument, a cigarette warning label created by the US Government (see Figure 3.3). This is one of a series of labels that have been proposed to replace the surgeon general's warning, but current litigation has not settled whether the labels will actually be used.

When analyzing visual arguments, like any others, it's useful to begin with the basic elements of the rhetorical situation. In this case, the label's purpose is to discourage women from smoking during pregnancy. From the stated reason, "Smoking during pregnancy can harm your baby," we can infer that the thesis of the label is "Don't smoke when pregnant." There may also be secondary claims, such as (1) "Don't smoke around pregnant women"; and maybe even (2) "Don't smoke in the presence of babies." The illustration of an apparently unhealthy baby implies a linkage between smoking and harm to infants, either born or unborn.

Figure 3.3

Cigarette Warning Label

How does this label activate reasoning, build credibility, and evoke emotion?

The primary audience is likely women who are pregnant or who are considering pregnancy, since the label explicitly warns about potential harm to "your baby." The label may also warn others about the dangers of secondhand smoke, particularly fathers, who might smoke in the presence of infants or pregnant women. To appeal to a younger audience, the creators may have chosen to use a comic book style, instead of the graphic photographs that other antismoking ads and labels use. Notice, too, that unlike the old cigarette warnings, the surgeon general's verification is not emphasized. Instead, a small copyright of the US HHS (Health and Human Services) appears in the background. Now the author of the government's warning appears to be the cigarette company or brand itself, whose name appears in large font at the bottom of the label. Suggesting that the message comes from the manufacturer rather than the government might be more persuasive for some audiences.

In this ad—like in many visual arguments—illustrations and emotion dominate the argument. In fact, the only support offered by the label is an illustration, a drawing of a distressed newborn baby in an incubator. The baby faces the viewer, crying out, with a breathing tube and electrodes. This disturbing illustration may evoke a strong enough emotional response to provoke action from smokers who probably already know about associated health risks—even though the argument presents no evidence or elaborate verification.

The argument's implications go beyond the risks of smoking that affect babies. By including a phone number, 1-800-QUIT-NOW, the label connects its message to a larger antismoking campaign and clearly states what the audience should do.

What other implications or questions does the label raise? For example, how might people respond to an argument that's literally in their hands? Would this label be powerful enough to dissuade consumers from buying a pack of cigarettes? Would it be powerful enough to persuade smokers to call the QUIT NOW hotline or stop smoking around children? Why might this labeling campaign be considered controversial?

TRY THIS ➤ Analyze a Visual Argument

For this exercise, find a compelling advertisement that argues with words and images, and then analyze the visual argument, using the following questions:

- What claims does the ad state or imply?
- What kinds of support are provided?
- How do the visual elements (images and document design features like color and font) work together with the words?
- What makes the argument effective, or not?

Responding to Arguments

Although reading may be your primary
means of learning in college, writing
is what typically provides evidence
of that learning. Your teachers will
often assign papers to test how well
you comprehend what you read.
They also expect that you can deepen
your understanding *as you write*
about a text, so they will ask you to
"respond" or "critique" or "analyze." You should begin by asking your
professor what he means by these terms, but a typical response assignment asks you to figure out what the text is arguing, either subtly or
explicitly (analysis), and develop some kind of reply.

To respond effectively to a reading, you should think of your
source as a catalyst. A good place to begin such a response is by evaluating the argument made by your source. Evaluation is not the same
thing as summary, which—as we explain on pp. 93–95—is a recap of
what an author says. Sometimes apprentice scholars summarize an
argument (that is, restate its most important parts) instead of evaluating it because they're reluctant to critique a published author, or they
don't know how to evaluate an argument, or they simply prefer the
easier task. Instead of regurgitating the gist of a message, evaluation
involves judging whether the writer's strategies were effective for her
intended audience and purpose (or for other audiences and purposes).
Again, when evaluating an argument, we're still not arguing with the
writer, but rather using her argument as a model from which we might
learn what choices are more or less effective. Once we're done analyzing and evaluating, we will understand our source well enough to
argue with it, to respond to it with our own opinion by agreeing or
disagreeing—or, preferably, by adding something new.

It's important to realize that simply agreeing with your sources
doesn't yield especially interesting results. Disagreeing is a bit more

74

interesting, but we want to avoid a simplistic "I'm-right-you're-wrong" kind of debate. So, whenever we're responding to an argument, we agree or disagree in order to *extend* the argument and contribute something new. Think about it: in any conversation, the most interesting person is the one who introduces a new idea, a fresh perspective on the topic.

However, you might believe you have little to say in response because you don't know much about the topic. Or you might have been trained only to comprehend an argument, not to engage in a conversation with it. Summary, analysis, and evaluation enable you to dig deeper into *understanding* your sources (what other scholars have already said) in ways that can yield something fresh to say. Another way to come up with a significant response is to do some brainstorming. The "Believing and Doubting Game" can deepen your understanding of what you read and, at the same time, give you plenty to write about.

Play the Believing and Doubting Game

This strategy offers an efficient place to begin because you start with what you already know and think, focusing your attention on the writer's arguments. The questions are inspired by a brainstorming and peer review technique called the "Believing and Doubting Game," which was developed by writing expert Peter Elbow. The Believing and Doubting Game helps you to think more carefully about how you relate to an argument as an individual reader (see Table 3.3).

The technique works like this: First, you "believe" the text fully by asking yourself questions that help you understand and extend the writer's ideas. Then, you "doubt" the text by asking yourself questions that help you challenge and even refute the writer's ideas. Running through these questions whenever you read can prepare you to design an argument of response, or even just to have more to say during class discussions of a reading.

Table 3.3   THE BELIEVING AND DOUBTING GAME

"BELIEVING" QUESTIONS	"DOUBTING" QUESTIONS
• What are the text's strengths? What does it do well? • Which claims do I agree with? • Which underlying values or beliefs do I share with the author? • How does the argument relate to my life? • What other ideas, examples, or scenarios fit the writer's argument?	• What are the text's weaknesses? • Which claims do I disagree with? • What are the writer's biases? • What does the writer overlook? What questions are left unanswered? • What claims need more support? • What linkages are faulty or missing?

Can you think of more questions that you could use to "believe" and "doubt" an argument?

TRY THIS ➤   Play the Believing and Doubting Game

In this exercise, practice playing the Believing and Doubting Game:

1. Read the essay "With Liberty and Justice for Some" by apprentice scholar Emanuel Grant (reprinted on pp. 270–278). Then, spend 30 minutes playing the believing game, in response to his essay: Practice responding to the argument by answering questions that help you extend Grant's ideas.
2. Spend 30 minutes playing the doubting game: Answer resistant questions that help you challenge Grant's ideas.
3. Write a blog post that responds to Grant's argument and designs an argument of your own. You won't be able to address all of Grant's points, so select a few that interest you and compose a response that extends the conversation about this topic.

Mind and Mine the Gaps

Arguments can never address a controversy exhaustively. Writers inevitably leave unanswered questions, alternative interpretations, missing links, and things left unsaid. These are opportunities for readers to join the conversation. We recommend that you "mind these gaps" just like subway riders do in New York City. *Minding the gap* means watching out for logical holes, missing examples, discrepancies, questions—spaces for you to insert your opinion. Along the same lines, once you find a gap, you can *mine* it: dig deeper, excavate the argument, and search for new idea "gold." When you plunge your shovel into the argument's holes, you can discover hidden gems and valuable never-before-seen insights.

So What?

We cannot expect that you will use every strategy we've presented every time you read. In fact, we hope you don't, because that would be inefficient. Just as expert writers adapt their process to the task at hand, so should you adapt your reading process to your purposes for reading.

Keep in mind that we can't enter scholarly conversations (make our own arguments) until we're familiar with *what* others have said and *how* and *why* they've said it. Once we understand the larger conversation surrounding a topic—through using active reading techniques—we can begin to find something compelling to contribute.

The concepts and techniques we've introduced can help you become a more efficient and effective reader who reads rhetorically, categorizes an argument's controversies, looks for gaps in arguments, and develops interesting responses. These lessons will pay off when you read and evaluate sources, which is the subject of the next chapter. In Chapter 4, we identify criteria for reliable and credible sources and recommend strategies for finding and using (summarizing, paraphrasing, and quoting) scholarly arguments. We also explain how to use sources as catalysts. Before we delve into the details, we describe how scholars typically consult sources early in their writing process and wait to finalize their thesis until they've done some research and investigation. This news might challenge you to reconsider your research and writing habits.

What's Next

Take what you've learned in this chapter and write responses to the following prompts:

1. **Online Reading Guide.** Reading onscreen is increasingly common. You might already use e-textbooks or do the majority of your reading on a laptop or tablet. Given what we've said about the importance of careful and critical reading, combined with the challenges of technology that Nicholas Carr cites, what problems might you encounter when reading electronic texts? Do you think e-readers help or hinder reading? What strategies could you use to combat any ill effects of reading online? What apps or resources might help you? Develop a list of strategies and resources for reading online, which you can share with your classmates.

2. **Multimedia Presentation.** Go online to the TED Talks website (http://www.ted.com/talks) and find a video of Matt Killingsworth's presentation, "Want to Be Happy? Stay in the Moment." The presentation covers many of the same arguments he and his coauthor made in their article, "A Wandering Mind Is an Unhappy Mind." Watch the video and answer the following questions:
   a. What did the presentation accomplish that the article could not? How did it do so?
   b. Did seeing and hearing the author make his arguments more or less credible? Why?
   c. What kinds of multimedia did he incorporate, and how did that enhance his arguments?

CHAPTER four

What's a Good Source

chapter checklist

- At what stage in the writing process should we locate and integrate sources?
- How do we find and evaluate credible, reliable, and useful sources?
- Why—and how—do we summarize, paraphrase, and quote?
- How can we manage the research process?
- How can we use sources to generate ideas?

You might wonder why we're talking about sources before we've developed an argument to write about. After all, scholars use sources to back up their arguments, so we need a thesis *before* we know which sources we need, right?

Not exactly. Scholars rarely begin writing an argument before they've reviewed the work of current and previous scholars. In fact, scholars almost always contextualize their own arguments in light of what others are saying or have said in the past. Although scholars frequently conduct research to update or corroborate previous work, our work won't be compelling if others have already answered our question or covered our topic sufficiently. So **starting with sources helps us:**

- Verify whether our work will yield something new
- Begin collecting information to answer our research questions
- Provide context for our investigation by relating our study to another scholar's work
- Borrow methods of investigation or theories that worked for other scholars
- Identify views, assumptions, or conclusions to build on or diverge from

What's most important is that we know what has already been said and can explain how our discussion or approach is different. Ideally, we want to offer readers some *news*.

An Elementary Way of Using Sources

To understand the process of finding and using sources, let's compare some different versions of writing assignments you may already know well. Scholarly apprentices sometimes get confused because their past experiences with "persuasive" papers and "research" papers make these two genres seem like they have little in common. Think way back to elementary or middle school, when you were probably taught how to write simple versions of a research report and an opinion paper. The process might have looked something like this:

Research report (Steps may not be in this exact order)
1. Pick (or be assigned) a topic, like *Bears*.
2. Find some convenient sources on that topic. Start with Wikipedia, of course, and begin assembling information like this: "There are

many kinds of bears, for example, polar bears, grizzly bears, panda bears, etc. Bears like to eat honey and baby seals. Some bears hibernate in winter . . ."

3. Take notes and/or cut and paste blocks of text and information into a document.
4. Organize your notes and information into an outline (optional) or rough draft (preferred).
5. Glue together sources with some of your own words, transitions, and so on.
6. Write an introduction that ties everything together, with a thesis or "main idea" that really doesn't make a substantial argument, like "Bears are very interesting creatures."
7. Restate your introduction as a conclusion.

Persuasive paper
1. Pick (or be assigned) a controversy, like *Gay Marriage*.
2. Choose a thesis based on what you already know and think about your topic: "Gay marriage should be [legalized or outlawed] because . . ."
3. Think of reasons why your thesis must be right.
4. Find sources that support your argument (only if required by your teacher).
5. Ignore sources that contradict or complicate your argument.
6. Write the equivalent of a five-paragraph essay (even if it's six or more paragraphs).

Okay, so that's a little exaggerated, but you get the point. (Exaggeration, also known as *hyperbole*, can be an effective persuasive technique. And it's one of our favorites.) To be clear: neither the research report nor the opinion paper is a good scholarly model.

As different as they seem, these kinds of "research" and "persuasive" papers do share a common ingredient. Each typically has a *thesis statement*, though each thesis functions differently.

A research paper thesis often functions like a topic sentence in a paragraph. It simply tells the audience what the paper's *all about*. In fact, writing expert John Bean calls this kind of assignment the "all about" paper. The thesis may seem somewhat argumentative (after all, not everyone finds bears interesting), but the argument itself isn't really very controversial or important. The audience is left wondering, *So what? Why would anyone want to argue about that?*

In contrast, although the persuasive paper *seems* very argumentative, if it lacks research (that is, outside sources), then it's really more like an unsupported opinion paper. How will you persuade a tough audience without something to support your thesis? A scholarly audience will wonder, *So what? Why should I believe this argument?*

CONSIDER THIS ➤   Introducing Sources

For this reflection, examine the way we introduced the quotation from John Bean. We called him a writing expert and used an "attributive tag" to introduce the phrase. Attributive tags like these help us clearly delineate between our ideas and other scholars' thoughts:

a. "According to the author, _____"
b. "The text states _____"
c. "The writer makes the point that _____"

You might also point out your sources' credentials (area of expertise, level of education, relevant accomplishments) like a lawyer would do for an expert witness. In this instance, did the amount of information we provided about John Bean make you trust him?

Writing that Follows Research

Experienced scholars combine the best qualities of the persuasive paper (a compelling argument) and the research paper (effective support), like this:

1. **Begin with a very specific problem or question** within your discipline that interests you: a catalyst.
2. **Review scholarly publications** to make sure that your question is worth asking or that your problem still needs solving, so that fellow scholars won't be wondering *So what?*
3. **Design and conduct some kind of investigation** to solve the problem or answer the question, such as conducting an interview or distributing surveys. Chapter 6 includes additional guidelines for conducting original research.
4. **Report results of the research**, in the form of an argument, to colleagues in your discipline via a scholarly conference presentation and/or publication.

Because scholars create arguments *from* previous scholarship, original data, practical experience, and other inspirations, **writing typically follows research** for experienced scholars.

In fact, here's a little secret: experienced scholars often dread writing as much as students do. Most scholars find answering questions and solving problems more stimulating than writing papers about what they discover. Once they've answered their question, scholars can get bored and just want to move on to the next problem. The last thing they want to do is worry about APA citation styles and manuscript formatting, but they know they have to publish their work so others can use it—and they understand that they must present their work in certain established forms (genres and styles) that their readers recognize and value.

Apprentices can begin to practice scholarly writing by investigating problems and questions through the work that others have done. Often the problems will be assigned by instructors who already know the key issues and background well, and who can even provide sources through course readings.

Other times, you can choose your own questions and engage in what we call "library research." Rather than collecting and analyzing raw data (a "primary" source), scholarly apprentices mostly use information that has already been examined and reported by others ("secondary" or "library" sources). As you mature as a scholar, you might even be invited to conduct original experiments or study historical artifacts or archives as primary source materials.

For now, you will often rely on library sources—used as verification—to support your arguments. Since you'll be borrowing the credibility of more experienced scholars by citing their work, you'll need to choose your sources carefully.

Sifting through Sources

So how do we know which sources are best? Let's begin by considering our trusty Internet pal, Wikipedia.

As you've probably noticed, many teachers dislike or distrust Wikipedia. Why do they discount it as a credible scholarly source? There are several reasons:

1. **Stability.** Wikipedia content changes all the time, and therefore your reader may not be able to go back and find the same information that was there when you accessed it. Although folks are getting more used to the idea of dynamic, electronic publications, most readers still trust printed text more (though this may change with time).
2. **Credibility.** Anyone can write Wikipedia entries, and contributors do so anonymously (known as "crowdsourcing"). Scholars care about credentials, which is why they place more trust in authors with proven expertise. If they don't know you, they don't (yet) trust you. That's why apprentices must earn credibility as they go and borrow it from more established sources.
3. **Reliability.** Scholarly publications undergo a rigorous review process through which experts scrutinize quality. Wikipedia does have an editorial review process, but it's more organic and egalitarian. Contributors edit each other's entries, and there's virtually no pecking order of expertise, just rule by consensus.

Scholars generally don't trust unstable sources written and reviewed by anonymous crowds. So, if you're trying to impress a scholar, citing Wikipedia probably won't work (unless, of course, you're writing a paper *about* Wikipedia).

But here's another little secret: Most of us use Wikipedia anyway—experts and apprentices alike. Let's consider why.

Despite objections about its stability, credibility, and reliability, Wikipedia provides a vast, easily accessible, and *relatively* accurate storehouse of information about almost anything. It's useful as a reference for gathering background information—a good place to get a general sense about a topic, then dig deeper into other, more reliable sources. Notice that Wikipedia entries often contain extensive references and suggestions for "further reading," some of which might be trustworthy enough to use as scholarly sources.

CONSIDER THIS ➤ Wikipedia on Wikipedia

For this reflection, read Wikipedia's entry on Wikipedia and discuss the following in class:

- What other issues does the entry raise about Wikipedia's credibility?
- Which references in this entry seem most trustworthy as scholarly sources? Why?

So What's a Better Source?

As we say throughout this book, when it comes to what works in writing, everything depends on the particular audience, purpose, and context.

four   What's a Good Source?

As we suggest earlier, the most trustworthy sources for an audience of scholars will be those written by other scholars in reputable publications that use a rigorous review process, such as a reputable scholarly journal. Figure 4.1 shows a spectrum of sources in order of increasing scholarly credibility.

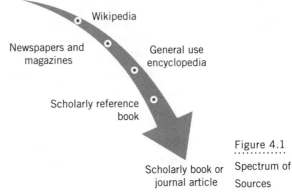

Figure 4.1

Spectrum of Sources

Can you think of why an urban legend might lack credibility, even if it's completely plausible?

Notice that we haven't claimed that any of these sources are necessarily invalid or incorrect. Urban legends, for example, are sometimes true and often believable. That's just our point: **Credibility depends on the particular audience and situation**. If you're arguing with a friend about sports, you probably don't need a scholarly source to seem convincing—maybe *SportsCenter* will do.

Even if they may not be the most credible scholarly sources, social media, the Internet, newspapers, and other popular sites can be good places to start searching for interesting topics to write about. Scholarly print publications lag behind popular and electronic media because it takes so long for scholars to complete their research and have it reviewed (and revised) for publication. So Wikipedia isn't necessarily a bad place to start.

Just don't stop searching after skimming the first few paragraphs on Wikipedia or the first page of Google hits, and remember to think carefully about what kinds of sources and evidence your audience will trust. Experienced scholars mistrust sources that haven't been scrutinized by experts, so if you want to communicate or argue with them, you need to be able to find, understand, and use academically credible references.

How Do We Find Credible Scholarly Sources?

Ask other scholars. When we're initially investigating a topic and looking for the best sources, we often start by asking other scholars to identify journals, books, or articles that experts in the field know well. These books and journal articles may even be on our colleagues' shelves. From these, we secure a clearer starting point, which can save us a lot of time. Also, when other scholars read our work, they will expect us to reference these key sources to prove that we know what we're talking about, or at least that we've done our homework.

You should do the same.

Instructors hold office hours for a reason: to help students. Take advantage of this time and meet with a professor who is an expert in the field that you're studying. For example, if you're writing a paper on alienation and the effects of social media on teenage girls, you might speak with an English professor specializing in feminist literature or a sociologist who studies gender, who could direct you to reliable and useful sources. This might seem intimidating and time consuming, but beginning your research in the right place can save you many hours of frustration.

Plus, most professors will be thrilled to help. Imagine how you'd feel if you spent years studying something like the feeding habits of Amazonian frogs, waiting patiently for that one student who showed genuine interest in your expertise.

We also consult reference librarians who can help us identify research techniques that will yield better results. Librarians work in research databases a lot more than we do, so they can share lots of techniques and shortcuts. For example, librarians can help us select appropriate databases for our topic or narrow our database search terms. They can also show you how to locate sources by proximity, since libraries and databases cluster sources by subject headings.

If we already have a handle on search techniques and want to work independently, we'll **explore a research database**, like Academic Search Complete. (If you don't have easy access to library databases, Google Scholar can help find scholarly articles in a pinch.) Since so many journal articles are stored online, we can access full-text versions of most. These databases only include material that has been peer reviewed, so we're usually confident that the articles are accurate and well researched, although they could still be biased or controversial. In addition to being reliable, many articles are searchable, so we can move through them quickly using the *find* function (Ctrl-f) to search for relevant sections of an article.

If we're looking for more general sources, like magazine articles or newspaper editorials, we'll **search online**. We might look at company websites, blog posts, or personal Web pages, depending on our purpose. But whenever we're viewing public sites like these, we shift our rhetorical thinking into overdrive. We ask ourselves:

- Who wrote this? What makes them credible?
- What are the authors trying to achieve?
- How do they support their claims?
- Is anyone profiting from this? Who? How might money-making efforts influence the content?
- When was this written?
- Will this still be here next month?

This kind of investigation is essential to determine whether an online source is credible and worth using. Sources need to convince us that they deserve a place in our argument. We expect to do a lot of hunting around, so we don't just settle with the first hits that our search engine picks. Settling is a rookie mistake. Unlike most online navigation that is quick and easy, searching for good sources takes time and patience. So don't just go with the first stunner you see; there are lots of fish out there, and the best catch might not appear until the third page of results.

TRY THIS ➤ Practice Sifting through Sources

In this exercise, practice searching for credible sources. As a class or in small groups, select a research topic that interests you—any topic that you're truly curious about. Then, search online for three to four credible sources.

1. If your library has access to research databases online, begin by entering search terms in a scholarly database, such as Academic Search Complete.
2. Select the full-text version of an article that seems promising and use the *find* function (Ctrl-f) to search for subterms that will lead you to the article's most relevant sections. For example, if you find a long scientific article on the health benefits of meditation, you might search for words like "stress" or "relationships" to quickly find the sections of the article that you're most curious about. Jot down notes on the most interesting information and points you find.
3. Search online for high-quality public sources, such as articles from a reputable newspaper, magazine, or organization's website. Use the questions above to evaluate these sources' credibility.
4. Skim each of the source's Works Cited or References page for other articles and books that are worth checking out. Once you've found some promising leads, try following that "paper trail" or at least make a list of additional sources to consult.
5. Wow your classmates by sharing your fascinating discoveries.

What's the Best Research Container?

Another criterion that you should consider when sifting through sources is *scope*. Look for the right-sized research container for the scope (the breadth and depth) of your argument. If your topic is broad, begin with a source that has enough room to meet your needs. **Big topics need big research containers**.

Here we're not talking about *Encyclopedia Britannica* or Wikipedia, either. If your topic has been studied extensively, you might find a more exhaustive and credible reference book on the subject in your school library. For example, for a topic as broad as World War II, our school's library holds several scholarly encyclopedias (including the five-volume *The Encyclopedia of World War II*) that could help you discover exactly what you want to write about.

Once you narrow your topic a bit, you might search your library for more manageable, medium-sized sources. Scholarly books, which are often 200–400 pages, focus more narrowly than most novice scholars might think. Our library has hundreds of books on more focused World War II topics, including *The African American Experience in World War II* or *London at War, 1939–45*.

BROAD SUBJECT

NARROWED TOPIC

RESEARCH QUESTION

Scholarly journals publish cutting-edge research, so they usually present specialized topics for subject matter experts. Most journal articles are about twenty to thirty pages in length, with an appropriately narrow scope that "fits" into that page count. For example, a journal article about World War II would have a very specific focus, like "Replacing Battleships with Aircraft Carriers in the Pacific in World War II," published in a discipline-specific journal, *Naval War College Review*. One advantage of a recently published journal article—as opposed to a book or an encyclopedia—is that it reflects the most current debates in a field.

Novice scholars sometimes think that journal articles are the quickest read because they are the shortest. Wrong. They might be short, but due to their specificity, they often require prior knowledge about a subject before they can be useful. That's why it's usually smart to educate yourself with a "bigger" source before diving into a dense journal article.

If you want to write about a contemporary controversy, you might also consider starting with online sources that examine topics from multiple angles, such as *Issues and Controversies* or *Opposing Viewpoints in Context*. Much like encyclopedias for a big topic, these sources can help you narrow a broad topic. Say, for example, you're interested in comparing educational standards in public versus private schools. You might begin with *Issues and Controversies* and from there, find a book like *Keeping Them out of the Hands of Satan: Evangelical Schooling in America* or an even more specific journal article, such as "School Vouchers and Student Attainment: Evidence from a State-Mandated Study of Milwaukee's Parental Choice Program," from *Policy Studies Journal*.

Following a research process like this one, which moves from "large" research containers to "smaller" ones, can help you narrow your scope, minimize frustration, and learn a lot more.

How Do We *Use* Sources?

Scholarly writing is a conversation. When scholars join that conversation, they listen awhile to get their bearings before they speak. Before trying to solve a problem or answer a question, scholars typically review what others have already discovered. They don't want to unnecessarily repeat research that has already been conducted or pursue questions that have already been answered. As they review the previous work, scholars often *summarize*, *paraphrase*, and *quote* other scholars in a "literature review" or "research review," which they publish with their findings to help their readers enter the conversation and share background information.

Why Do We Summarize, Paraphrase, and Quote?

Using written sources requires skill in three techniques: summary, paraphrase, and quotation (see Figure 4.2). Summary is the most important and common technique, and incorporates paraphrasing and sometimes quotation. Scholars use summaries to *distill* a source—either all or part of a text—into a more condensed, selective version. In practice, scholars typically summarize just the parts they need, such as a source's findings or the methodology. While a summary is a scaled-down version, a paraphrase is typically about the same length as the original passage.

Summarize

- To capture the whole text in a smaller amount of space
- To identify the most important parts of a larger text
- To condense

Paraphrase

- To represent a portion of the text in your own words
- To restate an idea in a different style but maintain the original length
- To translate someone else's words into your own phrasing
- To avoid quoting too frequently, in order to maintain a consistent tone

Quote

- To express a specific idea verbatim
- To credit an author's original term, phrase, or controversial statement
- To boost your credibility

Figure 4.2

The Rationale for Summary, Paraphrase, and Quotation

How would you decide when to use each of these techniques?

Why is it important to understand this distinction? Because you'll need to use the technique that best suits your purpose.

In many classes, you'll need to report on your library research by summing up major theories and significant previous research on your topic. In these cases where you're describing something long and complicated, a summary will allow you to *select* main points and *condense* the original. However, if you're restating just a paragraph or a sentence, a paraphrase will allow you to *translate* the original into your own words—not just do a synonym swap—while maintaining a similar length.

Generally, scholars prefer summarizing and paraphrasing over quoting. That's because both of these techniques allow the writer to maintain his voice and display his grasp of the material. Think about it: We can't condense or translate something unless we really know what it says, so when we summarize and paraphrase, we demonstrate that we understand the source. Simply quoting doesn't give us the opportunity to display this depth of understanding.

Quoting less also makes your writing smoother because readers don't need to transition repeatedly from your style to other writers' styles. Quoting is more acceptable or even necessary in English or writing classes because those disciplines care most about language. Scholars writing in the sciences or business, on the other hand, may quote rarely, if at all. Still, you can bet that in most scholarly writing you'll be doing a lot more summarizing and paraphrasing than quoting. These techniques leave a lot more room for your own ideas and arguments than if you flood your writing with quotations.

But summarizing a source can be difficult.

How Do We Summarize?

The task requires us not only to understand *what* the text says but also *how* it says—how it's structured, how it builds its argument, how it achieves its purpose, and so on. After we understand the original in its entirety, we can select the most relevant details. We focus on main claims and don't get bogged down in the details. Just like someone who builds model cars or airplanes, we construct a scaled-down version of the original that will fit the size of our paper. We also have to consider the proportions of the original: If the original is twenty pages long, we can't spend one-third of our summary on the first two pages. We don't have room for every detail, but we can't leave out any major parts, either. So we look carefully at the original and how all of the parts fit together before we decide what to include and what to leave out.

To select the right parts, it's helpful to get in the "believing" mindset: give the author the benefit of the doubt and try to understand exactly what he is trying to accomplish. Imagine how all of the parts could possibly fit together (even if they seem unrelated). Assume that the author's intentions are logical. Remain unbiased in your judgment of the ideas. Withhold evaluation and see the absolute best in the text so that you can write fair and nonevaluative summaries. There's plenty of time to discount ideas, reject messages, and tear apart evidence in assignments that call for analysis or response. But, when summarizing, we try to be nonjudgmental and play the role of an objective messenger. To do that successfully, we follow these steps:

1. **Read the text** carefully, paying attention to the genre of the original and how it's organized. For example, if you're summarizing a research article and you know how they're typically organized (described in Appendix B), you know where to find the main claims and support. Reading is the most important step because if we don't understand what we read, we can't summarize it well.
2. **Create a "reverse outline," or schematic, of the text's layout.** This technique comes in handy whenever you're reading complicated arguments, and even when you're revising your own writing.

To compose a reverse outline, first write down the main claim of each paragraph, either in the margins of the text or on a separate sheet of paper. You might be able to find a topic sentence, or you might need to express the main ideas in your own words; aim for one phrase or short sentence per paragraph. Forcing yourself to identify each paragraph's main claim helps you break down a complex argument and recognize its many parts. Then, write those points in outline form so that you can see the progression of the ideas on a single page, if possible.

3. **Select the most relevant points.** Study the reverse outline, and figure out the most central points—the blueprint of the text—the ones that someone who hasn't read the source would need to know in order to grasp the text's purpose and argument.

4. **Write a summary** that aims to be unbiased, clear, and proportionally accurate but shorter than the actual text. The first time you write the summary, it might still be pretty long. Don't worry about that; you can condense it further later. Just try to clearly convey all of the text's main points.

5. **Revise the summary** to make it even shorter. Now's the time to make the most brutal cuts. Figure out what deserves to be there and what can be left out. Beware also of any inaccuracies, judgmental language, or quotations that need citations.

How Do We Paraphrase?

How do we paraphrase appropriately, without running the risk of plagiarism (stealing another person's words or ideas)? The key is to represent the source closely without using the author's style or phrasing. To do so, follow these steps:

1. **Read carefully** the paragraph or sentence that you want to paraphrase.

2. **Think about what it's saying**. Mull it over. Chat with yourself about the ideas. (Experienced scholars talk to themselves all the time.)

3. **Rewrite the gist of what the source says**, without looking at the original paragraph or sentence. Resist the temptation to glance at the author's exact wording; otherwise, you might be influenced by the author's style and find it difficult to rephrase. The only reason to return to the original is to get a clearer grasp of the content. If you review the original, then repeat Step 2 before trying to write again.

4. **Double check the original** to ensure your paraphrase is accurate and significantly different from the original, in terms of sentence structure, word choice, tone, and possibly even length.

5. **Cite the author** with an in-text citation or use an attributive tag. We talk more about citation styles and practices, along with quotation techniques, in Chapter 9.

TRY THIS ➤ Practice Summarizing

In this exercise, practice summarizing by reading and summarizing the essay "With Liberty and Justice for Some" by apprentice scholar Emanuel Grant (printed on pp. 270–278). The essay contains approximately 2,400 words. Use the techniques we've covered so far to write a summary of it. Use your word processor to track how many words you use. Maximum word count = 240, or 10% of the original. Then, in class, compare your summaries with your peers: How similar are they? Which parts are different? How did you decide which details to include and which ones to omit? Did you include any quotations? How did you decide which quotation(s) to include?

After comparing your notes with classmates, condense your summary even further: eliminate 100 words so that you have one paragraph that contains only the most important claims and support in the essay.

Managing the Research Process

The process of sifting through sources can be overwhelming, and it's easy to get your sources confused. That's why it's imperative to **take good notes** throughout the process. Some writers record all of their notes in one place, like a notebook or research file. Other writers like to record information about each source on separate note cards or files.

When you find a particularly useful quotation, write it down in your research notebook or on a note card or type it into a document. That way, you can cut and paste quotations, along with their citations, into your paper easily and efficiently.

As you conduct your research, invest time in recording bibliographic information for all your sources: author, title, publication information, and page numbers for any quotations or paraphrases. **Keep meticulous records.** That way, you won't waste time shuffling through papers, trying to remember where you found a memorable phrase.

Using Sources to Generate Ideas

The process of conducting library research and summarizing other scholars' findings helps us discover a catalyst and begin collecting support for a potential thesis. You can also use the following techniques to help generate ideas:

1. **Play the Believing and Doubting Game** with each of your sources to discover new applications and arguments. Get in the habit of asking yourself these questions every time you read a new source.
2. **Find a source with which you strongly disagree**. Take note of everything you find fault with, which will help you clarify where you stand if you're unsure of your own position on a controversy.

3. **Create a table that compares and contrasts your sources**. You can use the table to do a number of things: (1) to outline the various perspectives; (2) to identify the heart of the matter, according to these sources; (3) to find points that the sources overlook; (4) to highlight central disagreements; and so forth.

4. **Pair two sources in conversation with each other**. Imagine what the authors might say to each other if they were together. Imagine what new insights they might reach, given the chance to converse. Predict the answers that one author might give to the other author's questions, given their respective positions.

5. **Look at one source through the "lens" of another source**. This strategy allows you to do a couple of things: (1) apply a theory that one source describes to another source's examples or case studies or (2) consider the implications of one scholar's argument on another scholar's position. For example, you could apply Darwin's theory of natural selection to an anticloning article, in order to discuss how cloning might enable survival of the fittest.

All of these strategies can prompt an original thesis, which we discuss in the next chapter. However, keep in mind that some of these strategies require you to speculate and build a case for your interpretation—in those instances, you'll need to explain and support your thinking. We talk more about how to support your arguments and use sources in Chapters 6 and 9.

So What?

Reading and using sources doesn't need to be drudgery. The process can come alive when we think of ourselves as conversing with interesting writers who are discovering fascinating things that might even change the world in some small way.

For instance, polar bears might not be here in 50 years. Scientists are investigating serious threats endangered animals face, and their work has significant consequences. Similarly, your state may be trying to decide what to do about gay marriage laws; perhaps your church— or you personally—are trying to decide your position on these arguments.

Our point is that jumping at the first answer trivializes an issue or a problem's significance. Well-educated people think carefully about how to read and process sources so that they come to sound conclusions.

Now that you have a strong grasp of the research process and scholarly ways of finding and evaluating sources, you're ready to begin thinking about a thesis. In the next chapter, we argue that the best way to develop a compelling thesis statement—one that your audience will want to read—is to pursue a stimulating question. We offer concrete strategies for finding important and inspiring questions, and we detail the steps of refining and narrowing a thesis statement to make it more complex. This chapter also recommends some thesis statements to avoid and gives alternative options like the evolving thesis and ones with a stylistic flair.

What's Next

Take what you've learned in this chapter and write responses to the following prompts.

1. **Read Further**. To see what other scholars have to say about this chapter's topic, read "Helping Students Use Textual Sources Persuasively" by Margaret Kantz, which is published in *College English*, Vol. 52, No. 1 (Jan. 1990), pp. 74–91. You should be able to find this article through your library's databases or in print form. Then, answer the following questions:
   - Who do you identify with more: Shirley or Alice?
   - What was enlightening about this article?
   - What particularly good advice does the article offer?

- What do you do with sources, in general? What could you do with this source?
- What genre of writing is this? What clues in the text do you notice?

2. **Using Sources.** Using our suggestions from this chapter to guide your search, select two reliable and useful sources on a topic of your (or your instructor's) choice. Then, use one of the five techniques we outlined for using sources to generate ideas. Record your brainstorming by taking notes, freewriting (see p. 104 for a description of this technique), or creating an outline or table.

3. **Credible Sources.** Create an annotated bibliography: a list and short summary of the best sources available on a specific topic. Select any topic that interests you, and then use what you learned about finding good sources to narrow down your source selection to five to seven credible sources. Summarize each of these sources in a paragraph and arrange them in the format of an annotated bibliography, as you would a Works Cited page, using your discipline's style guide (such as APA, MLA, or Chicago). Consult Chapter 9 for additional guidance on creating citations.

CHAPTER five

Where Can We Find a Compelling Thesis

chapter checklist

- How do we find a question worth pursuing?
- What are the right questions to ask?
- Can—and why would—you change your thesis?
- Does the thesis have to appear at the end of the first paragraph?
- What thesis statements should you avoid?
- How can you jazz up your style?

Even though you might have been taught to decide on your thesis *before* you start writing your argument, as an apprentice scholar you'll want to begin with a really good question. Remember, every argument answers a question.

Within Every Great Thesis Is a Stimulating Question

Scholarly inquiry builds new knowledge or understanding by posing questions, gathering information (conducting research), and processing that information to draw conclusions. When scholars publish their discoveries, they must "show their work" or build a case to support their conclusions. In their introduction or research review, scholars often tell readers explicitly what question they were trying to answer so the audience can focus their attention on whether the scholar has "earned" the conclusion by providing adequate support.

Ideally, questions grow organically from the work that scholars do. Scholars notice gaps in previous research, such as a historical archive or literary work that has never been examined, or an experiment that needs to be extended or updated using the latest scientific techniques. This kind of problem solving also applies to work outside of school: for example, when a business manager needs to develop a model for promoting her services to a new audience, or an engineer must design a factory to be as safe, sustainable, and cost effective as possible. While we may not always get to solve problems as significant or practical as curing Alzheimer's disease, scholars and professionals use similar methods to answer questions that matter to them and their readers.

Notice, though, that scholars, engineers, and business managers already have extensive training and experience in their field, which means they have the expertise to identify and solve these important problems. The originality of their arguments depends on that expertise. It's easier for a medical scientist to discover a cure for Alzheimer's if he's intimately familiar with state-of-the-art research trends and methods.

Lacking this expertise, how can an apprentice like you know what question to ask or problem to solve so that you can discover an original thesis? How can you possibly develop an argument that experienced scholars, like your professors, don't already know?

- **Keep reading.** Remember, scholars write from sources. Ask your scholarly mentor to recommend readings on your topic. Once you find a good source, scour its bibliography for related readings that will take you deeper or in new directions.
- **Apply your perspective.** You undoubtedly have knowledge or life experiences that your professor does not. Use that expertise to bring fresh perspective to a subject. Realize, too, that ignorance (meaning lack of information, not lack of intelligence) can be a strength. Knowing little about something may help you to ask questions or see things that are invisible to experts.
- **Make your own luck.** Just like seasoned scholars, apprentices sometimes stumble accidentally on a research topic, a piece of evidence, or an insight that others have overlooked. Discovery often happens by mistake, so be brave and curious.
- **Challenge yourself.** Arguments demonstrate evidence of thinking. Discovering something for yourself can lead to a good thesis, even if it's not news to experts.
- **Talk with others.** Conversation often sparks great ideas. Talking with trusted friends and mentors helps us refine fuzzy ideas and discover more original angles from which to approach a topic.
- **Try freewriting.** (See the next Try This exercise.)

Ask the Right Questions

Scholars cannot always identify significant questions and problems without some help. A great tool for getting started is to explore the kinds of controversies that arguments address, which we explain in Chapter 3. These five categories are all that we need to discover a great

TRY THIS ➤ Freewriting

In this exercise, experiment with a technique called *freewriting*, which simply means drafting with abandon. When freewriting, we don't stop to think about what we want to say or to edit; we just write. Freewriting is a great technique for getting started when you're not sure what you want to write about, and it's great for when you've read and thought a lot and just need to clean your brain. Freewriting is also a good cure for writer's block (which often happens to perfectionists who edit too much while composing). Here's a technique inspired by Peter Elbow's classic book *Writing Without Teachers* that you could try alone or in class:

Step 1: Open a new document in your word processor. Save it with an awesome manuscript title.
Step 2: Turn off your computer monitor and write for 15 to 20 minutes. (Laptops: swivel the monitor flat or cover with paper.) Don't stop writing for anything.
Step 3: Turn on the monitor. Save your work. Look down at the bottom left-hand corner to see how many words you've written. Gloat.
Step 4: Repeat Step 2 for another 10 minutes; then repeat Step 3.
Step 5: Spell check the document so it's readable. Do not edit. Save again.
Step 6: Close the document and take a 10-minute break.
Step 7: Return to your computer and read the document. Do not edit. Locate the most interesting, controversial, or promising sentence. Cut and paste that sentence into a new document and begin again at Step 1. Repeat until you get lightheaded or you complete a first draft.

question because most every argument you can think of falls under one of these categories. To illustrate how to use these questions to discover an argument or a thesis, let's work through another example.

Imagine that you want to write an argument about the media's influence on body image, but you don't know how to come up with an original thesis. You initially thought that you could write a thesis like "The media negatively influences teenage girls' self-image," but your professor told you that such an argument would be a cliché, because most people already know that. You're frustrated, and you don't know how to develop an alternative focus. Here's where you might start:

Develop a list of questions that you could ask about your topic, based on the five categories of controversies. Write down as many questions as you can. Your goal is to investigate the topic exhaustively so that you can find a question worth pursuing. Here's what a preliminary list might look like:

Categories of Controversy about the Media's Influence on Body Image

Controversies about existence or fact: (Is it true? Did it happen?)

- Does the media actually influence teenage girls? How do we know?
- Who else does the media influence?
- How much influence does the media have on teenage girls?
- Has the media always influenced teenage girls? Did this influence accelerate at a certain point?

Controversies about definition or interpretation: (Does this case fit the definition? How do we interpret this information?)

- What kind of "influence" are we talking about? Does the media influence girls' thoughts, choices, feelings, aspirations, values, or something else?
- What are the signs of media influence?
- What kinds of media (magazines, film, TV?) are most influential?
- What other cases would fit the definition of media influence?

Controversies about cause, consequence, or circumstance: (Was it intentional? Are there extenuating circumstances?)

- Who is to blame?
- Does the media intentionally target teenage girls? Why are teenage girls profitable targets?
- Do current problems like exercise addiction and eating disorders also result from the media's influence?
- Why are teenage girls particularly vulnerable? What other factors affect the media's influence?
- What are the consequences of this problem? What are the effects of a poor self-image? What other personal and societal problems are related?
- What theories (maybe from psychology) help explain why the media can have such a strong influence on teenage girls?

Controversies about evaluation: (Is it right or wrong? Is it serious enough to warrant our attention?)

- Are the media's influences good or evil?
- Should the media take some moral responsibility for its influence?
- Is this problem more serious than other issues adolescents face?
- Is the problem serious enough to warrant immediate action?
- Do we have a moral obligation to address this issue?

Controversies about jurisdiction, procedure, policy, or action to be taken: (What, if anything, should we do about it?)

- Should the government regulate media more closely?
- What can parents do to protect their teenage girls?
- How can teenage girls avoid or counteract the media's influence?
- What existing laws, policies, or solutions developed for similar controversies might apply?
- Should magazines develop a rating system like films do (G, PG, PG-13, R, NC-17) to limit adolescents' exposure to harmful messages from the media?

Once you develop a long list of questions, select the questions that are most stimulating and original. These are your starting points. From here, you can speculate on the answer to a question (develop a tentative thesis statement), or you can begin reading other scholars'

TRY THIS ➤   Practice Using the Controversy Categories

In this exercise, reflect on which controversy categories are most compelling, and then develop a list of questions yourself.

1. Review the media influence example and identify which questions are most interesting.
   - What makes these questions particularly thought provoking?
   - What categories of controversy seem to yield the most interesting possibilities? Why do you think so?
2. Following our example, select a topic that interests you, such as an issue related to your major or a problem that you have observed on your campus, and develop a list of questions using the controversy categories. Organize the questions in a table that outlines the controversy categories and then lists four to six questions per category. For example, you could brainstorm questions for any of these topics:

   - Cost of higher education
   - Admissions criteria
   - Extracurricular funding
   - Relationships in college
   - Campus diversity
   - Characteristics of "good" writing

   You might find it helpful to imagine stakeholders—potential audiences who care about this issue and would be affected by its implications. For example, students, parents, employers, legislatures, college administrators, and lenders might raise different questions about college funding.

---

views (verification) or collecting data (evidence). We describe methods for data collection in Chapter 6.

So What's a Good Question?

Believe it or not, you *can* ask a bad question, at least when it comes to creating a thesis. Some questions just won't lead you down a path toward an interesting argument. Bad questions can be too simple, too obvious, or just plain boring.

Good questions—ones that lead to good answers (strong thesis statements)—are challenging, compelling, and controversial. Keep these three Cs in mind when developing research questions:

Challenging. Scholars don't ask questions when they already know the answers. They pursue questions that require some kind of proof, scientific data, or investigation. These questions push scholars and their readers intellectually because they inspire careful, critical, and creative thinking. For example, compare the following:

- Already known: "Do students abuse Adderall and Ritalin to improve concentration and test performance?"
- Better: "Are universities morally obligated to create educational programs and policies that prevent students from abusing drugs and alcohol?"

Compelling. Good questions have significant consequences or implications for real people or real situations, even if the effects are mostly theoretical. The issues are important to the intended audience, and scholars are invested in finding reliable answers.

- Trivial: "Is the cafeteria's food service on weekends convenient for on-campus residents?"
- Better: "To what extent should colleges provide accessible and convenient services (beyond academic support)?"

Controversial. Great questions don't need to be scandalous (although they can be!), but they usually inspire some degree of disagreement among readers concerning the best solution to a problem or answer to a question. Selecting a question that has a spark of tension can lead to a more provocative argument.

- Pointless ("No duh"): "Is smoking unhealthy?"
- Better: "If smoking poses a public health risk, shouldn't it be illegal?"

CONSIDER THIS ➤ Using Examples

In this reflection, consider the challenge of using examples well.

Examples help us "show" our ideas, rather than only talk about them abstractly. But we have to think carefully about how audiences will interpret our examples, or they'll misfire. Consider the previous examples of "better" questions. Do you think they work? Do you understand and agree that the "better" examples are actually stronger? Can you think of more vivid examples than the ones we provided? How might you use examples in your own writing?

When you're brainstorming possible research questions, see whether they fit the criteria of stimulating questions by asking yourself:

- Which questions are most controversial, interesting, or complicated to answer?
- Which questions already have obvious, simple, or commonly known answers? (Avoid these.)
- Is this question expansive and sophisticated enough for me to fulfill my assignment's page requirement, yet narrow enough for me to investigate it deeply within the page limit?

- How might I answer this question? What methods (e.g., surveys, interviews, library research) could I use?
- Do I have the time and resources—such as access to relevant books and articles, labs, contact with experts—that I'll need to answer this question?

These practical questions help us determine what we can accomplish within the *constraints* of a writing task, which are:

- available time (for thinking, reading, research, drafting, revising),
- available knowledge (about methods, background info), and
- available space (literally, constraints of page and word counts, plus assignment guidelines, genre and style conventions).

When writers select a question or thesis that's simply too big, their arguments typically lack *focus*. Apprentice scholars oftentimes think they need a huge problem to fill the pages, but really they need a small problem to investigate deeply. Our advice: **Dig narrow and deep, rather than broad and shallow.**

It's difficult to demonstrate much thinking (develop a really good idea) if you're only scratching the surface of a problem. You'll likely just say stuff most people already know (obvious or uncontroversial thesis) or leave readers hanging (advancing a thesis that's more controversial than you realize, leaving holes in your argument). Instead, you need to select a focus that gets to the heart of an issue by unraveling layers of complexity.

"Great," you might say, "but how do I do that?" More insight into the kinds of controversy can help.

Picking Juicier Questions

As you might have noticed, controversies move from yes/no questions involving controversies of fact or existence (for example, "Do students cheat a lot? Check yes or no") to more complicated—and usually more interesting—questions involving definition, cause, evaluation, and policy (such as "Why do students cheat so much?" "Is cheating really unethical?" "What might be done about it?").

The questions in the latter categories are typically the ripest for picking because they're sweeter and more complex. Consider, for example, a yes/no question that examines a controversy of existence versus a question that involves policy:

- Simple question: "Should the drinking age be lowered to 18?"
- More narrow and complex: "What kind of public policies might protect young adults from the dangers of drinking while safeguarding their civil rights?"

The second question gets at the heart of the matter, the *So what?* Plus, it gives the writer a much clearer plan of attack. You can imagine exactly what the writer might research in the library, what she might include in her outline, and what pieces of evidence she might collect. The first question doesn't give the writer a specific focus, so she probably wouldn't know where to start.

So, to sum up: You can find the strongest thesis statements by

1. investigating a controversy thoroughly to identify the best questions that people haven't answered fully yet;
2. selecting challenging, compelling, and controversial questions; and
3. focusing on the later controversy categories.

Alternative Competing Hypotheses

Sometimes scholars develop multiple tentative answers, or hypotheses, to answer their research questions. For example, following the scientific method, early researchers may have used the following hypotheses concerning tobacco use:

1. Smoking improves health.
2. Smoking is unhealthy.
3. Smoking has no significant effect on health.

Next, researchers might collect evidence—by studying correlations between disease and smoking via health records, experiments on rats, or maybe just sitting around smoking a lot—and then measure which hypotheses have the most and least amount of support. The amount of support, of course, determines the strength of the conclusion (thesis). As evidence accumulates, the hypothesis intensifies from a possibility to a probability, and eventually from something we *suspect* to something we think we *know*.

CONSIDER THIS ➤   Using Humor

In this reflection, weigh the costs and benefits of using humor in your writing.

You may have noticed our occasional attempts at humor, such as suggesting that researchers might study the effects of smoking by "just sitting around smoking a lot." We try to use humor to enliven the text and give our reader a break from otherwise serious discussions.

While most people enjoy a chuckle, humor also incurs risk. Readers may read literally and become confused, or they might interpret the tone as inappropriate and not take us seriously.

Do you think our (sometimes lame) attempts at humor work? How do they affect how you read or process our ideas?

Investigating simultaneous, competing hypotheses helps scientists reduce bias. Even if a researcher favors a particular conclusion, the scientific method allows the evidence to speak for itself. Good researchers generate as many potential hypotheses as they can to increase their chances of discovering the best possible answer, which is sometimes something truly original.

Can I Change My Thesis?

Yes. Not only can you change your thesis, but you probably should.

The purpose of investigation is to *discover* knowledge, not just to reinforce what we already think. Experienced scholars allow their investigations to change their perspectives on a subject, which is why we begin with questions and hypotheses, rather than making up our mind before we begin our research.

Many inexperienced writers think that they should select a thesis early in their writing process and then stick with it at all costs. They see the thesis as an unchanging guide for the paper's direction. But this notion of a fixed thesis disregards the writing process that experienced writers follow. Scholars typically have a tentative thesis or hypothesis in mind when they begin researching and writing, but they refine and change their views as they encounter better evidence and other scholars' findings. **Their thesis ultimately *evolves*.**

For example, a writer might begin her first draft with a fairly simple thesis, like "SAT scores are unfair and unreliable predictors of college-level success." After some preliminary research, she discovers evidence that higher SAT scores do often correspond to higher college GPAs, so she revises her thesis: "Although SAT scores can predict many students' college-level success, universities should not value SAT scores over other aspects of a student's application, such as grades and extracurricular activities."

Then, in her next draft, she might refine those ideas even further by developing a solution, or proposal argument (a genre that we describe in Appendix B), for a specific audience of university policy makers:

> Colleges should use new technologies like FaceTime and Skype to interview applicants online, rather than relying primarily on outdated assessment tools that reflect students' abilities in very limited contexts, such as exam environments. To gain even more perspective on the "whole student," admissions offices might even employ current students to assist with the selection process.

Notice how the writer's final thesis is more specific and more original? It demonstrates the writer's *thinking* on the issue. Also, notice that this final thesis falls under the last category of controversies (controversies about jurisdiction, procedure, policy, or action to be taken). Not surprising, given what we said earlier about picking juicy topics. This final category is where you'll find your strongest thesis statements when readers already agree on the issues in the previous categories. Here's why: facts, as the basis of argument, are based mostly in the past; there's less to argue about because we know more about the past than the present and the future, which are still unfolding. Knowledge and beliefs (controversies about definition and evaluation) are juicier because we're still struggling to get a sense of them right now. Controversies about what we should do in the future are juiciest because we really don't know what will happen (it's anyone's guess).

In the case of our example, many readers would already know that SAT scores are inadequate predictors of college-level success, but they might be unsure about alternative criteria. The writer's final thesis would address the heart of the issue: "What should we do about this problem?" In her final draft, the writer may show how her thesis evolved, or she may just revise the original thesis by changing the introduction. Readers may never even know her previous thoughts on the topic. What's important is that she remains open to different ways of seeing a controversy so that she can understand its complexity and select a thesis that takes into account multiple perspectives and objections.

Why Would I Change My Thesis?

You might oppose such a flexible stance because of the extra time involved. After all, if you write your paper with one thesis in mind and then change your argument, you could face extra hours of researching and revising. How will you ever finish a paper if you keep shifting the focus of your argument?

Remember, the point of scholarly argument isn't only to finish a paper but also to discover and communicate knowledge. Scholars don't write for the sake of writing; they write to communicate (and sometimes discover) what they think.

Settling on a thesis before writing closes off opportunities to learn. Usually, you're not really *changing* your argument so much as *focusing* and *refining* so you can learn more.

How can you do so more efficiently? Spend more time reading and thinking and brainstorming *before* actually writing a formal draft. Anticipate problems in your thinking and objections to your position before they pop up in your paragraphs. Keep in mind, too, that for scholars, writing grows out of investigation.

Moreover, let's be honest: Most of us have trouble identifying exactly what we're trying to say until we talk it out. Drafting can achieve that. We might have a blurry idea of a thesis but once we start writing, we realize we really mean to say something different. Embrace that process. Allow yourself to discover first and organize later.

Peer review can also help us identify a good thesis. When someone reads a scholarly draft, the best question to ask is *What do you find most interesting?* (Consult Appendix A on "How to Benefit from Peer Review and Collaboration" for advice and additional questions to guide peer review.) Often, the most interesting—and thus potentially best thesis—lurks somewhere toward the end of a draft. This makes sense, if a thesis is really the conclusion of your thinking, right?

Because conventional scholarly arguments lead with the thesis, once you find it, all you have to do is put it at the beginning and pretend you knew that all along. It's like you're saying: *Here's what I discovered, now let me show you how I arrived there and why you should believe me.*

Alternatively, if you change your thesis midway through your writing process, you might want to tell readers how and why you've arrived at a new conclusion. You can do this with the "evolving thesis."

Writing an Evolving Thesis

You might be pleased to hear that there are other options available than leading with your thesis.

We're all familiar with the five-paragraph essay that keeps a consistent thesis throughout. Historically, though, the "essay" was exploratory and evolving. (The French word *essai* literally means an "attempt," "test," or "experiment.") Similarly, an argument with an evolving thesis builds and becomes more complicated, narrow, or detailed as the paper progresses. This kind of thesis offers different advantages, such as:

- **To show readers your evolving thoughts**. If you want to illustrate exactly how you've reached a particular conclusion, you can begin your paper with your initial hypothesis and then introduce counterarguments, evidence, or verification that influenced your thinking. By showing what has expanded and changed your thinking, you can take your readers on the intellectual journey that you followed while investigating the issues.
- **To build a complicated argument**. Sometimes you simply can't articulate your entire conclusion before you've explained its various subpoints. In these cases, you need to explain or prove one part

of the thesis before moving on to the other parts. The evolving thesis allows you to defend each claim separately and then—like a staircase—to build to the precipice, your overarching thesis. This strategy can make your logic clearer for your reader to process and understand.

- **To develop a controversial argument.** When you take a controversial stance, one that your readers might reject outright, it's smart to begin from a position that your readers are more likely to accept. That way, you can establish some common ground. Then, you can gradually evolve your thesis by proving claims one at a time, in the same way that you would develop a complicated argument. With this strategy, you essentially say to readers: "We can agree on X. Now let me explain Y. . . . After you agree with me about Y, I'll support Z. . . . Once you understand why I think Z is true, you might reconsider your position." The evolving thesis is useful when you need to persuade your audience gradually and methodically, when you want to get them on your side before fully exposing your position. For example, Charles Darwin used this technique in his groundbreaking book *On the Origin of Species by Means of Natural Selection*. Can you imagine why?

- **To keep the reader interested or surprised.** You can introduce an element of surprise and engage readers when you initially hold back a bit. We're not advocating that you mislead your audience or intentionally frustrate them, but you can unravel your ideas dramatically, like a ball of yarn. For example, instead of telling readers your full position in the first paragraph, you might give them a taste of it but leave out the complicated details. Then, you can incorporate the intricacies of your thesis as the paper evolves. This strategy is especially enticing when your reader expects you to take one position and you actually support a different one or when your topic might otherwise be dull.

117

As you might suspect, thesis statements raise ethical implications. On the one hand, showing your cards at the beginning of an argument can be more ethical because it's less sneaky. Because the audience already knows where the argument is going, they can evaluate evidence within that context, according to that purpose, as they go along.

On the other hand, the deferred or evolving thesis can also treat the audience as a partner investigator. If you present evidence without telling readers how to interpret it, they're free to draw conclusions for themselves. Of course, audiences might not reach the same conclusions as you do, so you lose some "control" over the argument. But that's okay if you consider your audience to be equals and remember that the point of arguing isn't just to win but to seek understanding and make the best decisions together.

Bottom line: Wherever you place it, the best thesis is somewhere you arrive, not a place to begin. A thesis states the results of thinking. Sometimes you need to investigate a topic, consider the controversies that surround it, weigh evidence, and activate reasoning before you know what to think. After all, jumping to conclusions often gets people into trouble.

TRY THIS ➤ An Evolving Thesis

For this exercise, study the structure and the strategies of an evolving thesis by reading the apprentice scholar's essay "With Liberty and Justice for Some" (on pp. 270–278) and discuss the following questions in class or with a peer:

1. What is the thesis? How does it change? To answer this question, mark each time the writer's thinking seems to shift.
2. What makes this evolving thesis effective?
3. What, if anything, doesn't work for you as the reader? What could the writer do differently?

Thinking carefully and considering all the available evidence and viewpoints? That's the work of scholars.

Titanic Thesis Statements

While the quality of an argument is always determined by its rhetorical situation (audience, purpose, and context), some arguments are just destined to sink. Two sinkers that we steer clear of are the "clichéd argument" and the "interesting argument."

- **Clichéd arguments** restate common wisdom ("We can learn important lessons from tragedies in our lives") or rely on an over-used idea ("Capital punishment is unethical"). Clichés don't work in scholarly writing because their life has already been sucked dry; there's nothing left to discover or add to the discussion. Also, clichéd arguments don't answer the *So what?* question. They may be interesting, but they don't solve an important problem or get to the heart of the matter. If we want to discuss an overly familiar topic, such as abortion or the legalization of marijuana, we have to find a compelling angle or an unanswered question that revives the discussion. Doing so is incredibly challenging.

- **"Interesting" arguments** essentially state that a problem or concept is interesting. Example: "J.D. Salinger's use of religious symbols in *The Catcher in the Rye* is interesting." This kind of argument can't be supported for an audience because it relies solely on personal opinion. Whether something is interesting is a matter of personal taste; it's not an argument that you can support with evidence. Don't get discouraged though. *Finding* something interesting is often the first step toward *saying* something interesting about it. Dig deep and think about why your subject interests you—find a catalyst—then tease it out into something others would also marvel about.

Infuse a Little Style

Thesis statements can engage readers through their ideas and through their form. **We aim for thesis statements that are both provocative and clear**: vivid in their expression and evident in their meaning. Actually, thesis statements can be more than one sentence long, and they don't have to be as dry and tasteless as cafeteria sheet cake. When we write—and rewrite—thesis statements, we search for words that convey our meaning clearly and lively with precise terms, language that will stimulate readers. We talk more about writing with style in Chapter 10, but for now, we want to encourage you to avoid boring, tasteless, and overly general statements that don't invigorate your reader.

"Although" Statements

One concrete way to engage readers is to use an "although" clause in your thesis statement, which positions your idea against an opposing idea. A thesis with an although clause looks like these samples:

- "Although many scholars support _____, new data suggest that, in fact, _____ is more accurate."
- "Although you might at first believe _____, once you see evidence to the contrary, you'll be convinced that _____."
- "Although it is true that _____, the real issue is _____, which many scholars have overlooked."

Try Something Unexpected

Another way to make your argument stand out is to select a purpose, audience, or genre that your reader may not expect. If you're having trouble writing a thesis statement because you can't find something interesting (original) to say, try to find an interesting way to say it. Specifically, try a style or genre that's different (like satire, or use a metaphor to structure your argument), or maybe pick a different purpose—for example, to amuse your readers or even to provoke them. You could direct the argument toward an overlooked audience who doesn't yet know they have a stake in the issue. Any of these strategies would put a different spin on the topic and bring something new to the conversation.

checklist for thesis statements
After you've composed a thesis statement, test its quality by making sure it meets these criteria:

- Answers a challenging, compelling, and/or controversial question
- Gets at the heart of the controversy
- Breathes new life into an issue and avoids overused, common wisdom
- Is appropriate for the argument's audience, purpose, and context
- Engages readers with specific and interesting content and style

So What?
How many times have you heard a friend make an argument that you've already heard a dozen times before? Contrast that feeling of boredom or exasperation with the way it feels to hear something new and think, "I've never thought about it *that way* before." Developing a significant question and compelling thesis is about finding that slightly different angle, fresh perspective, or personal twist that will give readers a beautiful "Aha" moment.

With a compelling catalyst, you're ready to begin building an argument. Although your argument might shift, evolve, and change as you go, you can begin thinking about how to support your arguments with verification, evidence, and illustration to make them more credible, logical, and emotionally appealing.

What's Next

Take what you've learned in this chapter and write responses to the following prompts.

1. **Analyzing Arguments**. Select a controversy debated in your community. Find two arguments (editorials, blog posts, opinion pieces, etc.) that express opposing viewpoints, and try the following:

   - For each argument, outline the author's main claims and identify which controversies each claim addresses. For example, what is the author's first main point, and is it an argument about fact, definition, cause, evaluation, or policy?
   - Compare the authors' claims: Do they address the same categories of controversy? Or are they arguing about different things (for example, one is an argument of fact, while the other is an argument of policy)? In other words, are they arguing effectively with each other, or are they arguing past each other?

2. **Writing for Social Media**. Publish a short argument online that raises awareness about a puzzling question or a significant problem. Demonstrate why it's worth pursuing or solving—address the *So what?* Then, reflect on the following:

   - How is publishing online different from the way you would typically write for class?
   - What did you have to take into consideration about your audience(s) as you were composing?
   - What are the unique rules and expectations of this genre and context?

3. **Using Sources as Catalysts**. Practice using sources to discover a catalyst. Review "Is Google Making Us Stupid?" and "A Wandering Mind Is an Unhappy Mind," and ask yourself:

   - How do these essays relate to each other?
   - What ideas, questions, viewpoints, etc. do they have in common?

- What issues are they both interested in?
- What might the authors agree on?
- Where might the authors disagree?
- What new questions or issues do you want to explore?

Develop three to five research questions or controversies that you could explore in an essay.

CHAPTER six

How Do We Support Arguments

chapter checklist

- How do we build credibility, activate reasoning or logic, and evoke emotion?
- What counts as evidence?
- How do we link support with claims to build an argument?
- How can apprentice scholars incorporate original research?

In this chapter, we'll explain some techniques that scholars use to collect and present various kinds of support. As we've discussed, scholars expect higher standards of evidence and reasoning than you might find in campaign ads or infomercials, but that doesn't mean that scholarly arguments can't include other kinds of persuasive techniques. Everyday arguments build credibility and evoke emotions that cannot be scientifically measured or predicted according to black and white rules of logic. Here again are the kinds of support that we introduced in Chapter 2.

Table 6.1 KINDS OF SUPPORT

EVIDENCE Something you can observe	VERIFICATION Something you can look up	ILLUSTRATION Something you can imagine
• Empirical data • Personal experience • Textual evidence	• Previous research • Law or precedence • Established theory	• Hypothetical example • Analogy or metaphor • Fictional narrative

Can you recall how different kinds of support activate reasoning, build credibility, or evoke emotion?

Building Credibility

Before most audiences will trust new information that we present, they must consider us or our arguments to be *credible*. We've already discussed how audiences find some texts more credible than others. For example, scholars take the *Oxford English Dictionary* more seriously than Dictionary.com. They see scholarly journals as more credible than Wikipedia.

Credibility, or what the ancient Greeks called *ethos*, usually comes from three sources:

1. **Verification,** borrowed from trustworthy sources. Verification relies on "secondary" sources, which means someone else has already analyzed or interpreted the evidence. By integrating verification into our arguments, we demonstrate that we've read and understand what experts have already said (as in a Research Review). We assume that our audience will trust us only after we prove that we know what we're talking about.

2. **Reputation,** or what the audience already knows and thinks about the author before they start reading (for example, if he's a respected scholar or celebrity washout). Readers trust authors whom they recognize as experts. Similarly, readers will trust arguments that appear in respected publications even before they begin reading.

3. **Presentation,** which involves using a style that's suitable for your audience and purpose. You probably wouldn't wear cutoff jeans and flip flops to a formal business interview. Similarly, we can project credibility in scholarly writing by using an appropriate style (effective tone, correct grammar and spelling, etc.) and by adhering to scholarly genres (clear organization, use of support, etc.). Careful editing also demonstrates that we care about our writing and our audience. Additionally, we demonstrate trustworthy character by considering different perspectives (including counterarguments), by acknowledging weaknesses in our own arguments, by treating sources respectfully (summarizing, quoting, and citing accurately), and so forth.

Activating Reasoning or Logic with Evidence

Evidence provides the strongest foundation for arguments.

To understand why, we must consider the concept of reliability, which indicates how closely the results of investigation come together to form a pattern. For example, if several professors graded the same paper differently, then we would consider their evaluation results to be unreliable. Reliability is a measure of consistency.

Audiences respond to evidence more reliably than they respond to credible and emotional appeals. We may not all laugh at the same jokes or cry at the same movies, but with the aid of instant replay and digital video, we can all agree when we see a football player stepping out of bounds. (Of course, without instant replay, referees generate lots of controversy.)

We're most "certain" of what we can observe and count because observing and counting don't seem like acts of interpretation. For instance, we're probably more confident in the conclusions we might reach if we conduct a biological experiment in a laboratory with carefully controlled methods than we might be confident in predicting next month's weather or developing a definitive interpretation of a Renaissance poem.

Quantitative Evidence

To seek reliable conclusions, scholars develop careful methods of investigation that will yield similar results each time. Scholars who engage in quantitative investigation use statistical analysis to test the quality of their results, which helps make statistics much more persuasive. Statistics also seem more precise. Compare, for example, the following statements:

- Most of Greenland's ice sheet has melted.
- 97% of Greenland's ice sheet shows evidence of surface thawing.

The apparent precision of the second statement seems more believable, right? The first statement sounds anecdotal—like something you might have heard from a friend who had a sister who knew some guy in Greenland who noticed a lot of melting. The second statement seems like something written by a scientist who might have planted a bunch of precise little instruments across Greenland, or, in this case, had access to sophisticated thermal satellite imagery. Also, "surface thawing" is more precisely stated than "melting."

Qualitative Evidence

Please don't think of evidence only as quantitative data. What "counts" as evidence varies across disciplines. In literary studies, "data" might be actual words (quotations) from a novel, or known biographical information about an author. Similarly, scholars of theater, music, or visual arts might use a performance or a painting as their primary "data." Sociologists and psychologists might observe and interpret human behavior.

Whatever their discipline, scholars are careful to design reliable and precise methods for collecting, analyzing, and reporting evidence. As you continue your scholarly apprenticeship, pay careful attention and ask your professors lots of questions about what "counts" as evidence in their disciplines, and how they determine whether that evidence is trustworthy.

Link Evidence to Claims

When arguing, scholars state or imply how their evidence supports their conclusions. Such connections between a thesis and its support demonstrate *linkages*. When writers leave out this important ingredient—the metaphorical glue or bridge that holds the argument together—readers must make logical leaps on their own. For example, imagine that a writer argues, "We should invest in clean energy (claim) because 97% of Greenland's ice sheet shows surface thawing (evidence)." The argument is difficult to follow because the audience has to supply the missing linkages: "Clean energy reduces carbon dioxide emissions, which reduces the climate change that causes melting ice sheets. So, if the ice begins to melt, we should invest resources in clean energy development and maybe avoid an environmental apocalypse."

In contrast, a scholar might connect his claim and evidence by saying, "We should invest in clean energy (claim) because excessive carbon dioxide is causing climate change (linkage), as demonstrated by the fact that 97% of Greenland's ice sheet shows surface thawing" (evidence). **Linkages provide the bridge that connects the claim with the evidence.**

Again, scholarly argument is case building. We want to "show our work" as much as possible so that the audience can follow along more easily.

Reader-Centered Writing

One way to show our work is to transform our arguments from author-centered writing (stuck in the writer's head) to *audience-centered* writing (focused on readers' needs and expectations). Reader-centered writing takes into account the experience the audience might have while reading: places where they could stumble, disagree, misinterpret, or need more explanation. Experienced writers view their writing from this audience perspective and build and clarify linkages between their claims and evidence. What's most important is to **help readers see the logical pathway that guides our thinking**.

Linkages elaborate all kinds of arguments because they make our assumptions more explicit. To see what we mean, look at the following example of a paragraph from an application essay. This first draft doesn't use much linkage at all:

> I am qualified for this job because I am hard working, I work well in teams, and I have top-notch experience in the field. During my senior year in college, I worked as an intern at Awesome & Super-Awesome Law Firm. During that time, I conducted research for one of the senior partners, filed confidential papers, and represented the firm at college fairs. I also have experience working extensively with my peers in group projects, and I studied abroad for six weeks during the summer.

The writer cites impressive experiences (evidence), but she expects the reader to do most of the linking—to understand *why* these experiences are valuable and *how* they make her a competitive candidate. She doesn't make an argument that would translate her experience into something meaningful.

Now, see how adding linkages (marked in boldface) can enhance the paragraph:

> I am qualified for this job because I am hard working, I work well in teams, and I have top-notch experience in the field. During my senior year in college, I worked as an intern at Awesome & Super-Awesome Law Firm. During that time, I conducted research for one of the senior partners, filed confidential papers, and represented the firm at college fairs. **The fact that the partners trusted**

me to preserve client confidentiality demonstrates that I am reliable, honest, and responsible. Moreover, the experience I gained as a company representative refined my presentation skills, **which shows that I am articulate and comfortable speaking in public.** I initially developed these professional social skills by working with my peers in group projects. **These assignments developed my ability to work independently and as part of a team, showing that I am both a self-starter and a collaborator. My self-reliance and my ability to handle adversity blossomed** when I studied abroad for six weeks last summer, **which required me to manage my own time, adapt to a new culture, and live independently.**

See the difference? Now readers know exactly why she is qualified for the job. The writer added revealing explanations that support her argument ("You should hire me"). These details fill in the gaps of her logic so that readers interpret her experience more like the writer intends. The evidence no longer stands alone, without any bridge to her thesis.

This elaboration adds something else, too: length. Not meaningless filler but substantive additions to the paragraph that also increase the word count. That's a win-win outcome, since many apprentice scholars worry about meeting an assignment's length requirement.

Scrutinize Your Linkages

We typically evaluate linkages between evidence and claims according to two criteria: relevance and sufficiency.

Relevance indicates the quality of the linkage. For example, grades are supposed to measure learning, but are they a relevant measure? Do grades accurately reflect learning?

In the sciences and social sciences, scholars carefully explain the relevance of evidence by making clear distinctions between correlation and causation. Just because, for example, Nicholas Carr sees a correlation (or linkage) between the rise of Google usage and a certain

---

TRY THIS ➤ Incorporate Reader-Centered Writing

For this exercise, select a paragraph in a paper that you are writing or have written recently (for this or another class). Imagine the paragraph from your readers' perspective, and ask yourself:

- Is it clear what I mean exactly?
- Where might the reader be confused? What could be misleading?
- How does this claim relate to my thesis?
- Where do I need to make the implications more evident?

Then, look for ways to connect your evidence with linkages.

---

kind of "stupidity" doesn't mean that we can claim for certain that Google is causing or "making" us that way. In this case, the evidence is circumstantial. And as we all know, any good defense lawyer will object to the relevance of circumstantial evidence against his client because the evidence might indicate something different.

Sufficiency reflects the quantitative strength of the linkage. We cannot claim more than we have evidence to support. Again, think about a courtroom trial. A jury will only find someone guilty if the prosecution offers sufficient evidence. In fact, in a criminal trial, where the defendant is "presumed innocent" until proven otherwise, guilt must be established "beyond a reasonable doubt." Chapter 7 explains methods to scrutinize evidence and linkages in greater detail.

Incorporating My Own Research

Apprentice scholars often rely heavily on "library research" to support their arguments with verification. However, scholarly arguments become more interesting when we can collect some evidence for ourselves. To do so, we use a reliable research methodology, present and analyze our results, and draw conclusions.

Research Methods

Many scholars use empirical research—that which is based "on the results of observation and experiment"—to support their arguments (*Oxford English Dictionary*). Scholars collect empirical data in the lab and in the field through various means, such as experiments, observations, case studies, and so forth. Even if you can't carry out elaborate experiments, you can conduct interviews and observations or distribute surveys to practice gathering reliable data.

You'll find it helpful to consult with a more experienced scholar, such as your professor, when developing your research methodology. The research question will determine the appropriate methodology. For example, if you wanted to learn how a scientist approaches the writing process in general, you might interview a biologist, a physicist, and a chemist using somewhat open-ended questions. To answer a more specific, narrowly focused research question (like "How much time do scientists typically invest in drafting a research article?"), you might survey several dozen different kinds of scientists.

To enhance credibility, we follow legitimate methods of data collection. Disciplines have specific guidelines and rules for conducting empirical research, which you might learn when assisting specific professors in their research. However, for many apprentice scholars, using legitimate methods mostly means following common sense:

- **Interviews.** Be courteous and respectful of your subject's time and expertise. Plan extensively beforehand, with carefully constructed questions, a clear sense of your purpose, and background knowledge about your interviewee. Record the interview, with permission, so that you can quote and paraphrase accurately.
- **Surveys.** Write clear and calculated questions that get at your research question but don't lead your audience too much. Invite a few peers to read over a survey before you distribute it to the masses so that you can catch any confusing phrases, misleading questions, or errors. Collect enough survey responses to have a representative sample size.

- **Observations.** When possible, remain inconspicuous and limit the amount of influence your presence creates. When drawing conclusions about an observation, consider the possible effects your presence might have had on the behavior you observed.

Keep in mind the strengths and limitations of different methodologies. Surveys may yield high reliability (consistent results) but lower validity: if a question is leading or confusing, the results might not really mean what we think. On the other hand, an interview or case study might yield high validity but low reliability or generalizability.

When conducting research that involves human subjects, most universities require a formal review and approval process to ensure that research is conducted with integrity, protects privacy, and keeps participants safe. Before conducting such research, consult with your scholarly mentor to learn more about the process and procedures.

Representing Results Graphically

Photographs, artwork, and other graphics can function as evidence, illustration, or verification in arguments. A photograph of damage to your car can provide evidence for an insurance claim. An original or borrowed drawing can illustrate a concept or evoke a specific mood or emotional response.

The Web is rich with image sources, many of which are free and widely reproduced. Remember, though, that scholars and professionals attribute their sources. Just as we would with other kinds of support like quotations and statistics, we provide a citation for where we found an image. Chapter 9 provides detailed guidance on how to integrate sources effectively and responsibly.

Charts represent information graphically and can help simplify large quantities of data, functioning like a visual summary. If our readers want to scrutinize data carefully for themselves, a table can make data explicit by organizing words and numbers into a format that's easy to read. However, charts are better for showing relationships clearly and simply.

We choose charts to suit the kind of message we want to present about our information.

- **Line charts** can show the relationship between two variables, such as the effort you invest in studying this book versus how much your writing improves. (We hope you discover a positive correlation.)
- **Pie charts** (like the one we use to show different parts of the writing process in Chapter 1) can show relationships among elements of a whole through percentages and proportionality.
- **Bubble charts** allow writers to illustrate three dimensions of data, like the one used in "A Wandering Mind Is an Unhappy Mind" (found on p. 259).

Other kinds of charts represent concepts, not evidence. For example, organizational charts, Venn diagrams, and flowcharts illustrate relationships and processes. Sometimes it's easier to explain a complex idea visually than in words. Simplifying concepts and making them vivid can also make messages more memorable.

TRY THIS ➤ Experiment with Graphic Design

In this exercise, experiment with different designs you could use to represent concepts.

1. Review the drawings, tables, and charts in this book, and choose one that you think might work better in a different format. Then, design two alternative graphics to represent the concept.
2. Select an important topic from this book that we did not represent graphically. Design a drawing, chart, or other graphic to represent the concept.
3. Compare your results with classmates and discuss which designs work best for representing different kinds of information.

Analysis

Once you've collected some data, you can begin to analyze it by asking yourself:

- What does this evidence suggest? What might it mean?
- How could this information help me answer my research question?
- Do these responses align with what other scholars have found, or are the results different?
- What questions remain? What else needs to be studied?

Be careful not to interpret your research results overzealously. Scholars hesitate to claim that their evidence "proves" their conclusions. Instead, they typically make limited claims about what their results "suggest." Again, remember the basics of argumentation: **Your claim can only be as strong as your evidence.** For example, interviews can help you to collect rich, detailed data, but their results cannot be easily generalized. And even if you surveyed 100 college students and they all responded "yes" to the same question, you can't generalize this response to say that "all college students agree." You can say, "100 out of 100 college students responded 'yes,' which *suggests* that this is a popular response among college students; however, more research is needed."

Again, more experienced scholars can help you with analysis.

Drawing Conclusions

Once we analyze our data, we integrate it into our argument and build a case. Of course, we don't just insert findings without saying something about them. In fact, what we say about data is often the most persuasive part of an essay: it's the place where we *amplify*—turn up, intensify, expand—our argument.

One technique we can use is *metacommentary*: explicit statements about our intended meaning, which clarify our message and address any confusion readers might have. Scholars use metacommentary to talk explicitly about what makes their evidence relevant, sufficient, and valid. They explain the methods they used to collect their data, the precise linkages between their claims and their evidence, and the thought processes that led to their conclusions. For example, we might say:

- What I mean by that is . . .
- The point I'm trying to make is . . .
- I'm not saying _____. What I am saying is . . .
- Let me clarify: _____ is my central argument.
- The gist of the matter is . . .
- In other words . . .

These statements allow us to interrupt the flow of our writing and step in as "The Author" to clarify any misunderstanding or speak directly to the reader. Metacommentary is similar to what narrators use when they interrupt a movie scene to explain something to viewers. We use metacommentary to talk about something we've just written or to refer back to a point we made earlier. We use it sparingly, though. Like any snazzy trick, we don't overuse it, for fear of diluting its power.

Evoke an Audience's Emotions

Evidence and credibility provide the foundation for scholarly writing, but like any form of human communication, scholarly arguments may also contain elements that arouse readers' emotions.

In everyday arguments, emotion often dominates. Consider, for example, television commercials that solicit donations for animal shelters by showing sickly, pathetic looking kittens and puppies. In fact, the term "pathetic" has roots in the ancient rhetorical name for a persuasive emotional appeal, *pathos*, which is also the root of the words "sympathy" and "empathy."

Emotion can be a powerful but dangerous force. Advertisers and politicians sometimes use emotional appeals to cloud their audience's judgment, to get them to act irrationally or to "go along" even when offered no logical reasons to do so. For example, cigarette ads might make teenagers think it's cool to do something that has potentially dangerous consequences. Political propaganda often uses emotions to motivate citizens to action, as in the World War I US military recruiting posters shown in Figures 6.1 and 6.2.

The potential abuse of emotional appeals makes scholars cautious about using them. Writers who attempt to manipulate their audience's emotions risk losing credibility.

Figures 6.1 and 6.2

Military Recruiting Posters

What emotions do these posters evoke?

Besides, emotional appeals tend to be the most subjective kind of "proof" available because emotional responses tend to vary among different individuals and cultures. Using facts and knowledge as evidence builds a more solid, objective basis for argument because most everyone trusts them and finds them persuasive. If we built a pyramid of persuasive appeals, we'd place evidence at the bottom, then credibility, with emotion at the top.

Think of this like a food pyramid: use emotion carefully, in small amounts. Just like sugar, butter, or seasonings in a recipe, a little goes a long way. In limited doses, emotion can amplify an argument, especially if you want your audience to *do* something, like admit you to college or adopt a business proposal.

What are some safer ways to use emotional appeals in scholarly writing?

- As long as you build the core of your argument with evidence and verification, you could consider adding a touching example in your introduction or conclusion that arouses your audience's emotions.
- Use vivid language and concrete imagery to illustrate your argument. Precise, fresh, lively words can stir interest and evoke an emotional response, even if the content isn't pulling at anyone's heart strings.
- Perhaps the most efficient means to invoke emotion is to use symbolic cultural references that you know will resonate with your audience. For example, you might arouse a US audience's patriotic values with an iconic reference, either an image (like Mount Rushmore or the American flag) or a verbal metaphor ("as American as baseball and apple pie"). Ancient Greeks characterized this persuasive technique as *mythos*, which still resonates with us, for example, through heroes

who are real (like Abraham Lincoln or Martin Luther King, Jr.) or imagined (think Wonder Woman or Captain America).

CONSIDER THIS ➤ Credibility and Emotion

For this reflection, study the military recruiting posters from earlier in the chapter, and choose a current television or magazine advertisement that piques your interest. As you examine the advertisements, reflect on the following:

- How do you think these advertisements were intended to play audiences' emotions?
- What specific visual elements do you think arouse emotions?
- Why do you think audiences would find these ads persuasive (or not)?
- What differences do you find between how these ads appeal to their audiences?

Personal Experience as Support

Personal experience can be used to enhance credibility or emotion. In our first chapter, for example, we explain that we (the authors) are both experienced writing teachers and tutors, assuming that information would increase your trust that we know enough to write this book. While less common in scholarly writing, in professional and everyday arguments, people often mention their experiences as credentials for speaking on a subject. Personal experience can also amplify an argument's emotional appeal by creating a vivid illustration or by demonstrating empathy for your audience.

In scholarly arguments, perhaps the most common use of personal experience is as evidence. For example, someone writing an argument proposing improved support systems for students with learning disabilities might describe his experiences with dyslexia. We're careful not to overgeneralize from personal experience—after all, our sample size is only one—but personal experience can bring a depth of detail and perspective that other sources cannot.

As a scholarly apprentice, you can use personal experience as a powerful primary source of evidence, credibility, and emotion. Just be sure to use it carefully and ask your audience (if available) when you have questions about whether it's appropriate for the kind of argument you're trying to create.

Narrating

One way to incorporate personal experience, to use a more intimate voice, and to entertain readers is to compose a narrative, which uses elements of storytelling. For example, you might have written a personal narrative statement for admission to college. Narratives like this contain implicit arguments (for example, "You should admit me to college because of A, B, and C"). You might use narrative in a creative writing class, in a cover letter, or in a graduate school application essay.

Researchers also sometimes think of their writing as a kind of narrative. A good research report "tells a story": we found this problem, designed this experiment, and discovered these results. Scholars also use "micro" narratives to arouse emotion or interest, especially in their introduction or conclusion. When employing narrative this way, scholars use narrative as a kind of evidence or illustration. For example, if arguing about homelessness, a writer might begin with a story about a real person and his experiences living on the streets.

Using narrative elements may seem like a no-brainer, but it actually presents its own set of challenges:

- **You can't forget the audience.** When you're telling a story, particularly a personal one, it's easy to get wrapped up in what you know. But you have to connect with readers and make your experience relatable and meaningful to them so that the implications are evident. The story needs to be captivating, with a source of tension, a *So what?* Just because an experience is life changing for you doesn't mean that readers will see its significance. That means you have to think about your audience the entire time, asking yourself:

○ Why should readers care?

○ What's the larger significance here?

○ What's the takeaway message (implications) that readers haven't already heard a hundred times?

You might consider answering some of these questions explicitly, at least in your draft, to keep your attention focused on your audience. If, in the final revision, you're confident that the audience will get your point, you can always remove those statements.

• **You need evidence.** You may think that a personal story doesn't require proof, but all arguments need support. Whenever you're trying to convince readers of something—to think differently about an issue, to change their attitude, to embrace your message—you're writing an argument that requires support. Narratives typically incorporate evidence in more subtle ways, but it's still there. Usually, it's in the details. Elements of the story help to support the conclusion, the overarching thesis or argument. To incorporate this evidence, ask yourself:

○ What story elements illustrate my message?

○ What details can serve as evidence to prove my point?

Be sure to layer in these proofs so that you're not only saying something enlightening but proving it, too.

So What?

Effective scholarly arguments use evidence and connect with an audience through credibility and emotion. However, each rhetorical situation requires a different dose of these supports. Scholars typically prefer evidence over credibility and emotion, but that's not to say that values don't influence how we investigate and reach conclusions—or that we shouldn't pursue questions that involve human emotion. As Aristotle taught, we must appeal to the whole person; while evidence provides a stable foundation, it doesn't always motivate people as powerfully as emotion.

Since writers support their arguments with appeals to reason, credibility, and emotion, arguments typically break down in one of these three ways. In the next chapter, we point out the gaps and faults that can weaken arguments. Problems like insufficient evidence, false authorities, and sensationalized claims can undermine a writer's purpose and deter readers, but they can also present opportunities for improvement. When we investigate an argument's cracks, we can discover holes to fill, new ideas to explore, and other hidden possibilities.

What's Next

Take what you've learned in this chapter and write responses to the following prompts.

1. **Analyzing Persuasive Appeals.** Find an everyday argument or persuasive text that interests you, such as an advertisement, political cartoon, letter to the editor, magazine article, etc. Map out the examples of evidence, verification, and illustration, and then consider how well they work: Are you persuaded? Why or why not? You might also consider creating a pie chart or another graphic representation that illustrates the ratio of evidence to illustration to verification.

2. **Metacommentary.** Review your favorite chapter in this book to find examples of metacommentary. Look carefully for places where we incorporated statements to clarify our meaning or address any

confusion readers might have. As you investigate, think about the following:

- What effects does this metacommentary have?
- Why do you think we chose to incorporate these statements where we did?
- What gaps in our logic would remain, without this metacommentary?

3. **Debate.** Have a debate in class about a controversial issue. As a class, list several potential issues, and then vote on the most interesting one. Next, divide into groups for each position on the controversy, and develop a plan for your argument. Develop a potential list of evidence, verification, and illustrations that support your position. You might spend time outside of class gathering more support and then present your arguments to the class. After each group defends its position, take some time to develop and present rebuttal arguments.

CHAPTER seven

What about Faults and Gaps in Arguments

chapter checklist

- How do arguments fall apart?
- What are fallacies, and how do we avoid them?
- How much can we rely on credibility and emotion?
- How do we anticipate and respond to objections?
- How do we elaborate to fill gaps?

Remember that scholars use arguments to expand the bounds of human understanding. Such lofty purposes call for rigorous standards, so scholars scrutinize each other's arguments to help improve the knowledge-building process. Receiving criticism on our writing is not always easy; you've probably had trouble accepting criticism during peer review or after you turned in what you thought was a stellar argument. But experienced scholars ultimately appreciate criticism because it helps us advance knowledge by contemplating many perspectives.

Since it's so difficult to anticipate every possible question or objection that an audience might raise, we have developed methods to help locate the gaps and faults in our own and others' work. Many of these techniques are rooted in the strong critical reading skills that we describe in Chapter 3.

Fallacies in Arguments

Arguments break down when readers discover weak linkages between a thesis or claim and its support. Scrutinizing these linkages is what most people mean by "critical thinking."

Arguments typically break down in one of three main ways: through faulty uses of

1. reasoning or logic (activated by evidence),
2. credibility (built with verification, reputation, or presentation), or
3. emotion (evoked by illustrations).

"Errors" in thinking can be categorized as various kinds of *fallacies*. You can learn about dozens of different kinds of fallacies in critical thinking or philosophy classes or via books and websites on the subject. For our purposes in this book, we are more concerned with describing some general categories and how they work rather than trying to cover every type of fallacy.

Weak Evidence

Arguments commonly fail when the audience does not consider the evidence presented to be sufficient or relevant. Remember, when thinking about arguments, that effectiveness depends on the specific audience: what one particular reader considers relevant or sufficient, another may not.

Insufficiency

Let's consider some examples of fallacies that involve *sufficiency*. You already know the most common one—the overgeneralization, sometimes called a "hasty generalization." In this case, a conclusion is reached before sufficient evidence accumulates.

For instance, in your automobile driving experiences, you might notice lots of cars with license plates from a neighboring state whizzing by you on the highway, swerving between lanes to pass cars like out-of-control giant slalom skiers. Observing a few dozen such drivers, you might conclude (or argue) that "Residents of _____ (insert neighbor state) drive like maniacs."

Of course, you shouldn't make such a claim after observing only dozens among *millions* of Neighbor State drivers, many of whom, we hope, drive more responsibly. But you can certainly imagine making this kind of mistake in your academic work or daily life. Like most fallacies, hasty generalizations are mental shortcuts, or tricks that we use to make sense of the world using whatever limited information we have at hand.

Just because a fallacy makes sense or seems persuasive doesn't mean that it represents sound logic and reasoning. Scholars and educated citizens avoid fallacies because they don't represent our best thinking: **Fallacies do not build the best possible case** for reaching a conclusion.

Still, whether or not the generalization matches reality, fallacies can certainly be persuasive, depending on the audience. If you present the Neighbor-State menace argument to another driver who has also witnessed such dangerous driving behavior, he might just agree outright, instead of rejecting your conclusions and chastising you for trying to get away with your hasty generalization. However, if your audience has not observed many bad drivers from Neighbor State—or if she's a skilled critical thinker who resists overgeneralizing about other people—she might accuse you of invoking a stereotype, which is another form of overgeneralization.

> **CONSIDER THIS ➤** Sufficiency Fallacies
>
> For this reflection, consider these sufficiency fallacies and reflect on the bulleted questions:
>
> 1. Students are lazy.
> 2. Professors lack common sense.
> 3. High school graduates make less money than college graduates.
>
> - What audiences do you think would find them persuasive? Why?
> - Which ones do you think are persuasive, and why?
> - How do you account for the differences in persuasiveness?

Unqualified Claims

Generally speaking, people don't change their minds easily. An audience that disagrees with an argument naturally tends to pick apart the argument, whereas when audiences hear arguments they already agree with, they tend to think less critically about the quality of the linkages and support.

What's difficult in creating arguments is knowing how picky or objective your audience will be. Generally speaking, you can assume that scholarly audiences will be reasonably objective and especially rigorous about sufficiency. You can avoid sufficiency fallacies, in your arguments and in your own thinking, by *qualifying* your claims.

A qualification is a stated restriction that limits a claim's strength. For instance, you might say something like "I don't know about *all* Neighbor State drivers, but I've seen lots of knuckleheaded ones in my neck of the woods."

Qualifying claims helps us to avoid exaggerating arguments. Let's consider ways to qualify the claim that "Students are lazy." We could do one or more of the following:

1. Weaken the verb: "Students *seem* lazy."
2. Narrow the subject: "*Some* students seem lazy."
3. Limit the object: "Some students seem *to devote inadequate efforts to studying.*"
4. Add support: "*Recent research indicates that* some students devote inadequate efforts to studying."

Notice that in these examples, the precision and length of each statement increases as the scope of the claim decreases. It's almost like scholars use more words to say less—but really, we're just careful not to overstate our claims.

One qualification that bothers many scholars is using the phrase "I think" to introduce a claim. (Even worse may be using "I feel" when discussing what you think or believe, rather than your feelings.) Beginning a claim with "I think" is probably why many English teachers ban "I" from student writing. It's not that they necessarily discount students' thoughts or experiences, either. As we discuss in Chapter 6, personal experience can provide very persuasive evidence. Teachers dislike "I think" because the phrase often precedes an assertion, or unsupported opinion. Students sometimes think they can avoid the work of building an argument (supporting their ideas and providing strong linkages) if they simply qualify their claims as "personal" opinion. Also, characterizing an assertion as "just my opinion" can shut down conversation for people who believe that "everyone's entitled to her opinion." For public arguments, especially scholarly arguments, audiences agree that everyone is entitled to her opinion—but they expect that writers will provide support and linkages for the audience to scrutinize.

Really, every claim contains an implied "I think" before it. Trust that your readers will know that: Take ownership of your arguments rather than "hedging."

> **TRY THIS ➤** Qualify Claims
>
> For this exercise, use the techniques you've learned here to qualify the other two claims from the previous CONSIDER THIS.

Irrelevance

Another main category of reasoning errors involves *relevance*. Even when there's sufficient support, the linkage between that evidence and the claim or thesis may be weak.

Correlation versus Causation

A common kind of relevance fallacy **confuses correlation with causation** (initially described on pp. 130–131). A famous example involves ice cream sales and drownings. As you can imagine, both increase in the summer, so we might see a *correlation* between increased ice cream sales and drownings. But that doesn't mean that increased sales of ice cream in the hot summer months actually *cause* more drownings. Folks just like to swim more when it's hot. More people frolicking in pools and ponds means more drownings.

Scientists and other researchers who use data to answer research questions employ statistical analysis to test the strength of the relationship between variables (like ice cream sales and drownings, or smoking and lung cancer). When a correlation becomes more than coincidental, the evidence becomes "significant." Scholars and others who have been well educated about quantitative methods habitually scrutinize scientific findings by asking questions like *How large was the sample size? What's the margin of error? What other variables may be involved?*

Changing the Subject

A second type of relevance fallacy intentionally introduces information that's only weakly related to the conclusion. Politicians often use this fallacy, changing the subject to avoid answering a question:

REPORTER: "Can you describe your proposed tax plan?"

CANDIDATE: "We need a tax program that supports the middle class and creates new jobs."

REPORTER: "Yes, but can you talk specifically about how your plan will accomplish those goals?"

CANDIDATE: "We must work together, across political parties, to solve these issues. I believe my track record demonstrates my ability to get things done in Washington."

In this case, the candidate simply changes the subject, or category of controversy, so as to avoid providing any specifics, drifting from the original question of *how* the tax plan will work to *what* it should accomplish, to *why* he's the person who can make things happen.

Philosophers who study informal logic or reasoning sometimes call the "changing-the-subject" technique a kind of "red herring" fallacy. (Supposedly, stinky fish were once used to distract or mislead hunting dogs from finding their quarry.) Generally speaking, scholars avoid extraneous information that might distract or mislead their audiences.

Straw Man Arguments

A third kind of relevance fallacy occurs when writers create "straw man arguments"—oversimplified, exaggerated, or simply inaccurate versions of opposing arguments—to make alternative perspectives seem weak, foolish, and easily refutable, like a scarecrow that we could easily knock over.

One of the most common straw man techniques is to misquote or use someone's words out of context. Another popular trick is to misrepresent or oversimplify opposing views. Think about the following examples of claims, drawn from straw man arguments we see and hear around us daily:

- "Pro-life advocates don't care about women's rights."
- "If you're not with us, you must be against us."
- "My opponent's tax plan will target the poor and destitute, while giving the wealthy a free ride."

We look out for the straw man whenever we're interpreting arguments, particularly opinion pieces, political ads, campaign speeches, and product advertisements. These sneaky moves tell us a lot about a writer and his message, mainly that his case probably isn't very strong if he has to weaken the other side in order to look good. We also scour our own arguments for faults like these.

> **CONSIDER THIS ➤** Mistreating Opposing Views
>
> For this reflection, think of a time when you or a friend treated each other's perspectives unfairly during a disagreement. Reflect on the consequences of mistreating different perspectives: How did this impact the way that you responded to the argument? What kind of character did you or your friend exhibit? Was the argument improved at all by downplaying the other side?

Truth as Support

Truth is a special category of support. Here we're not talking about facts or reality, but about a Truth that's not really open to question, such as religious beliefs or patriotism. Verifying an argument with a Truth can be very tricky; those who believe the Truth will probably believe the argument, but of course, not everyone believes the same Truths. Truths, after all, are usually matters of faith, not logic or evidence.

Invoking a Truth often shuts down arguments, because once a discussion gets down to matters that "aren't open to argument," there's little left to debate. Furthermore, in the United States, where we generally consider matters of faith to be private, scholars typically refrain from supporting arguments with Truths.

Whenever scholars can, they build their arguments on the least controversial, most accepted support available. When invoking values, public sources of verification make more effective scholarly arguments because they build on commonly held agreement. For example, Martin Luther King, Jr. critiqued racial injustice by invoking shared American values that had previously been articulated by the nation's founders and Abraham Lincoln. For an audience who shares those values, King's arguments are quite persuasive.

Relying Too Much on Credibility

Writers and readers commonly make mistakes with credibility, just as they do with evidence.

The first kind of mistake is agreeing with an argument because of the author's reputation, rather than the verification and evidence presented. We might make this mistake, for example, when thinking that everything we read in a textbook (like this) must be "correct." It wouldn't have been published otherwise, right?

Advertisements often use this kind of *false authority* fallacy because they know that consumers will buy products based on celebrity endorsements, rather than on what they know about the quality of the product itself or whether it really works. Of course, such endorsements can backfire with disastrous effects when a celebrity's reputation changes (think Lance Armstrong).

Credibility can also be used in deliberately or inadvertently negative ways. An *ad hominem*, or "against the person," fallacy intentionally emphasizes negative credibility, rejecting an argument just because of the arguer's reputation. This happens in politics when diehard

Republicans or Democrats refuse to consider the other side's arguments because of party affiliation, rather than evaluating the strength of support provided.

There's good reason not to be swayed or try to persuade others by relying too much on credibility. Think about it: credibility is a kind of oversimplification. Reputations are often inaccurate or not well deserved, and they can change or even be faked fairly easily.

Getting Emotional

Emotions provide the least reliable but most powerful kind of support. Consider how much money charities raise by showing cuddly puppies or starving children to evoke sympathy. Emotion can make the difference between an audience agreeing with an argument and doing something about it. However, emotion can also cloud good judgment, especially when those emotions become intensely positive or negative, so scholars employ emotions sparingly in their arguments.

The Usefulness of Fallacies

So what's the value of learning about fallacies? When reading or listening, recognizing fallacies can make us smarter consumers of arguments made by advertisers, politicians, bosses, and so-called friends. Education in this kind of rhetoric can be a kind of inoculation against being manipulated by others because we'll be more likely to think twice (or more) about whether we should believe an argument—especially when we're already inclined to do so.

Becoming more careful about fallacies in your own arguments can also help you to write more carefully in college and beyond. Arguments based on sound reasoning can withstand harsher scrutiny, and in most cases they can help us arrive together at more commonly acceptable answers to our questions and solutions to our problems.

seven   What about Faults and Gaps in Arguments?

TRY THIS ➤ · Identify the Fallacies

For this exercise, use what you've learned about fallacies to explain why the following statements might not persuade your professor:

1. None of the other writing classes are this hard and *their* teachers give all A's.
2. You only failed me because you don't like me.
3. My mom said this paper was really good.
4. I'm an "A student"; I don't deserve a B for this course.
5. This paper is just as good as the ones that earned me A's in high school.
6. Maybe my paper isn't that good, but I tried *real* hard.
7. What did you expect? I'm a math major.
8. If you fail me, it'll ruin my life.

Answers

1. Irrelevant: this is a "bandwagon" appeal that implies, "Because others are doing something, you should, too."
2. Confuses cause and correlation.
3. Appeal to false authority; what mom thinks isn't relevant.
4. Irrelevant: past performance is no guarantee of future results.
5. Irrelevant: high school isn't college.
6. Red herring.
7. Hasty generalization or stereotype.
8. Manipulative emotional appeal that is based in weak reasoning (slippery slope). This one's especially complex because it can be interpreted as any of three different fallacies: (1) it's an emotional fallacy, playing on the pity of the teacher not to harm the student with a bad grade; (2) it's a sufficiency fallacy, because one course grade typically does not cause success or failure in life; (3) it's a relevancy fallacy, because grades reflect performance in a course, not success or failure afterward.

154

But wait . . . there's more.

Humans don't simply operate according to cold, hard logic like robots or Mr. Spock. In fact, fallacies are often quite effective (that is, persuasive), even when audiences pay close attention. It takes practice and constant attention to recognize fallacies in everyday life, and, as humans, we often believe what we choose to believe. This isn't to say that you should willfully use fallacies to manipulate an audience, but you should also not reject arguments outright when they contain weak reasoning, either. Just be mindful of these faults as part of the larger picture.

Remember, too, that **fallacies aren't necessarily false.** Making a hasty generalization or invoking a Truth may very well be an error in reasoning, and using such techniques may cause a critical audience to question your conclusions. However, just because such fallacies use weak reasoning doesn't mean that they're false. For example, consider the fallacy "If you fail me, it will ruin my life." We can certainly imagine a situation where this might be true: perhaps a student is only at risk for failing this particular course, and he needs this course to graduate, and he's been offered the job of a lifetime but cannot be hired without the degree in hand. Still, his grade depends on his performance in the course, and nothing else.

Finally, consider the usefulness of fallacies as gems for further research. For example,

- You might think of a hasty generalization as a hypothesis worth testing.
  - You might notice red herrings as potential issues to investigate further.
  - You might use evidence to support an argument that typically evokes only emotion.

- You might search for credible sources to replace the false authorities that a weak argument relies on.

Anticipate and Respond to Opposing Views

Another way to make arguments stronger is to address alternative perspectives. When we fail to anticipate our audience's objections, readers are left thinking, "Yeah, but what about _____?" or "How could you overlook the fact that _____?" These omissions can annoy readers or imply that we haven't thought through our argument fully. At the very least, readers aren't fully convinced. At the worst, they're offended, angry, or unwilling to read any further.

Sometimes we feel this way when we view political ads that only show one side of the story, such as when a candidate attacks his opponent for one poor decision while disregarding all the good work he's done. This kind of *ad hominem* attack can diminish our trust in the candidate's good will.

This deliberately skewed perspective is troubling, and writers can make similar mistakes, whether they mean to or not. When this happens, readers want to proclaim, "I object!" like a defense lawyer on *Law & Order* does when the prosecutor asks an irrelevant question. There are several ways to avoid evoking this kind of response in readers.

Anticipate Objections

Imagining potential objections is one of the best ways to fortify our arguments against resistance. After all, it's much better to anticipate readers' objections before we release our words to the public than it is to hope that our readers won't think of that one counterargument that could unravel our whole case. Unlike in conversation, a piece of writing can't be supported or clarified any further once it's communicated. Once it's in print, we can't add or take anything back, so we use strategies like the following to *anticipate* objections.

Walk in the Reader's Shoes

In Chapter 8, we talk about Rogerian argument, which teaches us the importance of honoring our audience's perspective and their life experience. Whether or not we're writing a Rogerian argument to a resistant audience, we imagine what readers will think as they're interpreting our argument, what they value, what they know, and how they might respond to claims. We examine each of the argument's components from the reader's perspective and identify places where readers might object, asking ourselves:

- What elements of support are weakest and most vulnerable?
- What might readers have to say in response? If I were reading this aloud to another person, where might he stop me and say, "Wait a minute! What about _____?"

Identify the Potential Controversies

To avoid missing a key component of an argument, we make sure we've covered all our bases. We explore an issue comprehensively and identify different ways of approaching it by examining all five categories of controversy, which we outlined on p. 61. We figure out the heart of the issue—the place where our readers will likely disagree with us—before we start writing, or we review the various controversies as we're revising to identify alternative viewpoints.

Play the Devil's (or the Angel's) Advocate

Peter Elbow's "Believing and Doubting Game" that we mention in Chapter 3 helps us explore controversies from perspectives that differ from our own. It's worth spending time getting in the mindset of someone who thinks very differently from us because it can help us see an issue's complexity more clearly, rather than through our limited tunnel vision. We also ask trusted readers to play devil's advocates for us by directly challenging our ideas, pretending to support an opposing position, and pushing us to consider all the implications of our claims.

TRY THIS ➤ Locate Missing Objections

For this exercise, review a piece of writing that you have recently composed or are currently working on. Use the first two strategies we recommend (get in the reader's shoes, and identify the controversies) to discover alternative viewpoints and possible objections. Then, work with a partner to play devil's advocate for each other. Help each other identify possible gaps and faults in your arguments.

Respond to Objections

Once we pinpoint the objections readers could raise, we acknowledge and respond to them. Doing so demonstrates to readers that we've done our homework and understand the complexity of the controversy. Also, if readers have reasonable objections, we need to show how we've thought through those issues and reconciled our views. Basically, we have two ways of responding:

1. **We can concede.** When our readers' objections are valid, we typically acknowledge their legitimacy. We don't think of conceding as "giving in" or undermining our argument; rather, we concede to show readers that we're honest, open-minded, and reasonable. We're careful about the way we frame the concession, though, so that we don't *sound* weak or unsteady in our position. We use statements like the following to acknowledge the alternative view and then explain why our argument still works, despite an objection:

a. Scholars who claim _____ make a good point because _____; however, what they overlook is _____. This is actually more important because _____.

b. I concede that _____, but I still maintain my position because _____.

c. While _____ is a relevant concern, the heart of the issue is _____, which means _____ needs to happen.

d. It is true that _____. However . . .

Notice how many of the above statements contain words like "however," "while," and "although"? These terms are *conjunctive adverbs*. Also, most of the sentences contain two parts: a de-emphasized portion (the first "while" part, called a *dependent clause*) and an emphasized portion (the second part where our message comes through—the *independent clause*).

These examples show that sentence structure and word choice can bolster our message. We can emphasize our position by using conjunctive adverbs and a sentence structure that basically says, "I'll give you this minor thing, but look at what's more important." Subtle but effective, don't you think? We talk more about stylistic choices like these in Chapter 10.

2. **We can refute**. If we disagree with our readers' objections, we can explain how we've arrived at an alternative position. We articulate an opposing view and then present the evidence, verification, and illustrations that convinced us to think differently. We imagine this refutation as a mini-argument that needs support. Still, we maintain a respectful tone and treat others' objections fairly, without oversimplifying or inaccurately representing their views. Usually, this means that we summarize the opposing view in a way that shows we understand where scholars are coming from, like this:

a. Some scholars argue _____ because they interpret
   evidence to mean _____.
b. Many well-intentioned people have said _____,
   which is understandable because _____.
c. Another way of viewing this issue is _____.

After we give voice to the opposition, we explain and defend our
point of view. This refutation may take a few sentences, a paragraph,
or an entire section. It all depends on how relevant the objection is to
our central argument. To decide how much attention to give it, we
consider the building blocks of our case and what claims our readers
must accept in order to move forward in the argument.

Elaborate to Fill Gaps

We initially talked about "gaps" that exist in arguments on p. 77.
As we said, writers can never cover an issue entirely, so we can
always find more room for development. As readers, we can mine
these gaps to discover unanswered questions, missing evidence,
and places to insert our ideas. As writers, we can identify gaps in
order to expand and refine our arguments. For apprentice scholars
who struggle to meet an assignment's page length requirement, gaps
are a productive place to expand a draft. Keep in mind that if you
don't have enough material to fill the pages, chances are good that
you need to develop your argument by conducting more research or
digging deeper into your analysis. But if you're absolutely sure
that you have selected an appropriate scope for your writing task, you
can use the following strategies to enhance your argument. (Notice
that the last three suggestions can help you answer the *So What?*
question, too.):

1. Incorporate more examples.
2. Respond to more objections.

3. Relate the argument to real-life contexts.
4. Discuss the larger implications of your argument.
5. Make connections to other related issues.

Although these strategies help us expand our points, we do not "pad" arguments with unnecessary fluff. Like most audiences, professors typically would prefer that you get to the point and, if necessary, write less. Busy readers value conciseness almost universally.

So What?

As scholars and as citizens, recognizing fallacies can help us scrutinize arguments and avoid taking shortcuts with our thinking. Finding faulty linkages while reading can make us less gullible. Filling gaps while writing can make our arguments more convincing for demanding audiences in school and beyond. While we can't always see the faults and blind spots in our own arguments, we can ask others to review our work and help us refute counterarguments or elaborate and build stronger linkages.

Now that you have a sense of how to support arguments and how to avoid and resolve potential problems, you're ready to organize an argument's various elements. We recommend doing some preplanning before you start drafting, and in the next chapter, we offer several organizational strategies to use throughout the writing process. We encourage you to experiment with these and adapt them according to your (and your audience's) needs. We describe organizational "moves" that scholars typically employ, such as referencing other scholars' important discoveries, controversial claims, or shared knowledge at the beginning of an argument or proposing solutions at the end. The chapter also provides different patterns of development that you can use to structure arguments. Finally, we offer a few techniques for organizing your time so that you can finish a writing task and maintain your sanity.

What's Next
....

Take what you've learned in this chapter and write responses to the following prompts.

1. **Fallacies Scavenger Hunt.** Fallacies can be found everywhere. (Okay, maybe that's an overgeneralization.) Spend a day noticing as many fallacies as you can find—in the news, in advertisements, and in your daily conversations. Collect and analyze the most interesting examples. Then, bring your artifacts to class and discuss which ones you think are most persuasive, and why.

2. **Critical Thinking.** Imagine yourself in a job interview, and your potential employer asks you about your critical thinking skills. Write a page about how finding and fixing faults in arguments can help you solve workplace problems.

CHAPTER **eight**

How Do We Develop and Organize Arguments

chapter checklist

● How do we think rhetorically about organization?

● What techniques can we use to organize and develop arguments?

● What organizational "moves" do scholars make?

● How do we organize our writing process?

Communicating ideas accurately is incredibly difficult. That's why, when writing to others, we work hard to structure our ideas clearly and deliberately. Arranging ideas in a way that makes sense—and connects with our audience—increases the likelihood that readers will receive our intended meaning, rather than losing it in translation.

Therefore, we think about organizational elements more in terms of function than form. For example, rather than thinking of an introduction as paragraphs that just fill space at the beginning of our argument, we think of what we can *accomplish* with an introduction: introduce our topic and catalyst, provide background information, establish our credibility, and so forth.

Although we can structure claims, support, and linkages in many different ways, we design a deliberate plan for developing an argument so that we **put everything in its place for a reason**.

Organizing Rhetorically

Since there are many ways to arrange an argument, we must think carefully about our audience, purpose, and the linkages among our claims and supports in order to select the best structure. We don't have prescribed formulas that work in all cases. Sometimes apprentice scholars are tempted to use the five-paragraph theme, which is a helpful foundation for writing, but most college writing requires more than five paragraphs, and most arguments involve more than three main claims. Complex concepts and complicated arguments demand more sophisticated structures that allow us to expand our ideas, explore subclaims, and address readers' objections.

Before we start drafting—while we're brainstorming, freewriting, and outlining—we begin thinking about the best way to arrange our ideas, according to our particular audience and purpose. We analyze our rhetorical situation and ask ourselves:

- What's my purpose? What am I really trying to accomplish in this essay (for example, to change readers' minds, to offer a solution, to compare and contrast two theories, to help readers understand a key historical event)?
- What kind of audience will read this? Will readers likely resist or welcome my ideas?

- How are the arguments that I've read in this discipline typically organized? What kind of organization will my readers expect? Do I want to meet these expectations or surprise my audience?
- Am I conducting original research, such as collecting data or conducting experiments? How will I organize and present my results?

Rather than just picking a pattern that worked for us last time, we think strategically about what we're trying to do in the argument and who we're trying to reach. We aim to select a structure that meets our audiences' needs and helps us achieve our purpose.

Techniques for Organizing Your Thoughts

Different writing situations call for different strategies for organization. Sometimes we know most of what we want to say before we start writing. In those cases, we can compose an outline and pretty much stick to it. Other times, we lack a clear sense of our argument, so we need to begin writing, see where that takes us, and design a logical structure later. Still other times, we need to use organizational techniques that help us arrange and assemble our thoughts. Let's look at a few of those techniques next.

Visualize Your Organization

Every writing toolbox needs some techniques for conceptualizing your argument visually. One way is to imagine your paper as a building that has various rooms, each with a different function. We envision how the rooms (ideas, paragraphs) connect together in a way that will make sense to our readers. For example, if we imagined our paper as a museum that displayed ancient Egyptian artifacts, we could arrange the rooms chronologically (separate rooms for each time period), or we could organize the rooms topically. Either way, in the first room of our museum, we would want to greet visitors, arouse their interest, state our main claims, and preview the tour. After all, we would want to motivate our audience from the start and keep them from getting lost.

In addition, we would need to post clear signage (linkages) throughout the building to help visitors move easily through the various rooms. This would help the audience see how the rooms connect, how the contents of each relate to each other. Imagining the signposts that people would need helps us predict the linkages we would need to add to the argument.

Finally, we'd want to create a big finish in the last room. If, like many museums, our exhibit potentially overwhelmed our visitors with complexity and detail, we might want to summarize what they saw—tying everything together so they didn't miss the point. We might also want to answer the *So what?* question by elaborating on the implications of our argument, perhaps by showing ancient influences in modern-day Egypt, or even how ancient Egyptian art and culture has influenced the rest of the modern world.

Thinking metaphorically and visually about our argument helps us to imagine how its various parts fit together and to consider the paper from our audience's perspective so that they don't get lost, sidetracked, or confused.

Experiment with Maps, Graphics, and Software

While we're brainstorming, we oftentimes use idea maps, cluster diagrams, or technology to help us arrange our ideas. We might simply sketch out ideas on paper or use a word processor to design a graphic. We use visuals to help us explore an issue in depth, to discover various directions we could pursue, and to discover the linkages among our claims.

CONSIDER THIS ➤ Employing Metaphor

In this reflection, take a break from the chapter's content to examine and experiment with some choices that writers make.

We chose to use a museum metaphor for two reasons. First, similes and metaphors allow us to illustrate a concept using something that's already familiar, or relatable, to the audience. Second, metaphors are vivid; "showing" rather than "telling" will help our audience "see," understand, and remember an idea more accurately.

Using metaphors can be risky, though, because our audience might not recognize what we're referencing, or they may think we've oversimplified the issue. In our case, you might not be familiar with the typical layout of a museum. Even worse, you might apply the metaphor strictly and decide that all arguments are organized chronologically or topically. Despite these risks, we decided the benefits of vivid illustration outweigh the potential costs of misleading or losing readers.

Do you think the museum metaphor works? Is it placed wisely, or is there a better spot in the chapter for the metaphor? Can you think of another metaphor that would illustrate this concept? What does this example teach you about the complexities of using metaphors in your writing?

We can also use presentation software to give us a visual representation of our argument. For example, traditional software can help us generate a plan for organizing our argument if we think about each of our claims as a slide. We add subclaims and support in bullets under each slide's main claim. Then, we can rearrange the slides according to the most logical outline. We can transform our presentation blueprint into a paper by adding linkages and more in-depth support. Newer online presentation software alternatives can also be used for planning purposes because they allow us to organize ideas with more complicated structures and linkages. For example, we can illustrate how one claim connects to three subclaims that are all components of a larger idea.

TRY THIS ➤   Create a Visual Representation

For this exercise, create a concept map or other illustration as a way of developing and organizing an idea for an argument that you're working on.

Create a Reverse Outline

After we write a draft, we oftentimes outline what we've written to see whether the organization is working. This outline looks very similar to a prewriting outline, but it's called a "reverse outline" (described on pp. 94–95 in Chapter 4) because it's composed *after* a draft is written. Once we create the outline that reflects exactly what we've written, we can see whether our paragraphs are focused, our main claims are evident, and our ideas progress logically. Then, we make necessary changes.

Developing Your Arguments

Exploring an argument's various controversies, like we do when we're brainstorming, can also help us decide where to begin a paper and how to order our ideas. The hierarchy of these controversy categories (outlined in Chapter 3) offers a natural progression to follow. We can organize an argument around these categories by first addressing controversies about existence, then discussing definitions and consequences, then evaluating, and finally offering solutions.

This organization creates a logical progression of ideas, and it allows us to focus on the issues that are most controversial and interesting.

In fact, we typically don't cover all of these categories: we skip the issues that our audience already agrees with, knows, or understands. For instance, if we're writing about global warming, and we know that readers agree:

a. that climate change actually *exists*,
b. that it is *defined* as "an alteration in the regional or global climate" (*Oxford English Dictionary*), and
c. that it is *caused* by excessive carbon dioxide,

then we skim over the first three kinds of controversy (existence, definitions, causes) and get right to the heart of the matter to discuss:

d. whether climate change is *serious enough to deserve our attention* (evaluation), and
e. which *solutions* are most realistic and effective (policy).

We use the controversy categories as building blocks for larger arguments. Each category calls forth a particular kind of argument. For example, if we're writing an argument about women's changing roles since the turn of the 21st century, we recognize that we're writing an argument about existence (since we would be answering the question "Have women's roles changed since 2000?") and definition (since we would be answering the question "In what ways have women's roles changed?"). Once we identify what kind of argument we're developing, we can select the techniques that correspond to that category.

Arguments about Existence and Fact

Existence arguments can be difficult because audiences tend to hold stubbornly to what they think exists or is true or factual. Typically, existence arguments rely on observable evidence for support.

Consider, for example, how emphatically people who have witnessed UFOs believe in extraterrestrial life, while people who have not seen flying saucers tend to remain suspicious. Even within the scientific community, an experiment must be repeated again and again before there's consensus about a major discovery.

Because not everyone has a laboratory or can observe phenomena across the world, we often rely on verification to support existence arguments; we trust others to observe evidence for us. How else would we know about galaxies or subatomic particles that we cannot see for ourselves? So, if an apprentice scholar were writing an existence argument, say about President John F. Kennedy's assassination, she might draw from different historical accounts of the events of that day to speculate on what really happened.

Sometimes existence can be presented through illustration, as is the case with science fiction and fantasy art that, for example, develops a political critique or proposes an alternative future (think *The Hunger Games*). Michelangelo illustrated, through his drawings, the existence of flying machines long before we sent anyone to the moon. Illustrations can support arguments to bring into existence things we can only imagine.

Arguments about Definition

Many arguments begin with disagreements about how we define a term or concept. Arguments about abortion policy, for example, get bogged down before they begin if parties to the argument cannot agree on whether abortion is "murder." And arguments about whether abortion is murder also depend on when we define an embryo or fetus as "human"—that is, when human life begins. (Note how we use quotation marks to call attention to terms in dispute.)

Public controversies often hinge on the definition of a word or phrase. In a famous White House scandal, President Bill Clinton famously asserted that he "did not have sexual relations with that woman, Miss Lewinski," prompting vigorous debate about what specific kinds of physical interactions constitute "sexual relations."

Knowing that vaguely defined terms can cause arguments to stall, scholars tend to be very careful about the language they use, often explaining potentially controversial terms in the beginning of their arguments. Often, we present small definitional arguments as building blocks for larger arguments. For example, in order to argue against "corporal punishment," we would need to define what we mean by the term. Does spanking of children by their parents fit the definition? In most states, parents can legally use reasonable force to discipline their children. But what actions are "reasonable"? It's worth thinking through any terms that might be open to question before proposing a larger evaluation or proposal argument.

Usually, we argue whether a case fits an existing definition. But sometimes we discover a case that doesn't fit existing definitions, or we can't agree on a definition and need to create one. For example, we might redefine the term "marriage" by comparing different types of marriage and looking for patterns across groups.

Some definitional arguments can be so interesting, significant, and substantial that they can take an entire essay or even book to examine adequately. For example, rhetoric scholars Celeste Condit and John Lucaites wrote a book-length study of definitional arguments about the term "equality" in American history. Their book, *Crafting Equality: America's Anglo-African Word*, traces how public arguments transformed the very meaning of equality—from how the Continental Congress meant the word ("all men are created equal" but not women or slaves) to the present.

To craft a definitional argument, we must first settle on a definition that our audience will accept. Sometimes we can simply define a term explicitly and hope that the audience will accept our definition: "For the purposes of this argument, we will define 'reasonable force' as physical contact that does not cause bodily harm or long-term emotional damage."

Another strategy is to verify a definition with a credible source. Sparingly, we might use an everyday dictionary to validate our meaning: "*Merriam Webster's Dictionary* defines murder as. . . ." For a scholarly audience, a more credible place to start would be the *Oxford English Dictionary*, or *OED*, which gives a richer set of definitions and some historical background of how a word has been used over time. (Sometimes it's also interesting to see where words came from, what they originally meant, and how their meanings have evolved.)

For a more specialized scholarly audience, we consult specialized encyclopedias, like Thomas Sloane's 837-page *Encyclopedia of Rhetoric*. Scholarly encyclopedias are written by experts who provide extensive discussions and bibliographies to help sort out the nuances of key terms and concepts in a specialized subject. Check your local library's reference section for a range of scholarly encyclopedias, from the *Encyclopedia of Paleontology* to the *Encyclopedia of Management*.

Once we've established an agreeable definition, we then explain how our subject "fits" that definition using evidence and illustration. For example, a law that bans assault rifles will clearly define its characteristics so we can determine whether the Colt AR-15 fits the legal definition. If we wanted to argue that energy drinks are dangerous or unhealthy, we would need to explain what we mean by "dangerous or

---

TRY THIS ➤ Write a Definition

For this exercise, brainstorm with peers to identify an issue that is controversial due to people's conflicting definitions. For example, one controversy that arises regarding public funding for art is "What counts as art?" After you select an issue, write a one-page argument that develops and defends a specific definition of a term or phrase that is central to the controversy. Afterward, compare your definitions with your peers and discuss the implications of your definitions.

unhealthy" and then cite evidence that energy drinks have those effects.

Arguments about Cause and Consequence

Arguments that try to establish a causal link are one of the most difficult cases to make. That's because it's tough to definitively link a cause and effect without confusing cause with correlation. Oftentimes when writers try to argue about cause and consequence, they commit logical fallacies like the ones we discuss in Chapter 7. However, if you recall, Nicholas Carr built a compelling case against technology in "Is Google Making Us Stupid?" by arguing that the Internet is *causing* us to have difficulties concentrating and reading critically. If you look back at his article, you might notice that it's a causal argument.

> **TRY THIS ➤** Examine a Causal Argument
>
> For this exercise, review Nicholas Carr's essay "Is Google Making Us Stupid?" to analyze and evaluate it as a causal argument. If you've already studied it closely, you should be able to skim it quickly and identify specific techniques Carr uses to build his case. As you analyze the essay, consider the following questions:
>
> • Why do you think Carr organizes his article the way he does?
> • What are Carr's strongest points? Are they placed strategically?
> • Overall, does the organization work well?

Arguments about Evaluation

Like definitional arguments, evaluation arguments sometimes stand alone and sometimes become part of larger arguments. For example, an argument proposing a solution to international copyright infringement would probably begin by describing the problem and then explaining why copyright violations are wrong and deserve our attention (evaluate the controversy). This last part is especially important because ethical issues can help motivate an audience to act by highlighting an argument's implications.

We begin evaluation arguments by establishing criteria by which we will judge the case at hand. Those criteria must be based in values shared by the audience. Let's consider the argument against corporal punishment that we discussed earlier. In this example, the definition hinged on the phrase "reasonable force," which we defined as "physical contact that does not cause bodily harm or long-term emotional damage." Here, we're making a kind of evaluation argument, counting on our audience to share our belief that causing bodily or emotional damage to children is morally unacceptable.

Because evaluation arguments depend so much on values and beliefs, they tend to be complex and compelling, especially when they involve competing values. For instance, most Americans value national security and individual human rights, but the use of aggressive interrogation techniques on suspected terrorists (defined by critics as "torture") places security and rights in apparent conflict. In cases like this, we must argue why we hold one value more dearly than another.

To fully evaluate an issue, we might have to compare (find similarities among) and contrast (find differences among) components of the controversy. In fact, many arguments compare and contrast theories, texts, artifacts, events, concepts, and so on. For example, a research or literature review compares sources in order to describe and analyze the "conversation" about an issue. When using this mode of analysis, it's important to synthesize—bring items together in a new, enlightening way so that readers learn something new about a subject—rather than just look at each item or subject separately. **The structure we choose can help promote synthesis**. For example, if we compare similar items alongside each other, perhaps even within the same paragraphs, we're more likely to show off our good thinking by explaining exactly how we've arrived at our evaluation. Doing so can help us avoid the worst kind of comparison/contrast analysis—the one that says little more than "These things have some things in common but are still different." When we compare and contrast items in close proximity to each other, we can examine the intricacies of each, as they relate to the other.

TRY THIS ➤ Evaluate a Film or Restaurant

For this exercise, pick a film or restaurant that you want to evaluate. Before viewing the film or dining at the restaurant, identify a list of criteria against which you will evaluate your subject. Then, write a 500-word evaluation of the film or restaurant. Post your evaluation on a blog or a social network for others to read and comment on.

Arguments about Policy

We use this kind of structure when we write a proposal argument, which

1. describes a problem,
2. presents solutions, and
3. justifies a course of action.

We might not spend equal time on every section but instead think about the primary source of disagreement. For instance, if readers already understand the severity of a problem, we can focus more on the solution and justification sections. However, if readers don't recognize a problem, we need to spend more time proving that there's actually cause for concern. To determine which controversies you can skim or skip, do your research, test your arguments on a real audience (like a classmate or a writing center tutor), or ask your professor: *How much can I assume my audience already knows or agrees with my argument?*

Select Scholarly Arrangements

You can also experiment with some common "moves"—steps and strategies—that scholars use to develop arguments. For starters, you can follow the conventional argument structure of many disciplines.

As we've discussed, scholarly inquiry proceeds from a catalyst toward an answer or conclusion—also known as a thesis. Scholars often don't know what their thesis will be when they begin investigating, but they lead with the thesis when reporting their results, as if to say, "Here's what I've discovered. Now let me show you how I got there."

Although not all forms of writing follow this conventional structure, many of them still employ the generic moves and structure of the classical argument, which was developed by ancient Greeks and Romans. If you grew up in Europe or the Americas, this form of thesis-first argument should seem familiar. Other cultures sometimes meander toward their conclusions or don't proceed through their points in a straight line, allowing their arguments to unfold more like a narrative journey. In fact, some Non-Western cultures think we're rude for being so blunt, but American academic and professional audiences generally expect the "bottom line up front." Learning to get to the point early will serve you well not just in scholarly writing but also in business and scientific communication, where audiences don't want to work too hard or wait too long for you to answer the question, *So what?*

The conventional structure we offer next provides many options for moves we can make to organize an argument, but we never follow these lockstep. Rarely do we make *all* of these moves, or even sequence the sections in this exact order; rather, we thoughtfully select the ones that suit our rhetorical situation. Think of this structure not as a detailed outline to follow strictly, but as a series of options to use according to your audience's needs. Imagine the format as a menu to select from—deliberately and thoughtfully—when you're determining what your audience might need.

The Scholarly Model

1. **Introduction**
   - Identify the controversy, problem, or research question and its significance and relevance (catalyst).
   - Establish your qualifications to write about the topic.
   - Create common ground with readers.
   - Demonstrate fairness.
   - Arouse readers' attention and interest, often with an example or a personal narrative.
   - State or imply the thesis.
   - Forecast the structure of the argument.
2. **Background**
   - Summarize important sources and research on the subject.
   - Describe the subject's history and its theoretical foundation.
   - Give an overview of the situation or problem.
   - Explain the process you used to answer a research question or to study a problem (for example, methods used to collect and analyze data, or theories applied to a particular subject).
3. **Support**
   - Present verification, evidence, and illustrations that support the thesis, ordered in a clear and thoughtful pattern.
   - Explicitly link subclaims and support back to the thesis.
   - Report and tabulate data and results gathered through investigation, sometimes using figures and charts.
   - Analyze, interpret, and apply research findings.

4. **Consideration of alternative arguments**
   - Examine alternative points of view.
   - Note advantages and disadvantages of alternative positions.
   - Acknowledge limitations of your research or viewpoint.
   - Explain why your argument is better.
5. **Conclusion**
   - Briefly summarize and synthesize the overall argument.
   - Identify the implications of research findings.
   - Make clear what readers should think or do.
   - Add a strong emotional or ethical appeal.
   - Raise questions for further research.

Remember: This structure is a useful starting point that we approach creatively, adapting the template to our rhetorical situation. It's not a cookie-cutter model for all arguments.

Also, there is no prescribed formula for length. We might devote several pages to one section and only a few paragraphs to another. We select a ratio and scope that is appropriate for our purpose and audience. As an apprentice, you can practice these moves in different genres as you learn what different audiences expect.

Scholarly Moves

In addition to using the Scholarly Model, you can follow your professors' leads by modeling their organizational moves.

Move 1: Start with What Others Have Said
Most scholarly arguments begin by highlighting key contributions that other scholars have made. We do this for three reasons:

1. to familiarize readers with the context and place our argument within a scholarly conversation;

2. to verify our assumptions, methods, or the research question, as in a research or literature review;

3. to demonstrate that we've done our homework by reviewing previous research; neglecting to cite or at least refer to related scholarship damages our credibility.

The length and style of the research review depends on the paper's length and on the audience's familiarity with our topic. A formal review of previous research (or "literature review") can span several pages, or it might only appear in an opening paragraph that contextualizes the argument. Regardless of what the review looks like, **scholars rarely assert their own position before they've first acknowledged what others have said**. They situate their perspective within the larger scholarly "discussion" about a topic. For example, a writer might begin an argument by citing predominant theories that inform an issue and quoting important viewpoints. We describe these techniques for verifying arguments in Chapters 6 and 9.

These strategies allow us to present what is already known about a subject before complicating it. That is, we can establish what others have already "said"—what our audience knows to be true—before we challenge these perspectives, add our own discussion to the mix, and explore new questions.

Move 2: Highlight Agreement before Disagreement

As mentioned previously, sometimes we skim over issues that our audience already knows. However, jumping into the center of the controversy may be a strategic mistake when making arguments that are especially divisive or when we imagine that an audience will resist our thesis. In such cases, we first try to build some common ground with our readers. For example, we might begin by acknowledging opposing arguments to show our readers that we respect their perspective. This kind of move is typical in Rogerian argument (inspired by American psychologist Carl Rogers who coined the phrase "unconditional positive regard"), which focuses on negotiating and empathically listening to another side. Rather than blindly starting with our own position, Rogerian argument starts with the audience—prioritizing their views and building bridges to reach consensus—rather than pushing our own agenda in order to win or prove we're right. This example of an organizational move shows that the structure we choose can enable or undermine our purpose, and invite or alienate our readers.

Move 3: Put Your Best Foot Forward

If possible, we begin and end arguments with a bang. We lead and close with our strongest points so that we frame the argument with our most fortified claims. It's probably obvious why this works: readers enter and leave the argument with strong impressions. Plus, if you assume that readers' attention fades in the middle, that's a smart place to nestle weaker points. Alternatively, you could use the middle as a place to revive readers with a compelling point. Whatever approach you take, make it a deliberate choice that you select based on how you expect audiences to respond.

Organize Your Revision

Keep in mind that organization isn't only something we work on before we start writing. Oftentimes, when a professor asks you to revise your essay, one of the primary changes she expects you to make is the paper's organization. Here are some ways to improve an argument's organization while you're revising.

Add Transitions

Transitions can be easier when we think of them as signposts that direct the reader. Similar to a travel guide who points out important landmarks along the tour or a road sign that indicates when drivers need to exit, a writer guides her audience through her argument with strategically placed signposts. These markers tell readers, either explicitly or implicitly,

- what's coming next,
- how ideas are connected,
- when a change in subject or tone will occur, or
- how to interpret the argument.

Signposts make our writing clear and readable so that readers don't need to work too hard to interpret our meaning. Signals can be as simple as transition words like "however," "moreover," "similarly," and "on the other hand," or they can be as sophisticated as lengthy sections that clarify the relationship between one idea and another. What we don't want to do is just insert a transition word whenever we sense a gap. They're powerful tools, but transition words won't magically create a linkage where one does not exist. They're not love potion.

To create tighter connections between ideas, we consider the hierarchy of our claims—how they relate to one another—and we use signposts to highlight that relationship. It's important that we send the signal that communicates exactly what we mean. For example, we don't want to write *in addition* (which would connect two equally weighted ideas), when we mean *accordingly* (which would indicate a cause and effect). To be precise, we ask ourselves:

- How are these claims related? What is their relationship?
- Are these ideas equal, or is one a subpoint of another?

In addition to linking sentences, signposts can help paragraphs move smoothly from one to the next. Paragraphs typically begin by referring back to something familiar, such as the previous paragraph, a concept explored earlier, or the thesis. Readers are usually confused when they encounter paragraphs that don't clearly relate to something they've seen before. We can help readers feel comfortable in a new paragraph by beginning the paragraph with something *old*—something touched on earlier—and then using this reference as a bridge to *new* material. For example, review our previous paragraph, where we began by saying: "To create tighter connections between ideas, we consider the hierarchy of our points." Notice how the first part of this sentence is old information (because we made this point earlier)? The second part of the sentence introduces the new material, which is easier for readers to interpret within the context of the familiar statement. Imagine how the sentence would read without a reference to something already known.

Unify Your Argument

Another way to highlight connections is to repeat key words throughout an argument. We can weave in terms that are central to our argument to create a more consistent and memorable message. We're careful not to overdo it, though. In limited doses, these words can reinforce our argument and unify the paragraphs. For example, throughout this book, we've used the term "strategic" frequently to remind readers that writing should be deliberate. Has this word stuck out to you? Does it unify and reinforce our message, or has it been too repetitive?

When revising, we keep in mind how changes, even minor ones, can affect the paper as a whole. For example, if we change a paragraph's main point, we might have to alter our introduction. It's like the butterfly effect: changing the path of one idea can impact the course of the rest. That's why it's important to step back once in a while to review our argument's big picture and make sure the organization still works.

Design Your Document

How we arrange text on the page can also influence how our message comes across. By now, you've probably noticed that we regularly use headings and bulleted lists to make chapters easier to navigate. Titles, which are often underused by apprentice scholars, can also give writers some leeway for introducing a thesis more boldly than in the body of an article or essay. Remember how the title of "A Wandering Mind Is a Happy Mind" introduces readers to the article's main conclusion?

Other recognizable formatting techniques plainly signify to readers specific meanings or effects. For example,

- Headings and subheadings can break our writing into discrete, manageable chunks that help readers navigate content easily, as we've done in this textbook. Headings, in particular, make navigation easier, although they don't replace good sequencing and transitions. Different disciplines have their own expectations for where—and how often—writers should use headings. For example, science and social science papers (in APA style) generally encourage more explicit, standard design with headings. When you're taking research notes and writing early drafts, you can keep yourself organized by including headings, even if you remove them later.
- In most scholarly styles, hanging indentations indicate the format of bibliographic citations. (See p. 207 for examples.)
- Pull quotes reformat a short excerpt from the text to attract readers' interest. Magazine articles often contain these short quotations in the margins to emphasize an important take-away or a memorable phrase.

Bullets, like those above, provide a handy way to organize information. Because we read from top to bottom, readers assume that more important information comes first, but we can reinforce this idea by using a numbered or alphabetized list.

To organize categories of information multidimensionally, tables can be useful. Again, because we read from left to right, top to bottom, we assume that the most important information—such as labeling—will appear at the top and left. Placing information there signals emphasis.

Table 8.1   DOCUMENT DESIGN TECHNIQUES

DESIGN FORMAT	DESIGN FUNCTION
Headings and subheadings	Helps readers navigate content
Capitalized phrase in italics	Signals a book, magazine, or journal title
Paragraph with hanging indents	Indicates a bibliographic citation
Pull quote	Attracts reader interest

How do tables like this help present information?

Another powerful design element to consider is white space, or negative space, where there is no text or images. Margins, indentations, and spacing between lines can help readers process text more easily, with less clutter. White space can also be dramatic.

Like this.

Structure Your Writing Process

Just as we structure our arguments carefully, we organize our writing process in a way that enhances function. To be successful—and to maintain your sanity—we don't recommend tackling a large writing task at once, in one sitting, the night before the assignment is due.

The level of thinking and writing expected in college requires us to work in stages. Remember, writing is a process: We need time for our ideas to marinate, time to find sources, time to get feedback on drafts, and time to revise and edit. To reserve time for all of these things, manage writing tasks sensibly:

- **Break the assignment into a series of manageable tasks; then assign a deadline for each task.** For example, set a deadline for the outline and another deadline for the first draft. If you create a timeline that organizes your tasks, you can hold yourself accountable. You might use a daily planner for this, install scheduling apps on your smartphone or tablet, or find resources available online.
- **Break a long assignment into chunks.** For example, you could think of a twenty-page paper as four shorter papers, each with its own purpose. Thinking about the assignment in this way can make a daunting task more manageable. Focusing on smaller objectives, in stages, helps us be more productive and feel less overwhelmed. Consult the Scholarly Model on pp. 177–178 for ideas on how to divide large arguments into segments.
- **Get feedback along the way.** Assuming it's okay with your instructor, always have someone you trust read and respond to your paper before you hand it in. Your professor might be willing to do this during office hours. If you have access to a writing center, try working with a tutor who can help you think through an assignment's various parts, brainstorm ideas, develop a plan, and revise your drafts. Tutors typically see many different kinds of assignments, so they can teach you strategies and give you a different perspective than you may have considered.
- **Don't insist on following a fixed or linear plan.** Just because your argument begins with an abstract or an introduction doesn't mean you have to start on that section first. If you don't know where to begin—if you feel stuck or overwhelmed—start with something straight-forward: for instance, begin your Works Cited

185

page. Type up quotations that you might include in the paper. Format your document. All of these simpler tasks can get you started and alleviate some fear of the blank page. Remember, writing is difficult for everyone, and just because you're stuck doesn't mean that you can't find your way. Sometimes, in order to make progress, you have to jump around and then go back to reorganize or fill in the gaps.

So What?

The bottom line is that we structure arguments according to our audience's needs and put everything in its place for a reason. This means we need to know how each part of our argument functions. We can use various strategies to assemble our points in the best layout for our audience. For instance, creating an idea map might help us see the linkages among our thoughts, loosely following a common format might give us the structure we need, or reverse outlining our points might help us rearrange the argument. Since there are many techniques for organizing ideas, we recommend experimenting with different strategies to find ones you're most comfortable with. The larger your tool bag of choices, the more likely you will be to find a strategy that works when you get stuck or that gives you a starting point when you encounter a new writing task.

In order to develop an argument, we need to not only organize our claims and support but also incorporate "outside" sources seamlessly. The next chapter describes how we integrate sources smoothly into our writing and use them responsibly. All scholars are expected to write with integrity, so we explain how to borrow from sources and intertwine your ideas with other scholars. We show you how to create a conversation with sources by paraphrasing, quoting, interpreting, and elaborating on source material. We also explain some of the fundamentals of citation to help you decide when and how to cite sources in any argument that you're writing.

What's Next

Take what you've learned in this chapter and write responses to the following prompts.

1. **Examining a Publication.** One of the best ways to learn about effective organization is to study examples. To see how papers in your major are typically arranged, find a scholarly article that is published in one of your discipline's prominent journals.

   Your library most likely has access to these scholarly journals online; if so, you can begin by searching in a database like Academic Search Complete or EBSCOhost. You might also ask your advisor or a professor in your major to recommend an article that represents the typical features of scholarship in your field. For example, if you wanted to know what scholarly articles look like in writing studies, we would recommend examining articles in the journal *College Composition and Communication*.

   Once you've selected an article, look carefully at the organizational moves the argument makes and discuss the following in class or with a peer:

   a. How does the author begin? What "moves" does he make? For example, does he reference other scholars or raise important questions?

   b. How and where does the author address the argument's *So what?*

   c. Is the paper divided into different sections with headings?

   d. Are there major shifts in the paper between different topics? How does the author transition between different ideas?

   e. How does the author handle potential objections or different perspectives on the topic? Does she give voice to any opposition? Where?

    f. Are there graphics and charts? How do they relate to the text?

    g. Are there footnotes or endnotes? What purposes do these serve?

    h. What moves does the author make in the conclusion?

Now, write an e-mail to an incoming student who is planning to major in your discipline. Give him or her some tips for writing in your discipline, particularly for organizing and formatting scholarly papers. Provide links to useful resources and examples.

2. **Proposal Arguments.** Watch the film *An Inconvenient Truth* to investigate its techniques and evaluate it as a proposal argument. Consider the following questions:

    a. How is the film organized?

    b. How does the documentary convince readers that a serious problem exists? Are you convinced by the support?

    c. What unstated assumptions does the film rely on? What values and beliefs must the audience share?

    d. How well does the film respond to opposing views?

CHAPTER nine

How Do We Use Sources Responsibly

chapter checklist

- How—and why—do we write with integrity?
- How do we avoid plagiarizing?
- How do we quote and integrate sources?
- When do we cite sources?
- What are the fundamentals of citation?

Way back in high school, you might only have used sources to write certain kinds of assignments, like the dreaded Research Paper. In college, most professors will expect you to include sources—at least your class readings, if not "outside" library sources—every time you write.

For scholars, nearly every paper is a research paper. Or at least every paper presents an opportunity to conduct some kind of research, because for scholars, every paper attempts to answer a question through investigation. That's why professors care so much (sometimes it might seem like a little too much) about finding good sources and "documenting" or citing those sources in elaborate bibliographies or lists of "works cited." As scholars, we value each other's contributions and we leave a paper trail to prove it.

Write with Integrity

Anyone who's been interviewed by a newspaper or television reporter knows what it's like to have his words taken out of context or used to prove a point that he really didn't intend to make. Even if reporters try to use their sources responsibly, when they distill a long interview down to a pithy sound bite, the person being interviewed can feel cheated.

Scholars maintain their integrity by making a good faith effort not to "cheat" the authors whose words and ideas they borrow. That's why we work so diligently—using the techniques for careful reading and analysis that we've discussed in this book—to fully understand our sources' content, intended purpose, and persuasive strategies *before* we critique them, disagree with them, or use them to support our own arguments.

As a community of scholars, we must be able to trust each other's work and trust that our colleagues will use our work responsibly. That's where the idea of plagiarism comes from. Plagiarism is a kind of stealing, yes, but more important, plagiarism violates the trust of the scholarly community. How can we build upon each other's discoveries if we cannot trust the integrity of the work done to produce and communicate those discoveries?

Because we never know how our work will influence others, we take scholarly integrity very seriously. The results of "cheating" sometimes have obvious and immediate consequences. Imagine, for example, the potential health and safety risks caused by a medical researcher who takes shortcuts in testing a new drug. And think of all the previous research on which that medical innovation depended. Faulty research by a previous biologist or chemist or physicist might also have indirectly tainted the development of the new drug.

The credibility and integrity of our scholarly work is therefore *networked* and *interdependent*, which is why we cite our sources. We didn't design citation styles just to torture scholarly apprentices. Our specialized referencing systems (MLA and APA, for example) enable us to exhibit scholarly genealogies for our discoveries. Scholars who review our work can judge its credibility, in part, by scrutinizing the lineage of our work, which we present to readers through citations and bibliographies. So even though we don't expect you, as a scholarly apprentice, to begin "expanding the bounds of human understanding" just yet, we do expect you to acknowledge your sources from the beginning.

So far, we've been justifying why scholars cite their sources. The last, and perhaps most obvious rule of writing with integrity is simply that you do the work yourself and don't copy from other writers. Learning requires practice. **Copying from others denies you the opportunity to learn.**

Plagiarism

Most schools have formal honor codes that define various kinds of cheating. The term "plagiarism" typically means copying someone else's words or ideas without attribution. Buying a paper off the Web or copying someone else's writing is deemed the most serious of offenses and often carries the strictest penalties, such as failing the assignment or the course, or even expulsion from school.

You will also get into trouble for copying a passage from a source without quoting it. Remember to mark all quotations and provide proper citations as we describe below.

Students are often less familiar with other kinds of honor code violations, which may include the following: unauthorized collaboration and recycled writing.

TRY THIS ➤ Trace a Scholarly Genealogy

For this reflection, read and summarize an article that cites Matthew A. Killingsworth and Daniel T. Gilbert's article, "A Wandering Mind Is an Unhappy Mind."

   Killingsworth and Gilbert credit a number of sources in their bibliography that they built their research upon—their scholarly ancestors, so to speak. If you can access the online version of the article via your library's website, their citations are hyperlinked to the sources. Also on the website is a listing of subsequent research that grew out of Killingsworth and Gilbert's research—their scholarly descendants.

1. Choose one of the subsequent articles (scholarly descendants) listed on the website under the heading "This Article Has Been Cited by Other Articles." (If you can't access their article online, you can search Google Scholar for links to sources that cite the article.)
2. Read one article to see how it builds off of Killingsworth and Gilbert's research, and reflect on the following:
   • Where in the article do the authors cite Killingsworth and Gilbert?
   • How is the article related to "A Wandering Mind Is an Unhappy Mind"?
   • Can you imagine how Killingsworth and Gilbert's article might have been a catalyst for this article?
3. Then, write a one-page summary of the article, describing how it continues the scholarly conversation. Share your summaries in class to discuss the different threads that Killingsworth and Gilbert's "scholarly descendants" take up.
4. If you're interested in pursuing this further, read one of Killingsworth and Gilbert's "scholarly ancestors" to see how their work influenced "A Wandering Mind Is an Unhappy Mind."

Unauthorized Collaboration

Scholars rarely write alone. They usually discuss their ideas with others and ask colleagues to critique their writing. You should do the same whenever possible, with one caveat: **Always ask your instructor, in advance, about what kinds of collaboration she allows.**

Most professors, most of the time, will appreciate that you're using every available means to improve your writing. However, there may be occasions when you'll be expected to complete your work alone to demonstrate your own, individual learning. Seeking help from writing center tutors is usually acceptable, but to be safe, consider asking your professor first.

Recycled Writing

This may seem odd, but schools typically do not allow students to recycle papers. For example, you probably cannot dust off a paper you wrote in high school—however long ago that was—for use in a college class. This rule may not seem fair (after all, the paper is your intellectual "property," so you're not really stealing someone else's work), but handing in the same paper twice violates the primary purpose of academic integrity policies: **You can't learn something new if you don't do the work.**

If you want to reuse some words or ideas from a previous paper, ask your professor for guidance. She can probably help you think of ways to expand on your previous work. Scholars do this all the time as part of an evolving "research agenda," when they develop ideas over a series of research projects and publications. Tough questions and problems often take years to resolve.

Tips for Avoiding Plagiarism

- **Get to know your honor code** so you'll know how your school handles academic integrity. Ask questions when in doubt. Ignorance of the rules is typically not an excuse for breaking them.

- **As you read, pay careful attention to how writers use their sources.** Practice by imitating various styles. More skill with using sources will increase your confidence and lower the risk of plagiarism.
- **Maintain careful notes as you read and conduct research.** When taking notes, mark quotations with quotation marks, and keep track of page numbers and which material comes from which source.
- **Don't be tempted to write your paper and** *then* **go back to fill in the citations.** Doing so will only generate more work (retracing your research steps) and increase the risk of inadvertent plagiarism.
- **Don't procrastinate.** Looming deadlines cause anxiety that can cloud judgment. Don't be tempted to take shortcuts, and don't fool yourself into thinking that you write best under pressure. If, for some reason, you cannot complete your work on time, discuss your situation with your professor. Be honest, don't make excuses, and know that the sun will rise again tomorrow.

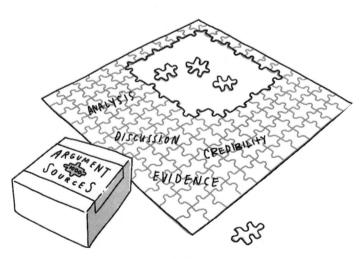

Quote and Integrate Sources

Most scholarly writing, including the kinds of assignments you're likely to encounter in college, uses published sources as verification to support arguments.

Every time you include a summary or paraphrase or quotation, you might think of that source as an expert witness in a trial. As the trial lawyer, you might borrow the expertise and credibility of a scientist, for example, to validate or refute DNA evidence. Then you'll have a conversation with that source—and with your audience—about what that evidence means (in other words, provide explicit linkages).

Unless your audience, the "jury," already knows your source (if he's Plato or Shakespeare, they might know him already), then they'll expect you to introduce your "expert witness" and explain why we should trust him. One of the best places to learn how to do this in nonscholarly writing is to study newspaper reporting.

Newspaper reporters seamlessly integrate other people's words into their articles, like in the following example:

> [S]ome experts note that as wealthy students abuse stimulants to raise already-good grades in colleges and high schools, the medications are being used on low-income elementary school children with faltering grades and parents eager to see them succeed.

> "We as a society have been unwilling to invest in very effective nonpharmaceutical interventions for these children and their families," said Dr. Ramesh Raghavan, a child mental-health services researcher at Washington University in St. Louis and an expert in prescription drug use among low-income children. "We are effectively forcing local community psychiatrists to use the only tool at their disposal, which is psychotropic medications."

> Dr. Nancy Rappaport, a child psychiatrist in Cambridge, Mass., who works primarily with lower income children and their schools, added: "We are seeing this more and more. We are using a

chemical straitjacket instead of doing things that are just as important to also do, sometimes more."

(Source: Schwarz, Alan. "Attention Disorder or Not, Pills to Help in School." *New York Times*, 9 Oct. 2012. Web.)

Reporters don't just assume readers intuitively know who their sources are. And they don't just insert a quote without any warning or description of the source's identity. Otherwise, readers might be confused.

Think of it this way: If you were sitting in your living room and someone just wandered in, without introducing herself or explaining why she was there, you would probably feel awkward or confused ("Hey, get out of my house!"). Similarly, readers are perplexed when a "stranger" (another source) appears in a paragraph. They want to know the identity of the source, what it's doing, and how it's related to the writer. So it's important for writers to *frame* their quotations with:

1. **an introduction**: usually an "attributive tag" (what some scholars call a "signal phrase"), like the examples we give in Chapter 4 ("According to . . ." or "The author states . . .") that clarifies who's speaking; and
2. **an explanation** that situates the "stranger" in the writer's space—explains why the source is relevant.

While newspaper reporters model the attributive tags we write in scholarly papers, they don't show us how to *converse with* sources. As

TRY THIS ➤ Study How Popular Sources Introduce Sources

For this exercise, collect several examples of popular sources (newspapers, magazines, etc.) and study how the authors introduce their sources. Create a list of rules or techniques that authors use.

you can see in the example, the reporter relies more heavily on the source to present information than is typical in scholarly writing. If you deleted the quotations from this excerpt, there would hardly be any content left. You can't really get away with that as a student because, as we keep saying, professors are typically more interested to hear what *you* think than what your sources say. So we'll describe how to create a conversation with your sources in the next section.

Create a Conversation

When we build sources into arguments, we not only clarify who our sources are, but we also create linkages by telling readers

a. why a quote is there,
b. what it means, and
c. how it's related to, or supports, our argument.

We don't expect our readers to figure this stuff out through ESP. For one, readers could misunderstand or misinterpret quotations. More important, readers wouldn't know what *we thought about* the quotation. We wouldn't be able to converse with our sources and with our readers. Instead of quoting a source and immediately moving on, we elaborate on sources in the following ways:

- **Interpret the source.** Unless a quotation's message is blatantly obvious, we typically offer some kind of explanation. Readers usually need help interpreting a quotation because we've taken it out of its original context. Especially when there's unfamiliar vocabulary or dense information, we translate the source's ideas into more accessible language. We add explanations directly after each quotation, such as:

"This passage suggests that . . ."
"In other words, . . . "
"Here, the writer explains that . . ."
"In this section, the author offers . . ."

197

- **Explain how the quotation relates to our argument.** Although the relationship between a quotation and our ideas might seem clear, readers often need us to highlight the linkage. We link a quotation to our paragraph's central point by telling readers exactly *why* and *how* the source is relevant. Quotations can serve as evidence that supports our point when we add commentary like:

"Dr. X illustrates my point exactly: . . ."
"Given what experts contend, it is clear that . . ."
"The author's views are relevant because they show that . . ."
"All of this relates to my point that . . ."

- **Tell readers what makes the quotation significant.** Since we only quote a source when it's necessary, we should know why a quotation is important. But readers need to understand the implications, too. They need to know what is meaningful about a quotation—why it matters—and what the consequences of its ideas are. To shed light on a quotation's implications, we say:

"This quotation is significant because it illustrates . . ."
"The author's ideas have important consequences, mainly that . . ."
"This is important because . . ."
"If we extend the scholar's argument, we can see that . . ."
"What makes this point particularly _____ (urgent, puzzling, thought provoking, valid, etc.) is . . ."

- **Consider ways to make a source our own.** Link a source to our argument by providing our own unique example, analogy, or related experience to illustrate the idea, like this:

"My own learning process matches the theories proposed by John Dewey in his book, *Experience and Education*. For example . . ."
"Nancy Sommers says that the writing process is like a 'seed' (384). A more fitting metaphor to describe my writing process would be . . ."

These strategies allow us to talk alongside our sources, rather than expecting them to speak *for* us. We can maintain ownership of the argument by preventing our sources from overpowering our own voice. We also gain some points with our readers—especially with professors—when we show off our analytical abilities and critical thinking skills.

TRY THIS ➤   Integrate Sources More Fully

For this exercise, review a piece of writing that you're currently drafting or that you recently composed, and look for places where you can introduce and elaborate on your sources more fully. Use the model phrases you learned to introduce quotations and explain, interpret, and/or contextualize your sources' arguments.

Paraphrasing

Paraphrasing is a difficult skill for apprentice scholars to master. To paraphrase effectively, you must closely read and fully understand your source, and you must practice, using the techniques outlined in Chapter 3. Here's another example of paraphrases using an excerpt from this chapter.

- **Original text:** "This may seem odd, but schools typically do not allow students to recycle papers. For example, you probably cannot dust off a paper you wrote in high school—however long ago that was—for use in a college class."
- **Proper paraphrase:** According to Schick and Schubert, colleges may consider resubmitting old assignments to be a kind of plagiarism (193).
- **Proper paraphrase with quotation:** Writing scholars Schick and Schubert warn students not to "recycle papers" from high school for college classes (193).

Writing scholar Rebecca Moore Howard coined the term "patch-writing" to describe "failed" paraphrasing, or what some honor codes call insufficient paraphrasing—source material that is neither quoted nor adequately rephrased. Here's an example:

- **Patchwriting:** It might seem weird, but schools typically prohibit students from reusing papers. You cannot hand in an old paper from high school in your college class.

Notice how the patchwriting changes a few words but retains nearly the same sentence structure as the original? It's not much better than a remix. Even with an accompanying citation, many colleges consider patchwriting a kind of plagiarism. Regardless of what an honor code says, patchwriting is a poor use of source text because it does not indicate that the writer has deeply processed or even understands the source. Students patchwrite more often when they are not familiar with the content or language of a source, so be sure to invest adequate time practicing the reading strategies from Chapter 3.

Citing Sources

We've waited until now to discuss the specifics of scholarly citation because too often students obsess about correct citation formatting. That's understandable for two reasons:

1. Because sometimes teachers obsess about citations, and you have to give them what they want, in order to get what you want (a good grade)
2. Because, as frustrating or foreign as citation formatting seems, the rules for citing correctly somehow seem more straightforward than rules for more complicated things like choosing a good topic or organizing your ideas. Unlike most things in writing, citations provide an opportunity for getting a right or wrong answer.

TRY THIS ➤ Practice Paraphrasing

In this exercise, reflect on the choices we make when paraphrasing, and write three different versions of a paraphrase. First, examine a quotation from page 384 of Nancy Sommers's article, "Revision Strategies of Student Writers and Experienced Adult Writers," which was published in a journal titled *College Composition and Communication*:

> The experienced writers describe their primary objective when revising as finding the form or shape of their argument. . . . When questioned about this emphasis, the experienced writers responded that since their first drafts are usually scattered attempts to define their territory, their objective in the second draft is to begin observing general patterns of development and deciding what should be included and what excluded.

Notice how we used an ellipsis (. . .) in the quotation? We did so to shorten the quotation, deleting this sentence: "Although the metaphors vary, the experienced writers often use structural expressions such as 'finding a framework,' 'a pattern,' or 'a design' for their argument." (Notice, too, in the previous sentence how we've marked quotations within a quotation using single quotation marks.)

Ellipses can be used to shorten a quotation so long as we don't significantly change its meaning. In this case, the deleted sentence simply expands on the previous one. If you had to cut more from Sommers's quotation, what more could you trim without changing its meaning?

Now, write three different versions of a paraphrase for Sommers's quotation. Include citations, as in our example. Compare your versions with a classmate and discuss the differences. Which versions do you think are most effective, and why?

So, why, you might wonder, do teachers obsess about citations anyway? And why do citation rules seem so picky in the first place?

Scholars value accurate citations because they illustrate the genealogy of our work. Missing or incorrect citations can hinder other scholars' efforts to evaluate the credibility of an argument or to relocate a source.

However, as important as citations may be for scholars who publish their research, experienced writers treat citations like they treat grammar and punctuation—as later order concerns that we described on p. 12—and you should, too. As an apprentice scholar, your writing will develop more quickly if you concentrate *first* on selecting good sources, analyzing and evaluating their content, and responsibly integrating their words and ideas into your own writing.

How Do We Know When We Need to Cite Something?

Here's the easy answer:

- **Always cite quotations and paraphrases**, and include the page number (if available).
- **Cite summaries, too.** If you're summarizing a small part of a source, include the appropriate page numbers. When summarizing an entire source, page numbers are not necessary.
- **Cite statistics, dates, and other details** that are not common knowledge.

Now, here's where it gets more complex: What exactly *is* "common knowledge"? We don't need to cite things that everyone already knows, right? As with most things in writing, that depends.

Before the Internet, teachers often told students that if you could find the same information in some arbitrary number of sources (three or five or however many different places), then you could consider that information "common knowledge," so you wouldn't need a citation. This general rule doesn't work so well anymore for two reasons.

First, the number of times some information gets published may or may not indicate anything about it being commonly known. Nowadays, websites often "borrow" information and text from each other without attribution. (Please don't follow their example.) Finding an urban legend repeated on fifteen different websites doesn't make it true *or* common knowledge. Just because the Internet operates as a public domain for everyone's benefit does not exempt scholars from citing what we find there, either.

Secondly, while the five-sources-equals-common-knowledge rule may have helped students before the Internet, the rule doesn't really get at the heart of the matter, which isn't really whether we need a citation but rather *When do we need to use a source to verify information in our arguments?*

The answer, of course, depends on your topic and audience: *How confident are you that your audience already knows what you're talking about?* For example, you can probably be confident that an audience educated in a US high school already knows what happened on July 4, 1776. But even a college-educated US audience would expect a citation if you were discussing the events of October 29, 1923 (the date when, according to Wikipedia, the modern Republic of Turkey was established). You can probably find the details of Turkey's history in hundreds of books, articles, and websites, but if your audience doesn't already know it—and *you* didn't before reading your sources—then they'll expect to see where you got your information. Otherwise, they just might not believe you.

Citation Fundamentals

Because there are so many different citation styles, we'll discuss some of the common features and concepts that most systems use. Scholars typically "document" their sources in two ways: bibliographic and in-text citations.

Bibliographic Citations

A bibliographic citation includes a complete list of information about each source. Bibliographic citations appear at the end of a scholarly article or paper as a list of "references" or "works cited" or as a "bibliography." **A bibliographic citation includes everything that a reader would need to know to find the exact source that you used.**

Each citation style formats the information a little differently, but the basic information is always the same:

a. author name(s)
b. title(s)
c. publication information (when, where, and who published the source)

Here's a bibliographic citation formatted in MLA (Modern Language Association) style, which literary scholars often use:

Schick, Kurt, and Laura Schubert. *So What? The Writer's Argument.* New York: Oxford UP, 2014. Print.

In-Text Citations

An in-text citation appears in the text, as opposed to in a separate list at the end of the paper. Specifically, **in-text citations appear right next to where you summarize, paraphrase, or quote from your source,** like in this MLA style citation:

> Some writing experts advise students to invest their energies in learning to use sources effectively before they "obsess about correct citation formatting" (Schick and Schubert, 200).

An in-text citation tells readers whose ideas are referenced, so the author's last name or other publication information (if an author is unidentified) goes in the parentheses. In-text citations point readers toward a specific source and, when needed, a specific place (page or pages) in that source. You don't need to repeat information in an in-text citation that you've already covered in an attributive tag, like in the following example:

> According to Schick and Schubert, there's no magical number of sources that distinguish information as "common knowledge" (203).

Although it might not seem like it sometimes, scholars try to follow common sense: If we've already told readers (at the beginning of a sentence) where an idea comes from, we don't need to repeat ourselves at the sentence's end.

Back in the day when scholars mostly cited books and printed journals articles, formatting citations was comparatively easy. Now, with so many different kinds of sources available, things get more complicated. You'll find it easier to make sense of citation formatting if you first understand the concepts behind the three main citation elements.

Author name(s). For printed sources like a book or journal (even when you're reading such publications online), the author or authors will be clearly listed. For other sources, the author is sometimes easy to find, like the person who wrote a letter or e-mail, the artist who wrote a song or movie script, or the author of a website.

When there's no clear author, you'll need to ask your professor or consult a citation reference guide for how to format this part of the bibliographic citation. For the in-text citation, you can use an attributive tag that identifies the publisher as the author, like this:

"According to the US Department of Energy website, ... "

Bibliographic citations always list the last name of the first author first and list the sources in easy-to-navigate alphabetical order.

Titles. Many publications have two-part titles (like *So What? The Writer's Argument*). Be sure to list the complete title in the bibliographic citation. What's a little more confusing is that many publications really have two different titles: one for part of the source (chapter, article, song) and another for the whole source (book, magazine, CD). Bibliographic citations include *both* titles.

Each citation system formats titles differently, but every style formats the part and the whole differently. MLA, for example, marks the part with quotation marks ("Is Google Making Us Stupid? What the Internet Is Doing to Our Brains") and formats the whole in italics (*The Atlantic*). These formatting differences may seem picky, but they help the reader know, in this example, whether you're referring to one specific article or an entire magazine.

Publication information. Again, with books it's easy to find where, when, and who published the source because that information is listed near the title page.

Publication information is different for periodicals, or sources that are published periodically, like magazines, newspapers, and scholarly journals. For those, the publication title (such as *Time* or the *Journal of Applied Behavior Analysis*) counts as the "publisher." Scholarly periodicals often have an additional system for identifying each issue, by number, as part of a volume. For example, MLA style includes the volume number followed by the issue number, like this:

Johnson, Kristine. "Beyond Standards: Disciplinary and National Perspectives on Habits of Mind." *College Composition and Communication* 64.3 (2013): 517–541. Print.

Bibliographic citations for periodicals also include page numbers.

Again, publication information gets more complicated with other kinds of sources. For example, different citation systems treat online sources differently. Some require the URL (web address) along with the date that you viewed (or "retrieved") a website, while others do not.

These rules might seem impossible to keep track of, but if you remember to collect the basic elements we've discussed—author, title, and publication information—as you conduct your research, you'll have whatever information you need to create your bibliography later. Bottom line: **Keep track of whatever details you or your reader would need to retrace your steps to find each source again.** Then, when you're reviewing your bibliography, ask yourself: *Is it complete? Does it contain all the required elements necessary for someone to locate the source again?*

So Many Styles . . .

Try to remember the main elements of a citation, but don't try to memorize the finer points of citation formatting. If you need to collect many sources, you might consider trying out an automatic formatting tool like RefWorks or EndNote. When you need to verify accuracy or format your citations manually, consult library resources (like the *MLA Style Manual* or *The Publication Manual of the APA*) or a reputable writing center website, like the Purdue OWL.

As you gain more experience in scholarly writing, it's worth paying attention to how citation styles reflect the kind of intellectual work done by the scholars who use them. For example, scientists and social scientists commonly use the citation system of the American Psychological Association, or APA style. Here's an APA style bibliographic citation:

Schick, K., & Schubert, L. (2014). *So what? The writer's argument.* New York: Oxford University Press.

When you contrast the APA style to the following MLA bibliographic citation, what differences do you notice?

Schick, Kurt, and Laura Schubert. *So What? The Writer's Argument.* New York: Oxford UP, 2014. Print.

In contrast to the MLA citation, the APA version exhibits some differences that seem designed only to frustrate students (see Table 9.1).

For example, APA capitalizes titles differently and insists that we don't abbreviate "University Press." But what about the other differences? Why do you think that scientists would abbreviate given names and move the publication date up to the front of the citation?

Scholarly style guides cover more than citation formatting. They also explain things such as how to format the title page and where to put page numbers. Style guides also help with less technical concerns, like how to use sources and make appropriate choices about writing style, so they're more useful than you might think.

Table 9.1   BASIC DIFFERENCES BETWEEN MLA AND APA CITATION STYLES

APA (used in the sciences and social sciences)	MLA (used in the humanities)
The author's (or authors') last name(s), date, and page number are included in the in-text citation, like this: (Schick & Schubert, 2014, p. 152)	The author's (or authors') last name(s) and the page number are included in the in-text citation, like this: (Schick and Schubert 152). No comma separates the author's name and the page number.
Authors' first names are not included on the References page. Only last names and first initials are given, like this: Schick, K.	Authors' first and last names are listed on the Works Cited page, like this: Schick, Kurt
Book titles are not capitalized, except for the first letters of the title and the subtitle, like this: *So what? The writer's argument*	Books titles are capitalized, like this: *So What? The Writer's Argument*
Quotations that exceed 40 words (called "block quotations") begin on a new line and are indented five spaces.	Quotations that exceed four lines (called "block quotations") begin on a new line and are indented two tabs.

What distinct disciplinary values do these subtle differences reflect?

....

TRY THIS ➤ Study the Chicago Citation Style

For this exercise, design a table that lists the basic features of Chicago citation style, especially those that differ from MLA and/or APA. To learn about Chicago style, consult the *Chicago Manual of Style*, which you might find in your campus library, or review reputable resources online.

....

So What?

We create arguments from sources by responsibly borrowing and building on the words and thoughts of other scholars. When in doubt, cite what's not already in your head. You won't be accused of plagiarism for citing too much. And remember, arguments should demonstrate *your* thinking. Use sources to support your arguments; don't let them dominate your writing.

Throughout the book, we've described writing as deliberate and flexible. In the same way that we select sources that our audience will find persuasive, we adopt a writing style that appeals to readers and suits our purpose. In our final chapter, we describe how to adapt your writing style to different rhetorical situations, including digital spaces. Rather than talking about strict rules, we explain the effects of stylistic and grammatical choices. We answer specific questions like "What is passive voice?" and "Can I make errors on purpose?" as well as share fun techniques you can try to vary your sentences, liven up your language, and add some pizzazz to your prose. Finally, we offer proofreading and editing advice that you can use on your own or with a trusted reader.

What's Next

Take what you've learned in this chapter and write responses to the following prompts.

1. **Using Sources in Scholarly and Nonacademic Work**. Find a scholarly journal article in your field on a subject that interests you, and investigate how the author uses sources. In three different colors, highlight quotations, paraphrases, and summaries. Then, find a magazine or newspaper article that also uses outside sources. Use the same colors to highlight the different ways the author uses sources. After you finish color-coding the articles, estimate the percentages and create a pie chart or other graphic to show your results. Compare your results with a classmate and reflect on the following:
   - How much does each author use each technique?
   - How much of the article is the author's thoughts?
   - How do the scholarly arguments use sources differently than the nonacademic ones?

2. **Citation Systems**. Look up the citation system that your discipline uses and practice formatting a few different sources' bibliographic citations. For variety, format a book, a scholarly article, and a credible website. Then, compare your citations with a few classmates:
   - What differences do you notice among styles?
   - What disciplinary values might influence these different details, such as the date placement?

CHAPTER ten

What about Style?

chapter checklist

- What are the features of style?
- How can we develop a range of voices and styles?
- How can we write more clearly and vividly?
- What creative choices can we make to improve style?
- How can we design effective documents?
- What about writing in digital spaces?
- How do we edit and proofread?

You may have learned "never" to use the first person ("I") in academic writing. But what should you do when a professor asks you to write about your personal experiences? When faced with a question like this, or another stylistic dilemma, keep in mind that "rules" for good writing are not universal or unchanging, because what works in one context for a specific audience and purpose might not work for another. In other words, **writing is a series of strategic choices.**

Writing with Style

What is stylistically appropriate in one argument might be a faux pas—or even a colossal blunder—in another situation. Just like you wouldn't wear PJs to a funeral, you probably shouldn't use slang in a lab report. But you might use popular colloquialisms in an article for the student newspaper because such language could help you connect with readers. So, like fashionable attire, what constitutes a smartly chosen writing style depends on the rhetorical situation.

Therefore, we define style as "thoughtful flexibility"—the ability to adapt our voice, word choice, sentence structure, rhetorical effects, and document design to different situations, expectations, or demands.

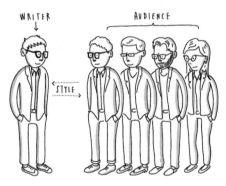

With practice, style is something that you can change and adapt, according to the needs of different audiences, purposes, and contexts.

Scholarly Style

When in doubt, you can adopt a scholarly style that exhibits the features listed in Table 10.1.

To be clear and precise, scholarly style doesn't have to be boring, nor does it require unnecessarily fancy expression. The universal rule for good style, in scholarly writing or elsewhere, is for it to *seem deliberate*, with every word and sentence carefully chosen for its particular audience, purpose, and situation. Effective scholars try to **write compelling prose that cannot possibly be misunderstood.**

While we can't offer foolproof advice for every writing situation, this chapter will help you think strategically about your stylistic choices. Before we delve into the details of style, let's focus on some fundamentals.

Table 10.1 SCHOLARLY STYLE

CLEAR AND READABLE	OBJECTIVE TONE	PRECISE AND CONCISE PROSE
• Smooth transitions • Free of unnecessary embellishments or linguistic devices that distract from meaning • Consistent verb tense • Lean sentences that aren't weighed down by extra prepositions or unnecessary words • Free of distracting and confusing mechanical errors	• Respectful treatment of sources • Unbiased language that doesn't invoke stereotypes or use potentially offensive terms • Third-person point of view (uses "I" only if appropriate)	• Active voice (as appropriate) • Free of filler phrases, like "there are" or "since the beginning of time" • Precise verbs and concrete nouns that convey specific meaning • Free of jargon and colloquial expressions

How would you classify the overall style of this book? How would you describe your writing style?

TRY THIS ➤ Categorize Characteristics of Good Writing

For this exercise, identify the distinguishing features of "good" writing, and then sort them as either higher order or later order concerns, using the following steps:

1. As a class, discuss the following question: "What are some defining qualities of 'good' writing?" List the characteristics on the board.
2. Assign each of the characteristics into one of two categories: higher order concerns and later order concerns. For example, if you decide that clarity is an important feature, which category does that fall under?
3. Discuss what you observe about labeling writing characteristics this way: Do any of the features fall into both categories? Which characteristics seem most important? What does this exercise teach you about writing?

Higher Order and Later Order Concerns

Scholars typically concentrate on big-picture concerns in early drafts and more minute concerns later. Revision focuses on higher order (or global) concerns—like focus, development, organization, and whether our ideas make sense. As we discuss in Chapter 1, experienced writers invest ample time in revising before we edit for later order (local) concerns, like grammar, punctuation, and so forth.

Here are three good reasons not to worry about polishing your prose until you have your ideas carved out.

1. **Perfectionism can cause writer's block**. Your mind has enough to do without trying to articulate your ideas perfectly the first time, especially when you're grappling with complex concepts and arguments. As an alternative, we like to freewrite (we describe this technique of drafting without editing in Chapter 5) during early drafts, which allows us to develop and organize our ideas before we nitpick over punctuation and sentence-level choices.
2. **Polishing can waste time and energy** while you're still sculpting. Every time you reorganize, add, or delete content, you'll have to refinish your writing.
3. **Editing while drafting is less effective** because it's difficult to concentrate on everything at once. Returning to our writing after putting it down for a day or more gives us a fresh perspective, which helps us find more errors and opportunities to improve style.

Remember that you don't have to proceed through the writing process in a linear, lockstep way. Still, we do recommend that you prioritize and try not to do everything at once. We prefer to read for content and organization first, giving less attention to mechanics; then, we can pay more attention to style and grammar, targeting the quality of writing. Once we get to the editing and proofreading part of the writing process, we review an argument multiple times, always with a specific, focused purpose.

Mechanics

Often we hear students clump all later order concerns together under vague headings like "grammar" or "flow." But these imprecise terms don't convey *exactly* what students are referring to: punctuation, transitions, sentence structure, verb tense, or any number of considerations.

Accurate, precise terminology can enable writers to think and communicate more carefully about their writing. For example, writers can ask for specific assistance from peer reviewers or tutors when they use terms that communicate their exact needs. Plus, we've noticed that writers who talk vaguely about their writing often are less sure about what they really need to work on. To be more precise, we use the term *mechanics* to refer only to sentence-level concerns, which include spelling, punctuation, capitalization, grammar, and usage.

Errors

Even though hardly anyone speaks or writes with perfect mechanics all the time, most educated readers expect standard academic English in formal writing. Sometimes mechanical "errors" significantly affect meaning. For example, consider how mechanics, specifically punctuation, can modify meaning:

- A woman, without her man, is nothing.
- A woman: without her, man is nothing.

Do you notice how these sentences mean something very different? This is the main reason why educated readers value proper mechanics: they value precise meaning and want readers to say what they mean clearly and deliberately. **Errors add confusion**. Errors cause readers to work harder to make sense of what we're trying to say.

Even when they don't seriously impair meaning, **errors diminish credibility** because of the potential for imprecision or miscommunication. Educated readers will likely interpret errors as signs of laziness

215

(like we didn't edit carefully and therefore don't care about our work) or ignorance (as though we don't know the rules). Just as when preparing for a job interview, when submitting a final draft, we make every effort to make sure our appearance is polished and professional. There's no reason to lose the job over a bit of toilet paper stuck to your shoe, or an errant apostrophe.

Grammar versus Usage

Grammar and usage are not the same, and experienced writers know the difference. Simply put, "grammar" involves the rules for how we use language traditionally or formally, while "usage" is how most people actually use language in everyday conversations.

Here's an example that explains the distinction. In Chapter 1, we mention that nowadays many scholars avoid sexist language by alternating between "she" and "he," or just using "she" (since "he" had his turn for hundreds of years). The same usage formula applies to the other forms of third-person singular ("him," "her," "his," and "hers").

Third-person plural makes matters more complicated. Grammatically speaking, personal pronouns should "agree" in number with the noun to which they refer. In the previous sentence, for example, "they" refers to and "agrees with" the word "pronouns." This gets tricky, though, when a pronoun refers back to a singular noun phrase. Take, for example, this sentence: "Every student should bring [insert possessive pronoun] laptop to class." From a strictly grammatical perspective, "every student" is singular, so the pronoun should be "his" or "her": "Every student should bring her laptop to class." However, because gender-neutral language has become popular for writers and speakers who are less finicky about grammar, people now commonly say, "Every student should bring *their* laptop to class." Experienced writers know this distinction and deliberately shift between formal and informal registers, or language styles, according to the particular audience, purpose, and context.

When you think about it, many errors don't significantly impair meaning. Because we usually read words and punctuation in the context of sentences, paragraphs, and pages, we can often make out what a writer's trying to say even if a word is misspelled, missing, or incorrect (substituting "their" for "there," for example). However, if you're writing something more formal, especially for a professor who knows and cares that "every student" is singular, then try to conform to standard academic English because mechanics affect credibility. In either case—informal or formal writing—try to avoid errors that confuse your reader.

You can find detailed discussions of mechanics in style handbooks and credible resources online, such as Oxford Dictionaries Online and Purdue University's Online Writing Lab (OWL). Even if you're not ready to memorize the rules for using *who* versus *whom* or avoiding dangling modifiers, we highly recommend finding helpful resources that you can consult on a regular basis.

Punctuation

Punctuation marks, like commas and colons, make our writing more readable: we can prevent confusion and reading fatigue by correctly punctuating sentences. Punctuation marks help us communicate clearly. In fact, these marks can even help us emphasize our argument and persuade readers subtly. When deciding how to punctuate a sentence, we ask ourselves: *How are the ideas in these sentences related? What level of connection do they have with each other?*

Punctuation marks create a spectrum of connections between ideas. For instance, periods offer complete separation, whereas commas produce a tighter relationship between similar ideas. If you think of a paragraph as a group of people, imagine how sentences mingle with and relate to each other.

1. A **period** is used to show full separation between ideas. Each sentence can "stand" on its own, independently.

EXAMPLE: "Experienced writers know that sometimes they have to write first to discover what their argument will be. Oftentimes they allow writing to inspire their thinking, rather than the other way around."

2. A **dash** is used to set apart—especially to emphasize or to elaborate—one portion of a sentence. Often, dashes direct the reader's attention toward the end of a sentence, but they can also highlight the middle portion of a sentence when two dashes are used like brackets (as in the previous sentence). Writers can also use commas or parentheses to mark off a part of a sentence, but the dash has a different effect. Putting commas or parentheses around something suggests that it's less important, while dashes are used to *emphasize* the separated portion.

   EXAMPLE: "Scholars typically take advantage of every opportunity to have someone read and respond to their work in progress—either their real audience or a peer who can play substitute."

3. A **colon** is used in two main ways: (1) to introduce a list (like we're doing right now); and (2) to combine two independent sentences, where the first part of the sentence introduces the ideas of the second part. The colon is placed after the introduction or the "spoiler" regarding what comes next.

   EXAMPLE: "A similar phenomenon occurs with writing: practicing effective habits can help them feel more natural, but practicing bad habits will further instill them."

4. A **semicolon** is used to connect closely related ideas that could be separated into two sentences but demonstrate a stronger connection when joined by a semicolon. The semicolon allows the writer to elaborate or clarify one idea with another closely related one.

   EXAMPLE: "You can build knowledge about writing through practice; however, practice alone won't make you a better writer."

Intentional Errors

As you've probably noticed through reading this book and elsewhere, writers sometimes bend or break the mechanical rules—especially rules of usage—for effect. This can be appealing, stylistically, so long as the audience knows you're doing so intentionally (and so long as it's appropriate for the purpose, genre, and context).

Like this, for example.

Sometimes we use incomplete sentences, extra punctuation, or one-word answers because the prose reads better with the intentional error. We like the way it sounds. Or the errors actually enhance the meaning or clarity of our message. We make these choices deliberately, after we've considered the full effect of our style selection, based on how we expect our audience to respond.

Since professors normally expect proper mechanics, apprentice scholars should incorporate intentional errors sparingly, when you decide that the effect magnifies the message.

Like any writer who reads her audience carefully, you have to figure out whether your creativity will be praised or scorned. These decisions provide practice for the judgment calls you have to make when composing work e-mails, communicating with clients, and writing online in public spaces. The style you choose determines the way you present yourself, and carefully selected intentional errors can demonstrate your rhetorical dexterity.

To be on the safe side, you can show your professor that you know what you're doing by pointing out intentional errors in your paper (mark them with asterisks, or add footnotes or penciled comments to explain), or you can always get permission ahead of time.

Voice

You've probably heard teachers talk about finding your authentic "voice" when you write. Readers in the humanities often like to "hear" a human writer as they read. In other disciplines, such as the sciences, audiences commonly expect a more objective sounding, "voiceless" style.

Neither approach is wrong. In fact, the more styles writers can master, the more flexibility they have to adapt to different situations.

Verbs make a big difference in how readers "hear" our writing. Scholarly writing often employs active voice, where the doer of the action (the subject) comes before the object, like this:

EXAMPLE: "The scientist (*subject*) conducted (*verb*) the experiment (*object*)."

Passive voice reverses the sentence order, placing the object before the verb and the subject, like this:

EXAMPLE: "The experiment (*object*) was conducted (*verb*) by the scientist (*subject*)."

Neither order is grammatically incorrect, but **many readers prefer active voice because it's usually clearer and easier to read**. In active voice, the action progresses in the order that it occurs—from the subject, through the verb, to the object—rather than placing the result before the cause. This linear order creates a steady rhythm that keeps readers moving forward. On the other hand, passive voice is often more wordy, which increases the reader's workload and slows him down.

In addition to being cumbersome, passive voice can be vague when the subject is missing because we may not know who performed the act. At its worst, passive voice intentionally hides the person responsible for the action. Consider, for example, the notorious statement "Mistakes were made," which doesn't indicate *who* made mistakes. The culprit can evade blame.

The bottom line is that scholarly writing values agency, clarity, and full disclosure. We aim to write sentences that help writers move smoothly and understand both what happened and who is responsible.

You can pinpoint passive voice in your own writing by spotting sentence structures like the example above (object - verb - subject).

Another trick is to notice the way the verb changes in passive voice. Passive voice always uses a "to be" verb (am, is, are, was, were, be, being, been) along with another verb in its past participle form (usually ending in -ed or -en).

To transform passive voice into active voice, ask yourself, *Who is responsible for this action? Who is performing this action?* Then, place the doer, or the cause, before the action or result.

TRY THIS ➤ Transform Passive Voice into Active Voice

For this exercise, practice transforming the following sentences into active voice.

1. Well-educated people know that everyone's perspective, including their own, is limited by ignorance and bias.
2. In college, you will often be judged more on how you develop and defend your ideas than the ideas themselves.
3. Arguments are built on a basis of acceptance or agreement.
4. Opinions can be shared by many, but are understood as subjective, or open to interpretation, debate, and revision.
5. As an apprentice, you will get to practice the same active approach to reading that scholars take, one that is fueled by curiosity, authentic motivation, and a desire to respond.
6. If your mind is not actively engaged, you will not remember what you read, let alone be able to comprehend or analyze new information and difficult text.
7. Experienced scholars mistrust sources that haven't been scrutinized by experts.
8. Scholars don't want to repeat research that has already been conducted or pursue questions that have already been answered.

Does changing voice change the meaning? If so, how? Which versions sound better? Why?

Now, inspect a piece of your own writing for signs of passive voice, and rewrite sentences that would be clearer in active voice.

Clarity and Vividness

Although imitation can help writers develop style, sometimes apprentice scholars try to emulate the dense, highly technical style that they read in published scholarship. Trying too hard to sound smart can sacrifice clarity. The result is wordy, convoluted, confusing prose that overworks readers.

Remember, the point of writing is to communicate. If our style interferes with our ability to communicate, we've adopted the wrong style. To avoid an overly academic, pretentious style, consider the following suggestions.

Use Strong Verbs

Sometimes writers nominalize verbs by turning them into nouns. For instance, "express" becomes "expression," and "communicate" becomes "communication." Nominalized sentences can become clunky or unclear because they are overloaded with prepositions and excessive words. Helen Sword from the *New York Times* (July 23, 2012) calls nominalizations "zombie nouns," which "cannibalize active verbs," leaving the sentence desiccated and lifeless.

To see what we mean, consider which of the following sounds better:

- "The study of rhetoric is *the investigation of* how persuasion and communication work."
- "Rhetoric *investigates* how persuasion and communication work."

Nominalized verbs sometimes help us express abstract ideas or vary our sentence structure, but nominalizations can also make our writing less lively, concise, and readable than using the original verbs.

Notice, too, how the first example sentence uses the verb "is" with the nominalization "investigation." The verb "to be" is not inherently evil, but it rarely enhances clarity. As a general rule, editing "to be" out of our writing can help us avoid using passive voice and nominalizations.

Replacing "to be" with more precise verbs that reflect our exact meaning makes our writing more engaging and fluid.

TRY THIS ➤ Eliminate Nominalizations

For this exercise, practice translating nominalizations into active verbs, and then look for nominalizations in a draft that you're currently writing.

To practice reviving stilted language, turn the following sentences into more lively constructions:

1. The demonstration of her character was shown through her consideration of others.
2. The examination of multiple views made the essay interesting.
3. The discussion of the issue was resolved through consideration of everyone's viewpoints.

Now, look for nominalizations in a draft that you're currently writing. Replace as many nominalizations as you can find with more lively, precise verbs. To make the process easier, try using the "Find" function in your word processor to search for word endings like -tion, -ism, and -ity.

Remember, Less Can Be More

While explanations and descriptions are necessary to communicate our full arguments, most readers appreciate when we spare them from wading through more words than necessary.

Vivid and Precise Language

Using descriptive language and varying your vocabulary choices can help you incorporate details into your writing that help readers feel, see, and experience your message. However, this style doesn't work in every situation. When the audience values brevity and clarity, as is often the case in business or scientific writing, literary flourishes fail. Chemists don't want flowery lab reports, and bosses don't necessarily like business proposals that rhyme.

So we are very careful not to overembellish our writing if the genre or audience calls for concision. But that doesn't mean that we can't use vivid and precise language. In fact, readers generally prefer specific and clear phrasing, details, and examples that express ideas precisely—so long as every detail is there for a reason.

For example, consider a vague word like "beneficial." It doesn't communicate much. If we said our course was "beneficial," readers wouldn't know exactly what made it beneficial. Was it informative? Intellectually challenging? Motivational? Transformative? Who knows?

We use descriptive language to select words that transmit our exact meaning without interference or distortion. Think of this as "showing" readers exactly what we mean, rather than just "telling" them. The difference is in the level of detail. When we "show" readers, we give them something concrete to grasp—evidence of our intended meaning. When we "tell" them, we claim more abstractly.

Telling and showing come together like a claim and support. For example, if you "tell" your audience to vary their vocabulary, then they might need for you to "show" them how.

Telling: "You might use synonymous phrases . . ."

Showing: ". . . for example, refer to a puppy as a 'wee canine.'"

See how the second version is more precise and even livelier because it's less abstract?

Creative Choices We Make to Improve Style

The best news about improving style is that it's something you can practice on your own.

Imitation

One way to develop a range of styles is to practice imitating other writers whom you admire.

Imitation is an ancient and useful technique for learning to write. Imagine, for example, that you were going to apply for a job but had never written an application letter or resume. Unlike in school writing, your audience (a prospective employer) would likely not provide detailed instructions for this assignment. Your best bet would be to ask someone who's recently been on the job market (and who scored a good job) to borrow her application documents to use as a guide.

Scholars often do the same thing when they want to write an article. Once they find a journal that their intended audience reads and that fits their topic, they study articles in the journal to create a set of instructions:

- What's the typical length of articles?
- How are they usually organized? For example, how much space do authors devote to reviewing previous research?

TRY THIS ➤ Practice Imitating

For this exercise, select a short piece of writing by an author whose style you admire. Study the passage carefully, noticing the author's voice, word choices, and tone. Then, write a paragraph about any topic of your choosing, trying to adopt the author's style. In class, compare imitations and describe the style you were trying to mimic.

- What style is typical? Do writers tend to write more or less formally? Are there lots of graphs or charts?

Sentence Variation

Another technique for improving style is sentence variation, which was popular during the Renaissance and used by great writers like Ben Franklin.

You can begin with a statement (like "I love ice cream"), then write multiple versions of the sentence, changing the style each time. Here are a few strategies for revision:

- **Rhetorical variation**: Change the audience, purpose, or context.
- **Amplification**: Elaborate, exaggerate, or use an analogy, metaphor, or simile. (Example: "I pine for ice cream like reality stars crave drama.")
- **Linguistic variation**: Substitute vocabulary or rearrange the order. (Example: Yoda from Star Wars might say, "Ice cream, I love" to emphasize the object.)
- **Genre translation**: Rewrite the sentence in verse, or as a Tweet. (Example: "Can't wait to eat this bowl of rocky road! #homemadeicecream")

Sentence variation helps writers assemble a richer stylistic toolkit, which can help them write more engaging prose. It also helps writers develop effective paraphrasing skills. And sentence variation can make writing more fun. Even with boring assignments, playing around with style can make the writing process more stimulating: If you can't write something interesting, write interestingly.

Figures of Speech

Rhetorical "figures" are useful tools for enriching style. You probably learned some while studying literature, for example:

- *Metaphor*: "the stench of fear"
- *Analogy:* "quiet as a mouse"
- *Hyperbole* or exaggeration: "a pea-sized brain"
- *Sarcasm*: "I never let schooling interfere with my education" (Mark Twain)

Brigham Young University's "Forest of Rhetoric" website (*Silva Rhetoricae*, http://rhetoric.byu.edu) provides scores of other examples and explanations to expand your repertoire.

Scholars sometimes use metaphors and analogies to introduce radically new concepts to each other or to explain specialized ideas to nonscientists (for example, explaining atomic structure as a solar system of subatomic particles).

Figures of speech can incur also some risks, such as:

- **Reference failure.** Much figurative language depends on the audience being familiar with specific cultural references. The common analogy "as annoying as nails on a chalkboard" may no longer make sense to younger students who've only used whiteboards and digital projectors.
- **Inappropriate style.** Using figurative flourishes in a lab report might not go over well with an audience that wants an objective tone and "just the facts."
- **Misinterpretation.** Attempts at humor, especially through sarcasm, can fail when the audience takes them literally.
- **Clichés:** Because audiences expect figurative language to explain something in fresh terms, overused expressions can seem stale and bland.

Still, using figures of speech can create fresh understanding and even be used beyond the sentence level as argumentative techniques. For instance, *anticategoria*, the "I'm-rubber-you're-glue" argument, turns a thesis back on the person making it. After the 9/11 attacks, for example, President George W. Bush condemned al-Qaeda as terrorists, to which Osama bin Laden responded by accusing the United States of acts of terrorism in the Middle East. This example raises the most important risk of using rhetorical figures:

- **False comparison.** Using figures of comparison to make an argument (example: "America's involvement in Afghanistan is like the Vietnam conflict") may provide a new way to make sense of your topic, but it might also cause an audience to claim that you're using fallacious reasoning (that is, you're using irrelevant support for your argument).

In any case, think carefully about your audience's background and expectations when using figures of speech. If you think there's a chance that your figures will misfire, provide more explanation—or maybe just take it down a notch.

TRY THIS ➤ Sentence Variation

For this exercise, restate the sentence "This assignment is challenging" in at least thirty different ways, keeping similar meaning but changing the style at least 50% each time. Try using several of the sentence variation techniques we described in the previous two sections. Then, share your work with a classmate, and explain how you varied each sentence.

Visual Design

Style isn't only cultivated in the language we use. Carefully crafted visual elements can help us compose arguments in clear, vivid, and compelling ways. Document design not only helps us present information, but it can itself become part of the message.

As with the writing process, sometimes it's useful for less experienced writers to focus on a few techniques, rather than trying everything at once. For many assignments, professors will still accept (or expect) a traditionally formatted document (words printed with black ink in twelve-point Times New Roman font using one-inch margins on plain white paper). However, since technology now gives writers easy tools for designing documents like professionals, you might consider ways to integrate visual elements when appropriate. In some subjects, like the sciences, writers typically have no choice but to use visual elements because it's difficult to support arguments without relying on tables and charts to present evidence.

Even some simple document design techniques can make an impact. Word processors and presentational software allow writers seemingly endless options to format text for persuasive effect. Choosing a more contemporary, traditional, or even playful font can influence how credible our arguments seem to different readers.

Verdanna, for example, gives a clean, modern look, which many designers recommend for online publication.

Georgia looks more traditional and may be better suited for print publication.

Comic sans is fun, but it may not be appropriate for more serious, formal occasions like college assignments or resumes.

We can use CAPITALIZATION, **bold**, *italics*, or even special formatting for emphasis, like this:

END ~~POVERTY~~ NOW.

As we explain throughout the chapter, stylistic techniques can enhance our writing, but like any kind of support, we think carefully about whether our audience will understand and appreciate such elements. Experienced scholars use such formatting consistently, in limited doses, for deliberate effects.

Writing in Digital Spaces

We make creative and deliberate choices when writing online, too. Contrary to what some people might think, digital writing is still writing. The fundamentals of argument remain the same, even when communicating online requires more complicated considerations of audience, purpose, and design. "Writing" online—whether it's a website, blog, e-mail, video, or social medium—is best when it's straightforward, engaging, and mindful of its rhetorical situation. We can easily get carried away with all of the tools and toys at our disposal online (weather apps, Web polls, counters, animations), but usually less is more. When in doubt, we keep it simple and remember what we know about rhetoric: Design with audience and purpose in mind.

How Is Writing Online Different?

For starters, it's *hypertextual*, so the Internet facilitates foraging more than careful reading. Online, you can certainly read articles or books that were written for print publication. Such documents will mostly look like they belong on paper: large blocks of black and white print without elaborate document features or images. Authors and publishers design such documents to control the audience's experience. Even though readers may skip around to find what they're looking for, print texts usually unfold in a linear way: writers expect readers to start at the beginning and read all the way through.

When designed well, online writing invites audiences to create their own reading experience (a "hypertext") by the choices they

TRY THIS ➤ Investigate What Makes Websites Work

For this exercise, examine several different websites written by different "authors," such as a school, a government agency, a business, and a person. Choose one or two that you use frequently and a few that you've never seen before, and then answer the following questions:

- What are the audiences and purposes for each site? How can you tell?
- Does each website's design (color, font, images, tone, etc.) seem effective for its intended audiences and purposes? How so?
- How does each site organize information?
- Which features do you find most and least effective?

make. Each reader can browse a website differently, choosing individual webpages on that site or following hyperlinks to other websites, depending on her interests and purposes. Some readers will wander the web like shoppers in the mall, while others will run into a website for a specific item like customers in a hardware store do.

We can use the Internet's labyrinth to our benefit when we embed images, videos, and links to other Web pages and sources in our writing. Hyperlinks provide a seamless and dynamic way to integrate our writing with other works, allowing us to converse much more effectively with other sources. For example, unlike an argument printed in hard copy, online, we can link to a source that verifies our claims, so readers can see the article for themselves—right away—as in the bibliographies in *Science Magazine* articles posted online.

Instead of writing a long footnote, we can link to a related website that extends the scope of our argument. But we need to be careful about how—and how much—we use hyperlinks. We don't want to give readers a chaotic reading experience, and we don't want to risk losing their interest.

Online writing is always public. Everyone from your dentist to your future mother-in-law can read your work. If you think that privacy restrictions add security, you're setting yourself up for potential problems. Yes, there are ways to make it harder for strangers (and "frenemies") to read your work, but these are not foolproof. You're better off expecting your future employer to access your silly photos and quirky top-ten lists. Since you leave traces of yourself on the Internet, ask yourself: *Will this posting, picture, or comment damage my credibility in the future?* For example, *Will that spontaneous status update come back to haunt me later?* Once something is online, it's permanent and it's public.

For most online writing, we have to consider many more audiences than for conventional publications. For example, a company's website must be designed with several potential audiences in mind: customers, shareholders, competitors, regulators, and so forth. Crafting a message that appeals to so many audiences is difficult, so websites sometimes have portals for distinct audiences. Your school's website might have a separate gateway for faculty, prospective students, current students, and alumni. Whether or not you design separate sections for different audiences, you'll need to imagine your work from different readers' perspectives.

Audiences move quickly. Generally, readers prefer efficient prose online so they can quickly scan and find what they're looking for. Plus, they might be reading on a small screen (smartphone, e-reader, or tablet). For these reasons, we write as concisely and design as clearly as possible. We use short sentences and paragraphs, when possible. We also know how irritating it is to scroll endlessly, so we typically limit the amount of text on a webpage to fit on a computer screen.

Remember, too, that online we're competing with pop-up advertisements, social media alerts, the alluring pages in neighboring windows, and other distractions. Keep in mind that hypertext probably brought your readers to your work in the first place, and hypertext can propel them out just as quickly. In this way, the reader drives the reading experience. So arguments need compelling design to maintain readers' attention. Tools abound, though, for making your writing (and your images, video clips, sound bites, etc.) a delight to the mind and the eye. We can use any of the following stylistic features to improve the readability of our writing:

- Navigation bars, headings, and subheadings help readers scan and find content easily.
- Bullets, pull quotes, and text boxes can break up long sections of text and direct readers' attention to the most important parts.
- Lists and charts will order and prioritize information.
- Boldface, color, italics, underline, and other text decorations (used in moderation) can highlight your prose.

Effective website designers employ "usability testing" to check whether a website will seem intuitive for their intended audiences. Just as with a draft essay, asking a peer to review your website or blog and provide feedback can be invaluable.

The Web is big and noisy. Among countless websites, blogs, e-mails, and tweets, it's difficult to be heard. Besides the joy of expressing yourself for your own amusement, think carefully about why you're writing online and what you're trying to achieve. Thinking rhetorically about the following questions will help you make intentional and smart choices:

- Why am I writing this? What am I trying to accomplish?
- Who are my readers? What kind of audience am I targeting?
- Why would anyone want to read this?
- What style (tone, level of formality, level of specificity) is appropriate?

Writing E-mails

Whether or not we blog regularly or create websites, we write many e-mails in school and in the workplace. To use e-mail effectively, consider the following suggestions.

Choose an appropriate style. Electronic mail can be as formal as a letter or as informal as a note. When we use e-mail to conduct professional business or to communicate with people we don't know well, we tend to write more formally and explicitly. Some general e-mail conventions include:

- **Explicit greetings**, including our reader's title or name (example: "Dear Professor Jones"). We usually don't just burst into writing unless we're engaged in an ongoing e-mail exchange. E-mail is not text messaging.
- **Some introduction** of who we are, if unknown to our audience, and why we're writing. Example: "I'm a student in Professor Smith's first-year writing class. Dr. Smith recommended that I contact you to ask for some research leads on a topic that I'm writing about."
- **An explicit question or statement of what you want or need.** Example: "Would it be possible to meet with you briefly next week during office hours to discuss my project?"
- **A polite closing.** Example: "Thank you for your time. I look forward to meeting with you soon. Sincerely . . . "

Write like it's official. Like anything that travels across the Web, e-mail is permanent—more permanent, really, because unlike a website that resides on the Web, many readers archive e-mails offline. While e-mail isn't yet typically considered as official as a written letter, sending something in an e-mail counts as putting it "in writing," meaning that e-mails can serve as a permanent legal or professional record. When you commit to something in e-mail, your audience will hold you accountable. And if your e-mail originates from your school's, company's, or agency's domain (.edu, .com. .org, .gov), readers may think that you represent that organization and hold it accountable for what you say.

That's why we're especially careful about what we include in e-mails and how we phrase our intended meaning. Indeed, e-mail presents lots of opportunities for misinterpretation. You've probably known someone who got into an argument over a misunderstood text message or felt embarrassed after autocorrect mangled your message. The same can happen with e-mail, especially with issues of tone. So we review and edit e-mails extra carefully, and if there's any question that a reader will be confused or misinterpret our mood, we ask a colleague to review our draft.

Unfortunately, though, no matter how much you labor over an e-mail, there's no guarantee that your reader will read it carefully. As with anything written in digital spaces, we therefore use document design features such as bullets, boldface, underline, and other formatting tools to help our audience read quickly and effortlessly. Audiences prefer not to read long or complicated e-mails, so complex discussions are better held face to face, on the phone, or with synchronous Web applications (live video chat). You can always follow up with an e-mail to document whatever everyone agreed to, follow up actions, and so forth. Again, as with any writing in digital spaces, the best rule of thumb is to keep things simple whenever possible.

Proofreading and Editing

Reading your writing aloud is a very effective technique that doesn't require much expertise but yields great results. Doing so slows down your reading and exercises more parts of your brain and body (eyes, ears, and mouth), so you can be more successful editing for clarity and correctness.

Hearing your own sentences can also help you better imagine how your reader will experience your writing. Reading aloud may be unnerving at first, but it can be a tremendously helpful way to detect confusing sentences, grammatical errors, or just an awkward tone.

Reviewing with Others

You can also **invite a trusted friend, classmate, or writing center tutor to read your work aloud**. You can check whether your main points come across clearly by asking the reader to pause after each paragraph and paraphrase or summarize what she just read.

We also ask reviewers questions like:

- How does the writing "sound"? Is the tone appropriate?
- Are there any sentences that are confusing, awkward, or otherwise unclear?
- Are there any word choices that are vague, confusing, or overly technical?
- Where can the writing be more concise? Where can I reduce unnecessary wordiness?
- Where should I combine or divide sentences?
- Where do you see mistakes, such as missing commas, subject-verb agreement problems, or misspellings?
- Where, if appropriate, might I add more personality, through humor or vividness or other stylistic devices?

Appendix A, "How to Benefit from Peer Review and Collaboration," offers more guidance for giving and receiving feedback.

Using Technology

Technology can help with editing, too. Spell-checking tools can be useful, though they usually won't catch things like homophones (their/there) or misused contractions and possessives (its/it's). For help with that, some word processors offer advanced proofing features, with options for activating grammar and style checking. In the settings, look for where you can select features you want your word processor to check, from spacing after punctuation to passive verbs and clichés. Some style checkers will also find sentences overloaded with prepositions (of, to, for, with . . .), accidental instances of "I," and other oversights. Just be sure to **think carefully before you take your word processor's advice**. Computers are careful readers, but they're not as smart or subtle as we are when it comes to writing.

Speaking of which, **be very careful with your word processor's thesaurus**. Synonyms carry similar but not equivalent meaning. Don't use words unless you know how to use them. Trying to sound smart by using words you really don't know often brings the opposite effect.

We also **use the "find" function** to identify boring verbs (is, are, have . . .) and grammatical mistakes we are likely to make, such as incorrect uses of "their" or "affect." The find function will search for any of these examples, giving us the opportunity to make changes.

Taking these extra steps makes it less likely that we'll annoy or exasperate readers. We all know readers who experience a visceral reaction when they encounter a split infinitive or a missing apostrophe.

Developing More Style

Good writing connects with its reader. We begin creating that connection when we select a question or problem that matters to us and our audience, and then write an argument that generates fresh understanding.

Still, in school or at work, we often cannot choose to write about a topic that naturally inspires our audience or us. However, what appeals to readers almost universally—and can make any writing more compelling to write or to read—is craftsmanship.

There's beauty in an instruction manual that explains how to assemble a barbecue grill with precision and clarity. A research assignment about a topic that seems uninteresting can become elegant when we imagine it as an opportunity to learn a particular style or a genre shared by a community of scholars, a way of making sense of the world that we would not have otherwise known.

Successful writers never stop collecting and perfecting their toolkit of writing skills and knowledge. You can grow as a writer throughout your life through continued practice.

- Always *read as a writer*, mining everything you read for new argumentative moves, organizational patterns, sentence structures and stylistic techniques, vocabulary and punctuation.
- Always *write as a reader*, considering how your intended audience will respond. Take every opportunity for others to read your work and help you to improve its effect.

So What?

Style is part of the message; it is central to how we connect with audiences. Although many of the components of style are later order concerns, their impact can be just as powerful as an argument's organization or support. Improving writing style is a lifelong pursuit, one that you can continue developing by experimenting, practicing, and exposing yourself to new genres and audiences.

What's Next

Take what you've learned in this chapter and write responses to the following prompts.

1. **Magazine Profile.** Investigate the style of a magazine that you like to read, and then compose a report that describes and analyzes the stylistic conventions of this magazine. To write your report, scrutinize the magazine overall and read a few sample articles.

Consider the magazine's purpose and audience, along with the following features:

a. Tone
b. Voice
c. Use of intentional mechanical errors
d. Level of detail and vividness
e. Figures of speech
f. Visual design

You might also compare the print version of the magazine with its online version, if available. Then, compose a two-page report that informs your classmates how to vary their style in order to write for this magazine.

2. **Style Makeover.** Select a piece of writing that you want to dramatically alter in style. Use many of the strategies we describe in this chapter to edit the punctuation, voice, language, sentence structure, figures of speech, and other stylistic elements. To help you focus, you might begin by selecting an alternative purpose or audience for the piece.

Appendix A

How to Benefit from Peer Review and Collaboration

THE ABILITY TO give and receive effective feedback may be the most valuable skill you can learn in life. You probably have a friend or relative who gives great advice, a person whom you and others trust, who listens carefully and provides help when needed. Employers and coworkers also value a person who can identify exactly what is and isn't working, and give useful suggestions for improvement. Such sharp critical thinking skills can benefit everyone and make you a sought-after colleague. Peer review is an excellent place to develop these skills and to practice these mental habits.

However, your experiences with peer review may be mixed. Think back on times when you've given or received feedback on writing: What worked, what didn't, and why? Compare those occasions with a time when you received excellent advice about something important other than writing. How was that advice given? What made the experience valuable for you? Now, consider what would be needed for peer review to be effective and for students to take it seriously.

The Advantages of Peer Review

In the following sections, we'll describe the benefits of peer review to you as a writer, a reader, and a collaborator; and we'll give you some suggestions for insightful questions and comments to offer during peer review.

Benefitting as a Reader

Becoming a strong, critical reader takes a lot of practice, and peer review can help you cultivate keen analytical skills that you can put to use right away in other classes. In college, you'll be expected to critically review (that is, read and analyze) a considerable amount of scholarly writing. Peer review gives you a chance to do that with essays that are typically more accessible than the professional scholarly writing you'll also encounter. Use peer review to strengthen your reading skills.

Benefitting as a Writer

Peer review lets you investigate other writers' styles, strategies, and pitfalls. You see approaches you might want to borrow and ones you definitely want to avoid. For example, reading your peer's vivid conclusion might inspire you to try a similar technique. Reading other students' work can also show you different ways to interpret an assignment, and such insight can give you a fuller understanding of the task at hand. If your peers' interpretations conflict, it's a great opportunity to identify potential questions, to talk with your instructor about his expectations, and to clarify the best ways to tackle the assignment.

The most difficult part of writing is imagining how an audience will interpret and respond to your writing. Participating in peer review gives you a glimpse into this perspective by showing you the effect of your writing on readers. Without that perspective, you can only guess whether your ideas are working.

Experienced writers take advantage of every available opportunity to have someone—either their real audience or someone who can play substitute—read and respond to their work in progress. To publish their writing, scholars submit their manuscripts to editors for feedback. Every once in a while, a scholarly journal will accept an article for publication with little revision, but much more often, editors respond with substantial feedback on how to improve the draft and a recommendation to "revise and resubmit." A demanding reader helps you better imagine your audience and then revise your essay to meet their needs.

An Unforeseen Benefit: Practice Collaborating

Practicing peer review will also strengthen your collaboration skills. You'll get to practice the interpersonal skills and social gestures essential for teamwork. For instance, when helping another writer find a better way to communicate a controversial idea or organize an elaborate proposal, you might have to soften your criticism with polite suggestions. Or you might have to help a writer avoid feeling embarrassed about a silly mistake or find a tactful way of saying that the thesis seems clichéd. Such honest communication is not easy. Tactfulness requires sophisticated conversation skills that must be learned through practice. Collaborating on writing is also tricky because you can't just rewrite portions of the paper for the writer. Instead, you have to help a writer help himself, meaning you give assistance but cannot write the paper for him. Examples include asking stimulating questions, highlighting problem areas for the writer to solve, or giving several options for the writer to choose among.

Providing Helpful Feedback

Right about now, you might be wondering, "How can I be expected to provide high-quality response if I'm not an expert writer who has read or written much scholarly writing?"

Indeed, many students find themselves saying things like "Nice job," or "I don't have much to add," or maybe "I think there's something fishy here but I'm not sure what," simply because they don't know what else to say. We understand that many students have had bad experiences with peer review and that you may feel unprepared to offer assistance, so we're offering you a model of questions and comments that can facilitate productive peer review. These questions are ones that you can ask each other and ask *yourself*, whenever you are writing.

Keep in mind that peer review shouldn't look the same during every stage of the writing process. In fact, you'll probably want to adapt the review process, just like the writing process and the reading process, depending on what the writer is trying to accomplish.

Prewriting Feedback

During the discovery stage of the writing process, it's helpful to have a conversation with your peers: talk about your ideas, pose and answer questions, serve as "devil's advocates" for each other, and identify possible plans for your papers. In this stage, you'll want to ask each other questions like:

- What interests you most about this assignment? What's the catalyst?
- How does this assignment connect to concepts you're studying in other classes, your personal experience, or other ideas you've thought about?
- What makes your topic controversial?
- Why would this topic matter to your reader? What are the implications?
- Who would care most about this topic? Who are other stakeholders?

Feedback on Drafts

Once you have a first draft, your instructor might ask you to review each other's drafts ahead of time and come to class prepared with questions and comments. Or you might spend time in class reading your drafts aloud and sharing feedback. A very successful technique that doesn't require much expertise but yields great results is for the writer to read her paper aloud, pausing every paragraph or two for the listener to summarize. This checks clarity, helps the writer better imagine her audience, and gives the reader practice summarizing. Reading your writing aloud or hearing someone else read it may be unnerving at first, but it can be a tremendously helpful way to detect confusing sentences, grammatical errors, or just an awkward tone. We hope you'll keep an open mind about such a useful exercise and be willing to try new strategies throughout the writing process.

When reviewing a draft, a smart place to start is simply to share your perspective as the reader. Writers need to know how their ideas are coming across, whether their points make sense, where their argument falls apart, and what the reader is confused about. Often the best thing you can do is to serve as an "ignorant" reader. You can point out questions that writers didn't consider, identify gaps in their reasoning, challenge their assumptions, and help them see where the reader might stumble. Essentially, you can give them a peek inside the mind of their audience so that they realize why readers might cringe over an insensitive comment, laugh at a lame example, or think of something they overlooked.

You might have noticed that we haven't yet said anything about helping with grammar. You might be tempted to pick the proverbial low hanging fruit of misspellings, punctuation problems, and grammar errors, but remember, these are later order concerns that you'll want to save for editing. **Early on in the process, try to concentrate on higher order concerns that will help the writer revise.**

In fact, one of the best things you can do for a writer, rather than nitpick or criticize, is to talk about what you *like* about a paper, what you think is really working well. Again, dig deeper than saying things like "nice job." Tell the writer *why* you think something works well for her intended audience and purpose, and suggest ways for her to build on that success.

Responding as a reader helps to adjust your expectations, both as a writer and as a reviewer, for how useful peer review will be. As an ignorant but curious reader, you really can't say something wrong or do harm (unless you're being downright mean, of course). You are the reader, and the writer needs to hear what you think and how you experience the text.

Responding with Questions

It's particularly useful to ask writers stimulating questions that help them discover what is and isn't working in a draft.

What is your purpose? Ask the writer what she is trying to achieve, and tell her what you perceive as her main points (You can say something like "I think what you're getting at is _____. Is that what you're trying to say, or am I missing something?"). This summary can help the writer see whether her message is coming across as intended.

Who is your intended audience? Talk to the writer about the audience he has in mind and why this audience is a good fit. Think about the background of these potential readers—their values, their experience, their knowledge—and talk about how they might respond to the writer's message. You can ask the writer why he thinks his writing style, analysis, examples, and so forth will work for this particular audience. Oftentimes a writer forgets to think about his audience's perspective, so you can help him imagine that reader.

What questions do you have for me about the ideas presented? Tell the writer how you understand her arguments, saying something like "So, what I hear you saying is . . ." or "Overall, I'm left with the impression that _____. Is that right?" Discuss any questions you have about the overall message, share your opinion on the issues presented, suggest other examples that might fit, and help the writer think more carefully about her ideas.

Is the organization working? Ask the writer why he organized his points in this way, and identify any places where you got confused, sidetracked, or lost. To help the writer transition between his ideas more smoothly, you can ask him: "What is the connection between these two points? How are they related? What do they have in common?"

What is significant about this issue? Ask the writer why her paper matters, why her readers should care. Sometimes, writers assume that the importance of an issue is obvious, but readers wonder, *So what?* You can help a writer identify the significance of her position by raising questions like "What are the broader implications of this idea?" or "Why do readers need to think about this topic?" or "What other concepts does this controversy relate to?"

Responding with Helpful Comments

All in all, you want to facilitate a *conversation* with the writer, not just search for grammatical errors. Remember, during this stage, your purpose is to critique and to help, not to edit. Be careful, though, not to overwhelm writers by giving them too much feedback. Instead, focus and prioritize your comments. Here are additional examples of helpful comments that offer a reader's perspective:

- "This section of the paper confused me because . . . It is not clear what you mean by . . ."
- "This argument may have more impact if you first start with your own experience, and then incorporate research and statistics."
- "I completely agree with your argument. The issues you raised related to _____ are important because . . ."
- "I see what you're saying about _____, but what kinds of evidence do you have to support that claim?"
- "I'm having a hard time seeing the significance of what you're saying. Can you tell me more about why this is important?"

Feedback during Editing

The kind of response that's needed while drafting and revising is usually very different from what writers need when editing. Reader response is a good place to start and will remain useful throughout the writing process, but it keeps the reviewer in the driver's seat. As you develop as a writer—and especially as you gain more control with and become more deliberate about adapting your writing process—take the wheel by asking your reader for particular kinds of response. During the editing stage, you can ask your reviewers questions like:

- How does the writing "sound"? Is the tone appropriate?
- Are there any sentences that are confusing, awkward, or otherwise unclear?
- Are there any word choices that are vague, confusing, or overly technical?
- Where can the writing be more concise? Where can I reduce unnecessary wordiness?
- Where should I combine or divide sentences?
- Where can I add more personality, through humor or vividness or other stylistic devices?
- Where do you see mistakes, such as missing commas, subject-verb agreement problems, or misspellings?

Accepting and Rejecting Advice

As we've said, the right kind of feedback can improve your knowledge about writing and help you develop expertise. But responding to criticism is not easy. Sometimes you will hear conflicting advice from different readers. At other times, you will disagree with a reader's suggestions. In both cases, you have to make decisions about how to revise. When deciding how to implement changes based on feedback, you should keep in mind that **scholarly writing is public writing**. Unlike writing that you may do simply to express your feelings or to record experiences for yourself, scholarly writing prioritizes the readers' needs, reactions, and preferences over your own. Like they say in retail, "The customer is always right." If several reviewers give you similar feedback, then they're probably right—even if you disagree. Keep in mind that it's more important for your readers to understand and be moved by your message than it is for you to keep a potentially unclear sentence, example, or style that you love.

Different cultures place different values on complex, ambiguous expression—the kind you might find in poetry or fiction. Unless you're writing literature, American academic readers expect writers to express themselves clearly so readers can expend less effort to interpret intended meaning. In other cultures, writers expect readers to do much more work: to draw subtle linkages, to fill in gaps, to think of examples, to know the source of famous quotations, and so forth. But, in Western writing, you'll typically have to do these things for your readers. This is why you need to add explanations and linkages or explicitly state your meaning when readers miss the point, even if the meaning seems obvious to you.

However, that isn't to say that you should just blindly take every piece of advice you're given. In cases of conflicting or questionable suggestions, for example, you should consider the source. Think carefully about the reliability and skill level of the reader and the impact or cost of making recommended changes. You might even want to get a second opinion: you could consult a trained writing center tutor or your instructor. The most important thing is to be thoughtful and strategic about revision—just as you should be during every stage of the writing process, knowing that good writing is all about good choices.

Collaborating Effectively

Collaboration skills have become essential in nearly every workplace. As a scholarly apprentice, you can learn effective strategies for social brainstorming by participating actively in class discussions or by visiting with your instructor during office hours. By using the techniques for peer review that we've discussed, you can also learn how scholars give and receive feedback on drafts.

Perhaps the most daunting kind of collaboration involves writing with others. At its best, group writing can help you create projects that you could not possibly write by yourself. But if you've ever done group work before, you probably know how frustrating it can be when things go wrong.

Here are some strategies to ensure a more successful and less stressful experience when writing with others:

1. **Plan ahead.** As soon as you get your assignment, meet with your group to develop a detailed, written plan for how you want to accomplish the project. Think carefully about how you will organize your time to give adequate attention to discovery, drafting, revision, and editing. Create a timeline with milestones to mark your progress, and allow extra time in case something goes wrong, like a group member getting sick.

2. **Decide on roles for your group members.** Most groups either write together, delegate tasks, or use some combination of methods. If it's convenient for members of the group to meet, either physically or online, then writing together can be a good technique, especially during the planning stage when many heads can be smarter than one. Drafting and revising can be accomplished together by using online tools, such as wiki spaces or shared online documents. Many writers find it easier to take turns when drafting together to avoid tripping over each other in the same document. If you can find a time and place to meet together with a big screen

or projector, group editing can be lively and help to achieve a consistent style.

Another common technique is delegated collaboration, which assigns different tasks to team members, usually based on their expertise and interests. One approach is to break the project into chunks: members each investigate and draft a portion that interests them the most.

Alternatively, you can assign someone who's good at research to take a leadership role for that portion of the assignment, and let those who are best at drafting and editing lead those efforts. You should also consider assigning a project leader to manage communications and deadlines and generally keep everyone on track.

Delegated collaboration can be more efficient than writing together, but this technique sometimes misses the opportunity for *synergy*—when collaborators create something better than the sum of their efforts. (This book, for example, is immeasurably better because we wrote most of it together.)

3. **Establish rules and expectations for your group.** Most collaboration horror stories result from disagreements among members or group members acting inappropriately. Collaboration is complicated. You cannot completely avoid problems, but you can minimize their negative effects by agreeing up front to some rules and expectations for how you will work together. Here's a checklist of questions to consider before you begin writing:

- How will the group make decisions when circumstances change (as they inevitably will)?
- How will the group handle missed deadlines or substandard work?
- How will you deal with a group member who doesn't pull his weight?
- How will the group respond to a member who's too bossy?

Another issue that's worth settling in advance is project evaluation. Many students cringe at the idea that their grade might be affected by other students' performance. If this is a problem for your group, ask your instructor if she wants—or will accept—separate evaluations for each member of the group. If so, then you could devise a system to document each member's contributions. Settle on criteria in advance (for example, level of effort, quality of work, collaboration performance, and so forth). When the project is complete, everyone should complete a self-evaluation and peer evaluations for each group member. Realize, though, that it's difficult to weigh collaborative contributions accurately, and that everyone will inevitably contribute at different levels.

Any time and effort that you devote to thinking about "what ifs" before you start writing will help you to avoid problems later. We recommend writing down your group's answers to the questions above, along with any others you can think of, in a shared document. You can begin the group conversation by asking each other: What strategies have you used in the past to make group projects work well? What problems or difficulties did you have?

Appendix B
Templates for Organizing Arguments

Classical Argument

1. **Introduction**

   a. arouses readers' attention and interest, often with an example or a personal narrative

   b. establishes your qualifications to write about the topic

   c. identifies common ground with readers

   d. demonstrates fairness (qualifications, alternatives)

   e. identifies the controversy and states or implies the thesis

   f. forecasts the structure of the argument

2. **Background** (this may be part of the Introduction)

   a. gives an overview of the situation or problem

   b. identifies the issue's significance and relevance

   c. summarizes important sources and research on the subject (literature review)

3. **Support**

   a. presents good reasons, evidence, verification, and illustrations to support a thesis

   b. orders ideas in a clear and thoughtful pattern (chronological, order of importance)

   c. clearly links support back to the thesis

4. **Consideration of alternative arguments**

   a. examines alternative points of view
   b. notes advantages and disadvantages of alternatives
   c. explains why your argument is better

5. **Conclusion**

   a. *may* briefly summarize the overall argument
   b. elaborates on the implications of the thesis
   c. makes clear what you want readers to think or do
   d. adds a strong emotional or ethical appeal
   e. demonstrates why the conclusion is in your readers' best interest

Proposal Argument

1. **Problem**

   a. Describe the problem.
   b. Explain why it deserves our attention.

2. **Potential solution(s)**

   a. Present one or multiple solutions, along with the costs and benefits of each.
   b. Remember that doing nothing about the problem is also an option.

3. **Justification**

   a. Explain how and why your proposed solution will work.
   b. Describe why the advantages will outweigh the costs or drawbacks.
   c. Convince readers that your solution is better than alternative fixes.
   d. Reference past similar solutions that suggest similar positive outcomes.

Research Article

The research article, also known as a scholarly paper, is somewhat different from the research papers you may have done before, where you used library sources or the Internet to learn about a topic. You'll write some of those papers in college, too, especially as an apprentice, but as you develop as a scholar you may begin to conduct research like scholars do, to enlighten the community of scholars. You might, for example, research a medieval poet or battle that no one else has studied before. Or you may investigate a very specific environmental or genetic cause of Alzheimer's disease. In either case, you will likely report the results of your research to other scholars in a recognizable genre containing the following elements, along with a title page:

1. **Abstract**: In this section, authors summarize their research so that readers can quickly preview the article. When reviewing previous research, scholars often sift through stacks of sources by scanning article abstracts.

2. **Introduction**: Engages the reader, establishes the significance of the research (why it's needed), and states the problem or research question.

3. **Research (or "literature") review**: Synthesizes what other scholars have already said about the topic so that readers understand the subject's history and its theoretical foundation. Along with the introduction, the research review establishes the *So what?* for the research question.

4. **Methods**: Explains the process used to answer a research question or to study a problem (for example, methods used to collect and analyze data). Typically, authors aim to provide enough information so that readers see their methods as valid and reliable.

5. **Results**: Reports and tabulates the data and results gathered through investigation. This section often uses figures and charts to report data. (Sometimes scholars report large quantities of data in a separate *appendix* at the end of an article.)

6. **Analysis and discussion**: Presents and makes sense of the findings. Though not necessarily the longest, this section is usually the most meaty—full of analysis, interpretations, and applications—and therefore often the most important part of the research paper. When readers trust the methods and results, they often skim ahead to the analysis and discussion, like peeking ahead to find out how the story ends.
7. **Conclusion**: Synthesizes the discussion, identifies the larger significance and implications of the findings, and/or raises questions for further research.
8. **Bibliography**: Gives credit to other authors and directs readers to other relevant sources. Sometimes called a References or Works Cited page, this section identifies the sources that informed and validated the author's work.

The research article is an appropriate structure for most research papers, especially for papers that showcase *primary source* data (collected through experiments, interviews, surveys, etc.). This format also works well for assignments that ask for portions of a research paper but don't require the whole kit and caboodle. The general structure of the research article can be adapted to fit different assignments and rhetorical situations.

A Research (or "Literature") Review

This kind of writing typically contains four main sections: Introduction, Research Review, Conclusion, and Bibliography. Professors assign research reviews when they want students to summarize, analyze, and synthesize prominent research on a topic. Research reviews help scholars understand and analyze what others have already said about a subject and then identify a research area, topic, or question that has not been fully explored.

A Research Proposal

This genre typically contains an Introduction, Research Review, Methods, and Bibliography. Scholars write research proposals to pitch research projects that they have designed. They describe the experiments or research plans they would conduct to collect data and answer a research question. Oftentimes the purpose of the proposal is to secure funding, support, or approval for a project, so scholars give readers an overview of their plans. A research proposal is a specific kind of *proposal argument* that offers or presents plans to solve an unanswered question or problem.

READINGS

"A Wandering Mind Is an Unhappy Mind"
by Matthew A. Killingsworth and Daniel T. Gilbert

Unlike other animals, human beings spend a lot of time thinking about what is not going on around them, contemplating events that happened in the past, might happen in the future, or will never happen at all. Indeed, "stimulus-independent thought" or "mind wandering" appears to be the brain's default mode of operation (1–3). Although this ability is a remarkable evolutionary achievement that allows people to learn, reason, and plan, it may have an emotional cost. Many philosophical and religious traditions teach that happiness is to be found by living in the moment, and practitioners are trained to resist mind wandering and "to be here now." These traditions suggest that a wandering mind is an unhappy mind. Are they right?

Laboratory experiments have revealed a great deal about the cognitive and neural bases of mind wandering (3–7), but little about its emotional consequences in everyday life. The most reliable method for investigating real-world emotion is experience sampling, which involves contacting people as they engage in their everyday activities and asking them to report their thoughts, feelings, and actions at that moment. Unfortunately, collecting real-time reports from large numbers of people as they go about their daily lives is so cumbersome and expensive that experience sampling has rarely been used to investigate the relationship between mind wandering and happiness and has always been limited to very small samples (8, 9).

We solved this problem by developing a Web application for the iPhone (Apple Incorporated, Cupertino, California), which we used to create an unusually large database of real-time reports of thoughts, feelings, and actions of a broad range of people as they went about their daily activities. The application contacts participants through their iPhones at random moments during their waking hours, presents them with questions, and records their answers to a database at www.trackyourhappiness.org. The database currently contains nearly a quarter of a million samples from about 5000 people from 83 different countries who range in age from 18 to 88 and who collectively represent every one of 86 major occupational categories.

To find out how often people's minds wander, what topics they wander to, and how those wanderings affect their happiness, we analyzed samples from 2250 adults (58.8% male, 73.9% residing in the United States, mean age of 34 years) who were randomly assigned to answer a happiness question ("How are you feeling right now?") answered on a continuous sliding scale from very bad (0) to very good (100), an activity question ("What are you doing right now?") answered by endorsing one or more of 22 activities adapted from the day reconstruction method (10, 11), and a mind-wandering question ("Are you thinking about something other than what you're currently doing?") answered with one of four options: no; yes, something pleasant; yes, something neutral; or yes, something unpleasant. Our analyses revealed three facts.

First, people's minds wandered frequently, regardless of what they were doing. Mind wandering occurred in 46.9% of the samples and in at least 30% of the samples taken during every activity except making love. The frequency of mind wandering in our real-world sample was considerably higher than is typically seen in laboratory experiments. Surprisingly, the nature of people's activities had only a modest impact on whether their minds wandered and had almost no impact on the pleasantness of the topics to which their minds wandered (12).

Second, multilevel regression revealed that people were less happy when their minds were wandering than when they were not [slope (b) = −8.79, P < 0.001], and this was true during all activities, including the least enjoyable. Although people's minds were more likely to wander to pleasant topics (42.5% of samples) than to unpleasant topics (26.5% of samples) or neutral topics (31% of samples), people were no happier when thinking about pleasant topics than about their

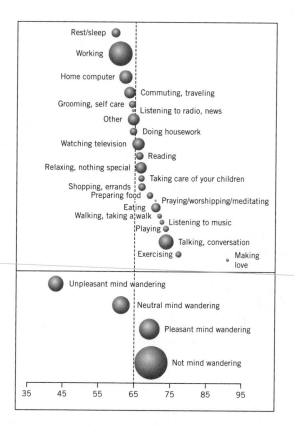

Figure 1.

Mean happiness reported during each activity (top) and while mind
wandering to unpleasant topics, neutral topics, pleasant topics or not
mind wandering (bottom). Dashed line indicates mean of happiness
across all samples. Bubble area indicates the frequency of occurrence.
The largest bubble ("not mind wandering") corresponds to 53.1% of the
samples, and the smallest bubble ("praying/worshipping/meditating")
corresponds to 0.1% of the samples.

current activity ($b = -0.52$, not significant) and were considerably unhappier when thinking about neutral topics ($b = -7.2$, $P < 0.001$) or unpleasant topics ($b = -23.9$, $P < 0.001$) than about their current activity (Fig. 1, bottom). Although negative moods are known to cause mind wandering (13), time-lag analyses strongly suggested that mind wandering in our sample was generally the cause, and not merely the consequence, of unhappiness (12).

Third, what people were thinking was a better predictor of their happiness than was what they were doing. The nature of people's activities explained 4.6% of the within-person variance in happiness and 3.2% of the between-person variance in happiness, but mind wandering explained 10.8% of within-person variance in happiness and 17.7% of between-person variance in happiness. The variance explained by mind wandering was largely independent of the variance explained by the nature of activities, suggesting that the two were independent influences on happiness.

In conclusion, a human mind is a wandering mind, and a wandering mind is an unhappy mind. The ability to think about what is not happening is a cognitive achievement that comes at an emotional cost.

References and Notes

1. M. E. Raichle *et al.*, A default mode of brain function. *Proc. Natl. Acad. Sci. U.S.A.* 98, 676 (2001).
2. K. Christoff, A. M. Gordon, J. Smallwood, R. Smith, J. W. Schooler, Experience sampling during fMRI reveals default network and executive system contributions to mind wandering. *Proc. Natl. Acad. Sci. U.S.A.* 106, 8719 (2009).
3. R. L. Buckner, J. R. Andrews-Hanna, D. L. Schacte, The brain's default network: Anatomy, function, and relevance to disease. *Ann. N. Y. Acad. Sci.* 1124, 1 (2008).
4. J. Smallwood, J. W. Schooler, The restless mind. *Psychol. Bull.* 132 946 (2006).

5. M. F. Mason *et al.*, Wandering minds: The default network and stimulus-independent thought. Science 315, 393 (2007).
6. J. Smallwood, E. Beach, J. W. Schooler, T. C. Handy Going AWOL in the brain: Mind wandering reduces cortical analysis of external events. *J. Cogn. Neurosci.* 20, 458 (2008).
7. R. L. Buckner, D. C. Carroll, Self-projection and the brain. *Trends Cogn. Sci.* 11, 49 (2007).
8. J. C. McVay, M. J. Kane, T. R. Kwapil, Tracking the train of thought from the laboratory into everyday life: An experience-sampling study of mind wandering across controlled and ecological contexts. *Psychon. Bull. Rev.* 16, 857 (2009).
9. M. J. Kane *et al.*, For whom the mind wanders, and when: An experience-sampling study of working memory and executive control in daily life. *Psychol. Sci.* 18, 614 (2007).
10. D. Kahneman, A. B. Krueger, D. A. Schkade, N. Schwarz, A. A. Stone, A survey method for characterizing daily life experience: The day reconstruction method. *Science* 306, 1776 (2004).
11. A. B. Krueger, D. A. Schkade, The reliability of subjective well-being measures. *J. Public Econ.* 92, 1833 (2008).
12. Materials and methods are available as supporting material on *Science* Online.
13. J. Smallwood, A. Fitzgerald, L. K. Miles, L. H. Phillips, Shifting moods, wandering minds: Negative moods lead the mind to wander. *Emotion* 9, 271 (2009).
14. We thank V. Pitiyanuvath for engineering www.trackyourhappiness .org and R. Hackman, A. Jenkins, W. Mendes, A. Oswald, and T. Wilson for helpful comments.

Excerpt from "Is Google Making Us Stupid? What the Internet Is Doing to Our Brains"
by Nicholas Carr

The Atlantic, July/August 2008

Over the past few years I've had an uncomfortable sense that someone, or something, has been tinkering with my brain, remapping the neural circuitry, reprogramming the memory. My mind isn't going—so far as I can tell—but it's changing. I'm not thinking the way I used to think. I can feel it most strongly when I'm reading. Immersing myself in a book or a lengthy article used to be easy. My mind would get caught up in the narrative or the turns of the argument, and I'd spend hours strolling through long stretches of prose. That's rarely the case anymore. Now my concentration often starts to drift after two or three pages. I get fidgety, lose the thread, begin looking for something else to do. I feel as if I'm always dragging my wayward brain back to the text. The deep reading that used to come naturally has become a struggle.

I think I know what's going on. For more than a decade now, I've been spending a lot of time online, searching and surfing and sometimes adding to the great databases of the Internet. The Web has been a godsend to me as a writer. Research that once required days in the stacks or periodical rooms of libraries can now be done in minutes. A few Google searches, some quick clicks on hyperlinks, and I've got the telltale fact or pithy quote I was after. Even when I'm not working, I'm as likely as not to be foraging in the Web's info-thickets reading and writing e-mails, scanning headlines and blog posts, watching videos and listening to podcasts, or just tripping from link to link to link. (Unlike footnotes, to which they're sometimes likened, hyperlinks don't merely point to related works; they propel you toward them.)

For me, as for others, the Net is becoming a universal medium, the conduit for most of the information that flows through my eyes and ears and into my mind. The advantages of having immediate access to such an incredibly rich store of information are many, and they've been widely described and duly applauded. "The perfect recall of silicon memory," *Wired*'s Clive Thompson has written, "can be an enormous boon to thinking." But that boon comes at a price. As the media theorist Marshall McLuhan pointed out in the 1960s, media are not just passive channels of information. They supply the stuff of thought, but they also shape the process of thought. And what the Net seems to be doing is chipping away my capacity for concentration and contemplation. My mind now expects to take in information the way the Net distributes it: in a swiftly moving stream of particles. Once I was a scuba diver in the sea of words. Now I zip along the surface like a guy on a Jet Ski.

I'm not the only one. When I mention my troubles with reading to friends and acquaintances—literary types, most of them—many say they're having similar experiences. The more they use the Web, the more they have to fight to stay focused on long pieces of writing. Some of the bloggers I follow have also begun mentioning the phenomenon. Scott Karp, who writes a blog about online media, recently confessed that he has stopped reading books altogether. "I was a lit major in college, and used to be [a] voracious book reader," he wrote. "What happened?" He speculates on the answer: "What if I do all my reading on the web not so much because the way I read has changed, i.e. I'm just seeking convenience, but because the way I THINK has changed?"

Bruce Friedman, who blogs regularly about the use of computers in medicine, also has described how the Internet has altered his mental habits. "I now have almost totally lost the ability to read and absorb a longish article on the web or in print," he wrote earlier this year. A pathologist who has long been on the faculty of the University of Michigan Medical School, Friedman elaborated on his comment in a telephone conversation with me. His thinking, he said, has taken on a "staccato" quality, reflecting the way he quickly scans short passages of text from many sources online. "I can't read *War and Peace* anymore," he admitted. "I've lost the ability to do that. Even a blog post of more than three or four paragraphs is too much to absorb. I skim it."

Anecdotes alone don't prove much. And we still await the long-term neurological and psychological experiments that will provide a definitive picture of how Internet use affects cognition. But a recently published study of online research habits, conducted by scholars from University College London, suggests that we may well be in the midst of a sea change in the way we read and think. As part of the five-year research program, the scholars examined computer logs documenting the behavior of visitors to two popular research sites, one operated by the British Library and one by a U.K. educational consortium, that provide access to journal articles, e-books, and other sources of written information. They found that people using the sites exhibited "a form of skimming activity," hopping from one source to another and rarely returning to any source they'd already visited. They typically read no more than one or two pages of an article or book before they would "bounce" out to another site. Sometimes they'd save a long article, but there's no evidence that they ever went back and actually read it. The authors of the study report:

> It is clear that users are not reading online in the traditional sense; indeed there are signs that new forms of "reading" are emerging as users "power browse" horizontally through titles, contents pages and abstracts going for quick wins. It almost seems that they go online to avoid reading in the traditional sense.

Thanks to the ubiquity of text on the Internet, not to mention the popularity of text-messaging on cell phones, we may well be reading more today than we did in the 1970s or 1980s, when television was our medium of choice. But it's a different kind of reading, and behind it lies a different kind of thinking—perhaps even a new sense of the self. "We are not only *what* we read," says Maryanne Wolf, a developmental psychologist at Tufts University and the author of

Proust and the Squid: The Story and Science of the Reading Brain. "We are *how* we read." Wolf worries that the style of reading promoted by the Net, a style that puts "efficiency" and "immediacy" above all else, may be weakening our capacity for the kind of deep reading that emerged when an earlier technology, the printing press, made long and complex works of prose commonplace. When we read online, she says, we tend to become "mere decoders of information." Our ability to interpret text, to make the rich mental connections that form when we read deeply and without distraction, remains largely disengaged.

Reading, explains Wolf, is not an instinctive skill for human beings. It's not etched into our genes the way speech is. We have to teach our minds how to translate the symbolic characters we see into the language we understand. And the media or other technologies we use in learning and practicing the craft of reading play an important part in shaping the neural circuits inside our brains. Experiments demonstrate that readers of ideograms, such as the Chinese, develop a mental circuitry for reading that is very different from the circuitry found in those of us whose written language employs an alphabet. The variations extend across many regions of the brain, including those that govern such essential cognitive functions as memory and the interpretation of visual and auditory stimuli. We can expect as well that the circuits woven by our use of the Net will be different from those woven by our reading of books and other printed works.

The human brain is almost infinitely malleable. People used to think that our mental meshwork, the dense connections formed among the 100 billion or so neurons inside our skulls, was largely fixed by the time we reached adulthood. But brain researchers have discovered that that's not the case. James Olds, a professor of neuroscience who directs the Krasnow Institute for Advanced Study at George Mason University, says that even the adult mind "is very plastic." Nerve cells routinely break old connections and form new ones. "The brain," according to Olds, "has the ability to reprogram itself on the fly, altering the way it functions."

265

The Internet promises to have particularly far-reaching effects on cognition. In a paper published in 1936, the British mathematician Alan Turing proved that a digital computer, which at the time existed only as a theoretical machine, could be programmed to perform the function of any other information-processing device. And that's what we're seeing today. The Internet, an immeasurably powerful computing system, is subsuming most of our other intellectual technologies. It's becoming our map and our clock, our printing press and our typewriter, our calculator and our telephone, and our radio and TV.

When the Net absorbs a medium, that medium is re-created in the Net's image. It injects the medium's content with hyperlinks, blinking ads, and other digital gewgaws, and it surrounds the content with the content of all the other media it has absorbed. A new e-mail message, for instance, may announce its arrival as we're glancing over the latest headlines at a newspaper's site. The result is to scatter our attention and diffuse our concentration.

The Net's influence doesn't end at the edges of a computer screen, either. As people's minds become attuned to the crazy quilt of Internet media, traditional media have to adapt to the audience's new expectations. Television programs add text crawls and pop-up ads, and magazines and newspapers shorten their articles, introduce capsule summaries, and crowd their pages with easy-to-browse info-snippets. When, in March of this year, *The New York Times* decided to devote the second and third pages of every edition to article abstracts , its design director, Tom Bodkin, explained that the "shortcuts" would give harried readers a quick "taste" of the day's news, sparing them the "less efficient" method of actually turning the pages and reading the articles. Old media have little choice but to play by the new-media rules.

Never has a communications system played so many roles in our lives—or exerted such broad influence over our thoughts—as the Internet does today. Yet, for all that's been written about the Net, there's been little consideration of how, exactly, it's reprogramming us. The Net's intellectual ethic remains obscure.

Google, says its chief executive, Eric Schmidt, is "a company that's founded around the science of measurement," and it is striving to "systematize everything" it does. Drawing on the terabytes of behavioral data it collects through its search engine and other sites, it carries out thousands of experiments a day, according to the *Harvard Business Review*, and it uses the results to refine the algorithms that increasingly control how people find information and extract meaning from it.

The company has declared that its mission is "to organize the world's information and make it universally accessible and useful." It seeks to develop "the perfect search engine," which it defines as something that "understands exactly what you mean and gives you back exactly what you want." In Google's view, information is a kind of commodity, a utilitarian resource that can be mined and processed with industrial efficiency. The more pieces of information we can "access" and the faster we can extract their gist, the more productive we become as thinkers.

In a 2004 interview with *Newsweek*, Brin said, "Certainly if you had all the world's information directly attached to your brain, or an artificial brain that was smarter than your brain, you'd be better off." Last year, Page told a convention of scientists that Google is "really trying to build artificial intelligence and to do it on a large scale."

Still, their easy assumption that we'd all "be better off" if our brains were supplemented, or even replaced, by an artificial intelligence is unsettling. It suggests a belief that intelligence is the output of a mechanical process, a series of discrete steps that can be isolated, measured, and optimized. In Google's world, the world we enter when we go online, there's little place for the fuzziness of contemplation. Ambiguity is not an opening for insight but a bug to be fixed. The human brain is just an outdated computer that needs a faster processor and a bigger hard drive.

The idea that our minds should operate as high-speed data-processing machines is not only built into the workings of the Internet, it is the network's reigning business model as well. The faster we surf across the Web—the more links we click and pages we view—the more opportunities Google and other companies gain to collect information about us and to feed us advertisements. Most of the proprietors of the commercial Internet have a financial stake in collecting the crumbs of data we leave behind as we flit from link to link—the more crumbs, the better. The last thing these companies want is to encourage leisurely reading or slow, concentrated thought. It's in their economic interest to drive us to distraction.

Maybe I'm just a worrywart. Just as there's a tendency to glorify technological progress, there's a countertendency to expect the worst of every new tool or machine. In Plato's *Phaedrus*, Socrates bemoaned the development of writing. He feared that, as people came to rely on the written word as a substitute for the knowledge they used to carry inside their heads, they would, in the words of one of the dialogue's characters, "cease to exercise their memory and become forgetful." And because they would be able to "receive a quantity of information without proper instruction," they would "be thought very knowledgeable when they are for the most part quite ignorant." They would be "filled with the conceit of wisdom instead of real wisdom." Socrates wasn't wrong—the new technology did often have the effects he feared—but he was shortsighted. He couldn't foresee the many ways that writing and reading would serve to spread information, spur fresh ideas, and expand human knowledge (if not wisdom).

The arrival of Gutenberg's printing press, in the 15th century, set off another round of teeth gnashing. The Italian humanist Hieronimo Squarciafico worried that the easy availability of books would lead to intellectual laziness, making men "less studious" and weakening their minds. Others argued that cheaply printed books and broadsheets would undermine religious authority, demean the work of scholars and scribes, and spread sedition and debauchery. As New York University professor Clay Shirky notes, "Most of the arguments made against the printing press were correct, even prescient."

But, again, the doomsayers were unable to imagine the myriad blessings that the printed word would deliver.

So, yes, you should be skeptical of my skepticism. Perhaps those who dismiss critics of the Internet as Luddites or nostalgists will be proved correct, and from our hyperactive, data-stoked minds will spring a golden age of intellectual discovery and universal wisdom. Then again, the Net isn't the alphabet, and although it may replace the printing press, it produces something altogether different. The kind of deep reading that a sequence of printed pages promotes is valuable not just for the knowledge we acquire from the author's words but for the intellectual vibrations those words set off within our own minds. In the quiet spaces opened up by the sustained, undistracted reading of a book, or by any other act of contemplation, for that matter, we make our own associations, draw our own inferences and analogies, foster our own ideas. Deep reading, as Maryanne Wolf argues, is indistinguishable from deep thinking.

If we lose those quiet spaces, or fill them up with "content," we will sacrifice something important not only in our selves but in our culture. In a recent essay, the playwright Richard Foreman eloquently described what's at stake:

> I come from a tradition of Western culture, in which the ideal (my ideal) was the complex, dense and "cathedral-like" structure of the highly educated and articulate personality—a man or woman who carried inside themselves a personally constructed and unique version of the entire heritage of the West. [But now] I see within us all (myself included) the replacement of complex inner density with a new kind of self—evolving under the pressure of information overload and the technology of the "instantly available."

As we are drained of our "inner repertory of dense cultural inheritance," Foreman concluded, we risk turning into "'pancake people'— spread wide and thin as we connect with that vast network of information accessed by the mere touch of a button."

"With Liberty and Justice for Some"
by Emanuel Grant

As Americans, we are in love with the concept of justice. Freedom and fairness are as integral to our identity as hot apple pie and cookouts on a summer's day. I feel downright lucky to be here—in a land of opportunity where the hardworking are rewarded. In my readings of the works of the greats of economic commentary (Milton Friedman, Steven Levitt, and Stephen Dubner to name a few), it has become quite clear that our nation's success is formally attributed to our warm embrace of democratic and capitalistic ideals. We are described as the world's wealthiest country in terms of GDP (Gross Domestic Product), yet what does that wealth mean? Who owns it?

In terms of financial wealth—described by UCSC professor G. William Domhoff as "total net worth minus the value of one's home"—in 2007, 42.7% of our nation's wealth is owned by the top 1% of our population and another 50.3% is owned by the next 19% in the economic ladder. With some simple number crunching, a shocking, unnerving statistic unfolds: the wealthiest 20% in our society own a whopping 93% of our nation's wealth. That leaves a paltry 7% of wealth to the bottom 80% of Americans. Maybe these discrepancies are a good thing. Maybe they prove that if you work hard in life, you're going to be living large. To me, however, these statistics spin a tale much different than that of the American dream. They bastardize any notions of equality, justice, and social responsibility that I once identified as truly American. Though no economic system is perfect, it seems the structure of the one present leaves the poor grasping for straws as the rich enjoy the fruits of their labor.

Unless you are in this top 1% bracket (in which case go ahead and burn my paper now; you won't find comfort here) or *at least* within the remaining 19% of wage earners, you should be furious! Why should a select few Americans live in the lap of luxury while the others are forced to live paycheck to paycheck? I'm no socialist nut; I agree that people should be rewarded for their hard efforts. But, there must be a way to narrow the gap, to spread the wealth a little more. 7% of our nation's wealth for 80% of its people just doesn't *sound* right. With this in mind, I plan to target the highest echelons of our society and find an alternative to the farce of economic justice that pervades our economic system.

A fun little riddle before we delve deeper: try naming one thing NBA, National Rugby League (NSWRL) and MLB players all have in common. If you can't think of an answer besides that they all are athletic and have ridiculous amounts of money, you're probably not alone. In the sports world, the commonality is known as a salary cap—there's a literal limit that a league sets on how much LeBron can make for a year of excellence on the court; in the real world, the same phenomenon has been called a wage ceiling or a maximum wage— a government set standard on how much an earner can take home. I believe the introduction of maximum wage policies is a solution for the income inequality we see in our nation. Yes, I said it; cue the USSR anthem and call up the retired McCarthyites to put me away for good. I think there's a maximum amount of money you should be legally allowed to make. Try your best to palate my words. Remain skeptical; don't trust me yet. But, I beg you to keep an open mind. Remember, I am no politician; I'm not trying to trick you with some underhanded rhetoric. I have a bona fide, genuine concern for the majority of Americans (i.e. the 80%) who are fighting an uphill battle in their "pursuit of happiness," and I will use the principles of Macroeconomics to fortify my argument and fight for you—the little guy.

Though I am arguing for ceilings on wage, I bet you didn't know that the government already built a structural roof on your earnings. You just happen to be standing on it. It's called a minimum wage. We all accept it. Whether you're serving up burgers at your local McDonald's or ripping up ticket stubs at the premier of Tarantino's next violent thriller, the government has already stepped in and said that there's a minimum amount you are allowed to earn for that job.

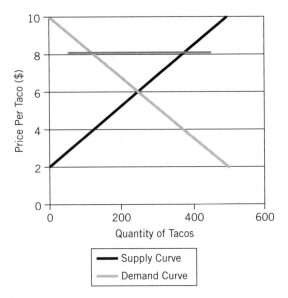

Figure 1
Bill's Taco Stand

While we generally accept this ideal, there are formidable consequences on the economy at large. These consequences make up the
roof of which I previously spoke. To see these consequences, we first
need to see how wages are decided.

British economist Alfred Marshall was the first person to depict a
complete picture for the determinant of price–what the market decides
as a fair amount for a good or service—in his creation of the laws of
Supply and Demand (Frank and Bernanke 65). Put simply, there is a
market for *anything*. On one side, there's a group of producers that creates a product (the supply) and wants to get as much money as possible
for it. On the other, there's a group of consumers that want a product
for as low as a price as possible (the demand). These motives are opposing; where the forces meet is the point at which a price is determined.
Take a look at Figure 1 for a fictional example of how much our friend

Bill will get for his tacos sold at his taco stand. The red line denotes the demand. At eight dollars, Bill would like to sell 400 tacos, but his customers are only willing to buy 100 at that price. If he refused to sell below that price, there would be an excess supply of 300 tacos (400 – 100)—the difference between the points of intersection of the horizontal line between the Supply and Demand curves. In a free market, this process goes back and forth until the lines intersect, at what is called an equilibrium price, where Bill's production of tacos meets his demand.

These same principles carry over to labor markets. The only thing that really changes is the label on the axes. What was once the price of a good or service is now the wage of a worker. What was once quantity now becomes employment, the number of jobs available. Again, there is a supply side and a demand side. In this case, employers are the supply while people looking for work make up the demand. A true free market economy would use this model to determine wage, and an equilibrium price (wage in this example) would be reached—this is how much a worker would be paid. However, this supposedly ideal scenario does not reflect reality; the government in an effort to help the lower class has instituted a minimum wage. Reflected in Figure 2, a serious problem emerges. Though the government may have altruistic motives, the minimum wage intrinsically expands unemployment. Companies can't afford to pay workers more than that equilibrium price a free market economy would set for wage, so what they do is simply higher less workers—this time, an excess supply of job seekers (and, thus, more unemployment) ensues.

Suffering an influx of unemployment, a minimum wage economy operates inefficiently; this economy is not utilizing its resource of labor to its full potential, since people that could otherwise be working are not (Frank and Bernanke 177). Regardless, it still seems necessary and just for workers to have some sort of minimum so that we don't have Americans bringing home just a couple of dollars a day, no matter how menial the labor. It becomes a necessary evil. America is not the only country that faces this dilemma. In Australia, there has

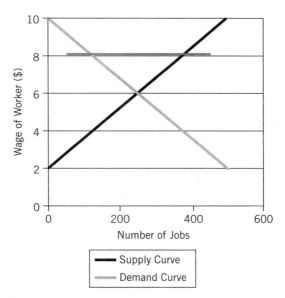

Figure 2

Labor Markets

been heated debate on this same issue. As previous chairman of the Australian Fair Pay Commission, Ian Harper posits that it is equally inefficient to pursue the abolishment of a minimum wage as it is to keep it, for it would evaporate the "safety net" on wage that these laws create (4). In his opinion, all that is necessary is the maintenance of some sort of minimum, anywhere below the equilibrium levels. I would challenge Mr. Harper to think outside the box; the solution that we both seek—one "economically efficient" as well as socially acceptable for wage redistributions—may lie in the additional adoption of a maximum wage, the exact opposite policy (5).

The target market for the implementation of this kind of law is American CEOs. They make the most. If the wealth distribution in America got you a little frustrated, go ahead and grab yourself a couple aspirins to calm down that heart of yours before we continue; the

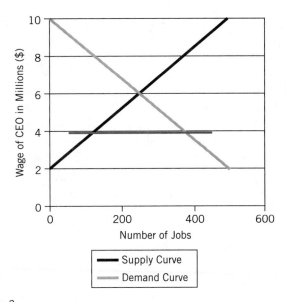

Figure 3

Proposed CEO Labor Market

magnitude of CEO salaries might just put you in a stretcher. Venkat Venkatasubramanian in a longitudinal analysis of wage distributions for Purdue University magnifies the following statistic in his research: while in the 70s CEOs made about 50 times as much as minimum wage workers, as of 2007 they now make on average 866 (that's right; *eight-hundred-and-sixty-six*) times as much (766). To put that into perspective, for every eight dollars a person makes in an hour, a CEO makes close to 7,000 dollars. If you're working an eight hour day, a minimum wage earner brings home about 64 dollars, while a CEO working that same amount of time brings home 56,000 dollars— more than that worker would make in two years working full time. These are just averages, many CEOs make much more than that. Do CEOs really work 866 times harder than their lowest employees? Emphatically, I answer "of course not!" Sure they have highly stressful jobs, but a free market approach to their salaries makes up a double standard (767). Why do we set wage laws for the lower classes that have proved to increase unemployment while simultaneously ignoring the opposite side of the spectrum? Let's turn the minimum wage graph on its head and show what a wage ceiling will do for our economy; look now to Figure 3. As we can see, a possible benefit occurs in the divergence away from equilibrium; there is now an excess supply of CEO job openings available but not enough CEOs willing to take the wage.

In an interview with James Madison University Economics professor Dr. Vipul Bhatt, I went over this theoretical framework for a maximum wage. Though he lauded the model in theory for what I was setting out to solve, he coerced me away from what I now see as naivety and explained what would happen in reality. "There will be a shortage of CEOs in your model," he said. Even if the government did put a cap on CEO wages, "they will always find a way to get money outside of their salary in the form of bonuses and stock options." On top of this, if they are not getting paid in full, their performance will decrease and more poor decisions will be made, and government "does not want to interfere with performance." Fine. But if a maximum wage isn't realistic, then what is?

As we can see, a chasm exists between economic theory and its practice. As Dr. Maureen Ramsay of the University of Leeds expressed in her "A Modest Proposal: The Case for a Maximum Wage," "it seems implausible that it is necessary to make some individuals hundreds of time richer than others in order to retain incentives" (207). But, we somehow continue to operate under that principle. If a flat out ceiling won't work, what else is there? I kept my nose to the grindstone, and the answer hit me in the face while reading Venkat's work: the greater the fairness of a company, the greater the entropy (capability for work) in that company (777). While he posited the idea of pay scales, why not simply tie the salary of the CEO to a set ratio of that earned by the lowest paid worker for the company, fusing the ideals behind a maximum wage with real world practicality (776)?

Two enormously successful companies have been built upon such a principle. Praised in *Time Magazine*, Ben & Jerry's ice cream and Whole Foods supermarkets, from their inceptions, tied the top of management to the bottom tier of workers (Fonda 63). Though Ben & Jerry's had to abandon the practice in the mid-90s to hire a new CEO, Whole Foods still operates on a maximum of a 14:1 ratio (63). Their CEO is only taking home 14 times more than the person that's bagging the groceries they sell (sounds much better than 866 times, right?). With this idea in practice, the bosses are still rewarded handsomely for their efforts, but the bottom tier workers do not feel alienated from their executives—growth in salary is still possible. You can have your cake and eat it too. As an added bonus, this practice would inherently boost productivity across the spectrum once implemented; anyone who works in the company, no matter what their rank, has the extra incentive to do their best at all times because any increase in the profitability of the company is shared directly with the worker. The *incentive* to do well serves as a catalyst for both the growth of the company and of personal salary.

Increased incentives for workers, no matter how important, lead to economic growth (Bhatt). While the flat salary caps remain regrettably implausible, the adoption of ratio driven salaries for corporate America has unlimited potential. I'll set a bar, middle of the road, in comparison to today's standards. If we required CEOs to be paid a maximum of 100 times what their lowest workers are getting, that's still a difference in a factor of 766 times what it is today. Think how much more wealth could be shared! Unfortunately, the biggest problem the implementation of a ratio-wage policy faces is founded in the culture of American greed that got us here in the first place: the wretched bedfellow of the free market. However, if our nation is the wealthiest on this planet, why should only a select few enjoy it? Possibly, there may be a need for a call for change—a change in the distribution of wealth in our society. The wealth of our nation should be our greatest benefit as Americans, holistically. That wealth cannot and should not be contained all within the grasp of an elite echelon of the top wage earners. I'm not here to spark a Marxist revolution in America, but I very well want to level the playing field—and expand social justice with economic policy, reframing what it means to be an American and to be free. At the end of the day, if both you and your boss can stand to benefit, what is there to lose?

Works Cited

Bhatt, Vipul. Personal Interview. 3 Nov. 2010.

Domhoff, G. William. "Who Rules America: Wealth, Income, and Power." *Power in America*. UC Santa Cruz, n.d. Web. 8 Nov. 2010.

Fonda, Daren, et al. "The Rumble Over Executive Pay." *Time* 163.22 (2004): 62–64. *Academic Search Complete*. Web. 8 Nov. 2010.

Frank, Robert H., and Ben Bernanke. *Principles of Macroeconomics*. 4th ed. Boston: McGraw-Hill Irwin, 2009. Print.

Harper, Ian. "Why Would an Economic Liberal Set Minimum Wages?" *Policy* 25.4 (2009): 3–7. *Academic Search Complete*. Web. 8 Nov. 2010.

Ramsay, Maureen. "A Modest Proposal: The Case for a Maximum Wage." *Contemporary Politics* 11.4 (2005): 201–215. *Academic Search Complete*. Web. 8 Nov. 2010.

Venkatasubramanian, Venkat. "What is Fair Pay for Executives? An Information Theoretic Analysis of Wage Distributions." *Entropy* 11.4 (2009): 766–781. *Academic Search Complete*. Web. 8 Nov. 2010.

Credits

Cigarette Warning Label: US Food and Drug Administration, Silver Spring, MD 20993

Destroy This Brute poster: Library of Congress Prints and Photographs Division, Washington, D.C. 20540

Join the Navy poster: Library of Congress Prints and Photographs Division, Washington, D.C. 20540

Block quotation from "Attention Disorder or Not, Pills to Help in School": Schwarz, Alan. *New York Times*, 9 Oct. 2012

Excerpt from "Is Google Making Us Stupid: What the Internet Is Doing to Our Brains": Nicholas Carr, *The Atlantic*, July/Aug 2008.

"A Wandering Mind Is an Unhappy Mind": Killingsworth, Matthew A. and Daniel T. Gilbert. *Science* Vol. 330, 12 Nov. 2010

"With Liberty and Justice for Some": Emmanuel Grant

index